PENGUIN

A SOUTH INDIA

Michael Wood, journalist, broadcaste..., ...m-maker, has been acclaimed for his hugely popular BBC tel...r... series and the accompanying books *In the Footsteps of Alexander the Great*, and *Conquistadors*; the latest is *India: a Journey in History*.

Michael Wood

A SOUTH INDIAN JOURNEY

PENGUIN BOOKS

PENGUIN BOOKS

Published by the Penguin Group
Penguin Books Ltd, 80 Strand, London WC2R ORL, England
Penguin Group (USA) Inc., 375 Hudson Street, New York, New York 10014, USA
Penguin Group (Canada), 90 Eglinton Avenue East, Suite 700, Toronto, Ontario, Canada M4P 2Y3
(a division of Pearson Penguin Canada Inc.)
Penguin Ireland, 25 St Stephen's Green, Dublin 2, Ireland (a division of Penguin Books Ltd)
Penguin Group (Australia), 250 Camberwell Road, Camberwell,
Victoria 3124, Australia (a division of Pearson Australia Group Pty Ltd)
Penguin Books India Pvt Ltd, 11 Community Centre,
Panchsheel Park, New Delhi – 110 017, India
Penguin Group (NZ), 67 Apollo Drive, Rosedale, North Shore 0632, New Zealand
(a division of Pearson New Zealand Ltd)
Penguin Books (South Africa) (Pty) Ltd, 24 Sturdee Avenue, Rosebank, Johannesburg 2196, South Africa

Penguin Books Ltd, Registered Offices: 80 Strand, London WC2R ORL, England

www.penguin.com

First published by Viking 1995
First published in Penguin Books 1996
This edition published in Penguin Books 2007

1

Printed in England by Clays Ltd, St Ives plc

ISBN: 978-0-141-03267-2

To Rebecca

Contents

CONTENTS

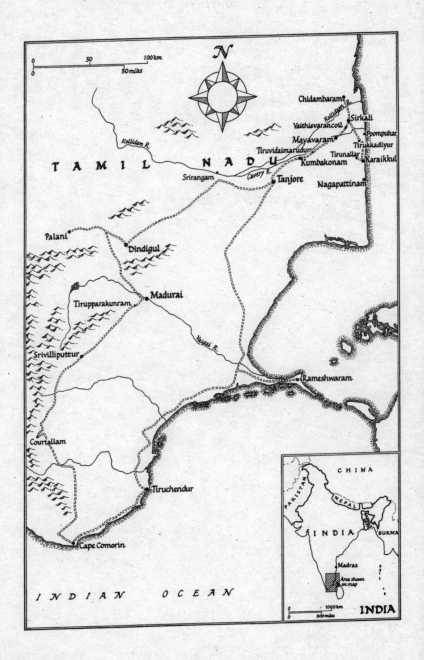

Introduction

This book tells the story of a series of journeys in Tamil Nadu, the southernmost state in India, which stretches down to the tip of the subcontinent, opposite Sri Lanka. This is a land which many visitors since Marco Polo's day have thought one of the most splendid and fascinating on earth, and my simple aim in writing was to give the general reader, and the traveller, a flavour of the beauties of Tamil culture, and of the southern landscape. I have called Tamil Nadu the last classical civilization, by which I mean a civilization in which a substantial element of the traditional ways of thinking – in belief, culture, music, and literature, for example – is still alive in the mainstream, however pervasive the impact of modernity and global culture may be in India today.

The book is also about a friendship between my family and an Indian family in a small town in India's deep south. This friendship came about as a result of a chance meeting with Mala and her family when my wife and I arrived in the ancient town of Chidambaram as travellers one Diwali twenty years ago. Hers is a traditional Saivite family belonging to the agricultural caste which supported the Cholan kings in the great age of Tamil culture in the ninth and tenth centuries, and who have devotedly carried down the beliefs and aspirations of their caste till today; people who are playing their part in the dynamic world of modern India, but who also still live in sacred time. In the epilogue this new edition brings the story of Mala and her family into the twenty-first century.

I would like to thank the many friends in Tamil Nadu who

helped me write this book and who, more importantly, gave me their friendship over a dozen visits to their country: chiefly M. Nagaratinam and family; R. Sushila and family, Lakshmi Vishwanathan; Dr R. Nagaswamy; the priests of the Nataraja temple, in particular R. N. Dikshithar and Rajdurai Dikshithar; the staff of Hotel Tamil Nadu, Chidambaram; Dr R. Baskaran and family, and all those who travelled on the 1992 pilgrimage to Tiruchendur and in 1994 to Palani. Lastly I would like to thank the staffs of the various temples in this story who kindly allowed a non-Hindu access to their shrines. To all my grateful thanks. I hope they will understand and forgive such liberties as I have taken in the story with time and place. In England I would like to thank Pru Cave, John Collee and Stuart Blackburn for their helpful comments and criticisms. I would also like to thank two scholars whose work has inspired all who love Tamil culture: Kamil Zvelebil for a title, and David Shulman, for a beginning; also Gabriella Eichinger Ferro-Luzzi for help with Mr Ramasamy's jokes: I hope all three will look kindly on my magpie borrowings. Last of all my greatest debt is to Rebecca Dobbs for her love, encouragement and understanding, and to our daughters Jyoti and Mina, without whom this journey would never have happened.

Prologue

For a long time when we came to Madras we used to stay in a room in a tower block, J.P. Tower, down Nungambakkam High Road. A ten-storey warren of flats and small businesses, it was only built in the late seventies, but already its yellow walls were stained black by the relentless heat and the monsoon rains. The auto-rickshaw would stop on the corner of a narrow dirt lane which led to the entrance to the building. You climbed out by a heap of rotting vegetation and soggy cardboard chewed over by a thin white cow which, like the rubbish, never seemed to move from this spot. Over the lane a new hotel was built in the mid-eighties with a liquor permit room at the back – Tamil Nadu was still a dry state in those days – and along with the cow, there would always be a doorkeeper in khaki fatigues and military beret on duty by the gate. Inside, when the clinging heat of the Madras night put its hand on your shoulder, there was chilly air-conditioning, and beer so cold it took your breath away.

Inside the tower block the foyer had a lingering aroma of DDT and incense. One lift was always out of action but, miraculously, one always worked. It was operated by a barefoot lift boy with a sweet smile, who never lined the lift up with the floor, so that you usually had to crouch to get out. (I never understood why; I had a crazy notion this was some kind of tactic because of the power cuts.) We used to stay on the fifth or sixth floor, I can't remember now: a cluster of rooms for travelling salesmen which was dignified by the name of the Krishna Executive Lodge. It had been booked for us by a Tamil friend who worked in an office on the floor below. The rooms were very clean, if mosquito ridden; the lady at the desk was very quiet and patient, always game to spend half an hour trying to get a trunk call for you, before disappearing to another floor to do the mysterious other job which occupied most of her day. The boys, on the other hand, were quite unsuited to running such an establishment; they were ever helpful and always smiling, but insisted on turning on the TV at full volume at the crack of dawn while they prepared cardboard toast and muddy coffee.

The place was handy for midtown: in ten minutes you could walk to the restaurants and bookshops down Dr Radakrishnan road, under the flyover, where the sleepers on the street live on concrete ledges inches away from the traffic, cooking their evening meals on wood fires at the feet of the huge, hand-painted movie hoardings which line the road. Near by was Mr Balasubrahma-nian's Carnatic Music Bookshop, a treasure house of traditional Tamil culture, its shelves sagging under texts of Thyagaraja and the other 'modern' greats of southern music. Here too were books on the classical dance and, in the back, stacks of literary, philosophi-cal and religious classics: grammars, glossaries, epics, poems on love and war, medieval treatises on literary theory, the songs of the saints (which are still memorized in traditional families). These are all part of a continuous two-thousand-year-old tradition which is virtually unknown in the West, one of the world's last surviving classical cultures. And as if to to remind you of its wellspring, in the front room of the shop was a a little shrine with puja lamp, bowls of camphor and incense, and a picture rail lined with old gilt-framed pictures of the gods. Here Mr Balasubramanian did his prayers every morning before opening.

Close by was the Music Academy, where you could go to concerts of classical dance, Bharata Natyam – an art form now enjoying a renaissance after its suppression in the temples by the British in the early years of the century. And round the corner there was Woodlands Restaurant, where the vegetarian tradition of the south could be sampled, eaten with the hand from plates of fresh plantain leaf. The enduring connections with the British period may give India a strange familiarity to the visitor from these islands, even in the most unlikely places, but the newcomer to the Tamil south does not have to venture very far from his or her hotel to see that this is a wholly different civilization, which has survived to take modernity on something like its own terms.

The best thing about J.P. Tower was the view. To see it you had to climb up the stairwell, glimpsing through open doors some of the strange clientele of the upper floors: one-room import–export offices, astrologers, shipping agents and a specialist in sexual problems ('MD, Mysore'). Past the room for the lift machinery there was an inspection door on to the roof. Outside you had to scramble over a jumble of air-conditioning pipes, building debris and pools of dried concrete, and then duck under washing lines snapping in the breeze which comes up from the sea in the late afternoon. At the railing you found yourself looking southwards over the wonderful urban landscape of south Madras: growth and decay intermingled, growing out of each other. Near by another tower block was going up: this was the beginning of the new boom years for the city. Labourers clambered barefoot over a forest of wood and bamboo scaffolding, baskets of bricks on their heads. Tiny white loincloths, red headbands, sweat glistening on ebony backs. The construction method can hardly have changed for a thousand years; temple towers and skyscrapers alike are thrown up with crazy webs of timber and bamboo poles lashed with coir rope, which look as if the slightest puff of breeze would blow them down.

Further out you could see a city of gardens, a green sea of palms dotted by the spires, domes and pavilions of the old British suburbs around Adyar Park, the Madras Club and the river. Looking southwards the first time, I found this view simply heart-stopping. And ever since then it has seemed to me like the threshold of a magical land. The sun sinks to the horizon, an orange ball, and the sky turns soft peach to the south-west, shading to a ripple of gold with translucent ultramarine above. Thirty or forty miles away on the horizon you clearly make out the red hills of Tirukalikundran, tipped by the spire of its ancient temple. There, every day towards twelve, two eagles come to be fed from bronze bowls by Brahmin priests in a mysterious ritual which was reported nearly four hundred years ago by European visitors. Always around midday; always two eagles – never one or three. It is one of those strange Indian fairy tales (like rope tricks, snake charmers and self-mortifying fakirs) about which we read in our childhood books – and which turn out to be 'true'. A foretaste of the wonders and illusions which lie beyond.

Those distant hills mark the gateway to the south. From Madras it is five hundred miles down to the tip of India at Cape Comorin, where the Arabian Sea meets the Bay of Bengal. To the west and north-west, the Tamil country rises to high wooded mountains, the Western Ghats and the Cardamom Hills, which still abound in wild beasts. There the British built their hill stations, like Kody and Ooty, to escape the ferocious heat of the plains. But the heartland of the south is the flat country of the Coromandel coast, cut by the rivers Pennar, Vellar, Cavery and Vaigai. This is where Tamil civilization grew and flowered – 'the most splendid province in the world', Marco Polo called it. It is a land of dazzling emerald-green rice fields and immense palm forests, where at almost every railway halt the temple gateways tower above the trees like petrified vegetation, ancient centres of myth and religion which are still part of a living sacred landscape, 'India's Holy Land'. It is still, for those susceptible to enchantment, an enchanted country: a 'land where it all comes back', as an old India hand once said to me, 'the stuff of your karmic dreams'. This is the story of a journey through that land, down to the southern tip of the subcontinent, through the landscape – physical, mental, imaginal – of the Tamil universe; one of the last – perhaps the last – of the

4

classical civilizations to survive to the end of the twentieth century. The journey started long ago, one Christmas. And it started with a prediction.

Part One
THE COOL SEASON

Mala's house lay in a dusty street of beaten earth, hard beneath the feet, heavy with sun. Chidambaram is really just a big village clustered round the temple; and hers is a village street lined with ancient wooden houses with thatched roofs, little latticed verandas and pillared porches. At the threshold of the house every morning she laid out a *kolam*, a pattern in rice flour on the swept floor: intertwined geometric shapes, a flower, a peacock, a maze, auspicious signs to protect the home. Here in the south, the unseen is always palpable, and is always threatening to break in upon the present; it can never be ignored.

It was Mala's choice to live here, so as to be close to the great temple of Nataraja. For south India's Saivites, devotees of the Great God Siva, this is the holiest of all shrines, where the god is enthroned as Lord of the Dance in the golden-roofed sanctum whose origins, it is said, lie back in the remotest antiquity. The immense rectangle of the temple dominates the town, and its towers can be seen for miles across the flat landscape of the coastal plain; at night, when their lamps are lit, they are landmarks to sailors out at sea. After her husband lost his sight, Mala returned here, to the place where she was born, to bring up her children, and to be near Nataraja. Sometimes her devotion drove the girls to distraction. There was nothing much for them in Chidambaram. Life would be better in Madras or Pondi. But as Bharati always said, 'Mother would never leave Nataraja'.

Every day without fail Mala would go into the temple at six in

9

the morning when the air is still cool, walking barefoot through the spacious courtyards to hear the music and see the flame lifted to Siva's eyes. And again at ten, for the offerings of honey, milk and coconut, and then in the evening when the age-old Tamil hymns are sung by the *oduvars*, hereditary singers from the middling castes like her own, who must stand outside the sanctum, for this is the preserve of the Brahmins with their Sanskrit rituals. Even when she was away, Mala could tell you to the minute which of the events of the temple's ritual day was under way. It was a rhythm as ingrained in her daily life as waking, eating and sleeping, and I suspect it gave her as much sustenance.

Mala's house was a few minutes' walk from the East Gate of the temple. She had a single room with a lean-to tiled roof around which lizards and rats scampered; a row of triangular air vents in the bricks allowed a little breeze in the hot weather. Inside there was enough space for a wooden bed, a folding camp bed, a metal chest for the family treasures, a treadle sewing-machine and a small table. When everyone was at home the children slept on the floor. On the walls she hung brightly coloured religious posters depicting her favourite gods and goddesses: many-armed creatures with kohl-dark eyes and dreamy smiles, garlanded with flowers, their saris seamed with gold. Above the bed was an out-of-date calendar from a sparking plug firm in Madras, with a picture of the god who is beloved of all Tamils, Siva's son, the divine boy-child, Murugan: a beaming cherub with a plume of peacock feathers. At the other end of the room there was a narrow kitchen space behind a five-foot-high brick partition; here she had a Calor gas burner, stone shelves for pots and pans, a vegetable basket, a grinding stone and pestle. Outside her door a communal passageway led to a latrine, a well and a small tank for rainwater. In this confined space, the surrounding streets and shops, and the temple itself, most of her daily routine passed.

It is like any other small southern town sweltering in the plain, but here the hot, brick-kiln blast of midday is always dissipated by the breeze which comes in from the sea in the afternoon. Just down the lane, past the thatched shed where Mr Ragavan mends broken-down auto-rickshaws, is a yellow-painted concrete water-tower. From here you can see the whole place laid out before you, from the golden roof of Nataraja's shrine over the temple gardens and out to the green and white minarets of the mosque on the Cuddalore road, where the town abruptly ends and the paddies begin.

It is a warren of thatched and tiled houses, shaded by palms and dotted with little exuberantly painted shrines. It has three mosques, a couple of churches and three big cinemas. There are tea stalls on almost every corner. The one I used to haunt is in East Car Street. It is run by an unlikely couple, a big albino man and his wiry little assistant. The small one does the mixing and pouring; like a conjuror playing to his audience, he throws his tea in a great arc from jug to cup and back again, never losing a drop.

Outside the albino's tea stall, beyond the shadow of his awning, a little lane runs up to the temple gate. Mala comes this way every day: it is full of people from dawn till midnight, walking to and from the temple, stopping to shop or to talk to friends. Here is Raja the priest's house, and Ravi the tour guide; there is the woman who sells pilgrim souvenirs, painted plaster geegaws of gods and pottery busts of movie stars. Further on is the lugubrious seller of almanacs and astrological texts who squats impassively under his sunshade. By the gate, next to the man who does door-to-door ironing, is the boy who looks after your shoes for a few paise when you go into the shrine.

On the other side of the temple courtyard is the bazaar. This is the oldest part of the town, and it grew up around the sacred precinct in the Middle Ages. Mala's father's house is in this part of town, and it is here that her oldest son Kumar is hoping eventually to set up in business. The daily fruit and vegetable market is here, the bank, the police station and the telegraph office. Near by you'll find the merchants, the goldsmiths and the importers of electronic goods from Singapore and Malaysia. You can see the new money here, as India's economy starts to open up. Fancy houses with marble floors and security gates nestle cheek by jowl with the decaying mansions of the old landed class (people like Mala's father). In their carports are brand new Ambassadors, chrome gleaming under protective sheets, bonnet insignia sheathed in little leather pouches.

During business hours this side of town is jammed with cycles, bullock carts and honking buses. At the 'Hackney Carriage Stand' horse-drawn rickshaws queue for business, little two-wheeled covered carriages which trot up and down at an alarming pace carrying veiled Muslim ladies home with their shopping, or ferrying the pot-bellied moneylender, dabbing his brow, to a rendezvous with some insolvent client. On the corner with Bazaar Street is the pan man, cross-legged at his table, absorbed in his ritual. Like an alchemist with his metal tray and cutting block, his silver tins and blades, he concocts explosive mixtures of powdered white lime paste, betel slivers, tobacco, cloves and cardamom. These he rolls up in the fleshy green betel leaves in the bucket of cold water at his feet to make a mouthwatering (and mildly narcotic) digestive. Like all good pan men he knows the individual tastes of all his regulars as they stop by his stand for a chat on the way home after work.

If you are heading further afield, the bus and train stations are down in the new part of town, east of the temple. Here, close to the statue of Mahatma Gandhi, are the cinemas, packed every night even at the late show. There are flower sellers, sweet vendors and *dosa* stalls, and a rank of black and yellow auto-rickshaws, little two-stroke three-wheelers which buzz around the dusty streets like cross bumble-bees. All day and most of the night the area round the bus stand is a hive of activity as the long-distance coaches roar in, plying between Madras and the deep south, and battered and windowless country buses lurch out to pound the lanes of the hinterland. Hang around here for a while and you meet the people who always seem to be on the move in India, whatever the hour: families coming home for the Diwali festival, itinerant holy men and women wandering between the great shrines and little bundles of people clutching their life's belongings, heading who knows where.

Beyond the perimeter wall of the bus stand is the canal which circles the town; on its banks live the poorest people, in thatched shanties, close by the steps under the bridge. It is dry for most of the year here, but perilously close to the flood when the monsoon comes and the water begins to rise. These people live by recycling everyone else's throw-outs: glass, plastic bags, bottle tops, bits of metal. Unlike Western society, nothing is ever wasted here, everything finds a new use, a new life. Their self-contained little world lies on the edge of Chidambaram. Cross the canal bridge and you soon reach the town limits. Before you the road snakes off over the tracks toward Annamalai University, past the long sun-baked platforms of the railway station, where a smudge of smoke hangs in the air from the 1230 Chingleput Passenger.

Just passing through, as most do, you might get the impression the town is dirty, inefficient and chaotic; corrupt even. (I have heard many Indian visitors, north Indians, overseas Tamils, say as much.) But once you have stayed in it for a while, you get to feel something of its real character, to discern its unseen patterns and hidden charms. Chidambaram is a small place, but bursting with life and vitality. In it there is an intricate, many-layered order which works in a way one feels no Western town ever could. At any time of day or night, for example, you can find hot tea, food and shelter. At any time you can travel on to another destination. Nothing is standardized, and hence nothing is ever monotonous. And for all the great variety of people, jobs, religions and castes, there is not the huge disparity in wealth and condition you find in the great northern cities of India, where the poverty is desperate and seemingly irredeemable. The man who bags bottle tops by the canal bridge has his own independence and economic being, and, no less than the tax collector and the town archaeologist, his own outlook and philosophy.

And in the centre, dominating the skyline and visible from everywhere in town, there is the temple; symbol of an older order, social, economic and psychological. The temple was the meeting place of earth and heaven, focus of a social and moral system which for thousands of years determined how people were born, lived, procreated and died. Now all around it the order is shifting: in the rich houses in the bazaar, in the huts by the canal, in the Muslim and Harijan villages in the hinterland. For the small-town *mafiosi*, the smugglers of gold, spices and videos; for the pan man and the moneylender; for the temple priests; and for Mala and her children, it is all changing day by day.

I

Mala

We first met Mala at the time of the autumn monsoon. We were heading slowly down the Cavery valley to Chidambaram, simply in order to see the temple. It is one of the greatest shrines in India, and is famous right across Asia wherever Hinduism has taken root. That first night, though, when we got off the slow train from Tanjore, everything appeared hazy and indistinct. A fog seemed to have enveloped the town, the aftermath of a typhoon in the Bay of Bengal. It was festival eve and fireworks thumped and cracked in the gloom as we walked past the bus stand; acrid smoke hung in the air like a tropical bonfire night. In the darkness of an unfamiliar place we had no bearings and were scarcely aware of what we saw, which made what followed seem all the more strange and exciting.

Eventually the pyramids of the temple towers reared up black against the cloud-filled night sky. We passed under a massive stone gate, carved with the poses of the sacred dance which announced the domain of Nataraja. Inside we found ourselves in a vast enclosure with columned halls and sacred bathing tanks stretching away into the shadows. We crossed the courtyard to where huge silver-studded doors opened into the interior down a granite stairway. At the bottom a forest of columns went off into the darkness; above were livid white neon strips. Camphor burning at the foot of the columns created the illusion that the stone was somehow magically on fire.

It was the eve of Diwali, and crowds of devotees were milling back and forth. From the inner sanctum came the sound of a bell, and then a swirl of drums and the sharp trill of trumpets. What we saw seemed almost to belong to the realms of science fiction. The inner shrines were ringed by a maze of pillared corridors, which that night were thronged with beautiful young men dressed in white, foreheads shaved, their long black shiny hair worn in a tight bun to the left side: these we learned were the Dikshithars, the hereditary priesthood of Chidambaram.

It felt as if we had been transported into another world and time, rather like entering a temple of ancient Greece, the Parthenon, say, or Eleusis, still intact, its altars still burning. The strangeness of it all: the smell of sacrifice, the fiery music, the languid young men with their women's hairdos and darkened eyes, their white loincloths discreetly hemmed in purple and gold. We were struck by the immaculate austerity of their appearance and comportment. Some called us over to talk. In answer to our questions, they readily explained: 'God is half-man, half-woman, and in token of this we wear our hair this way.'

In the very centre of the shrine was a strange building, unlike almost any other shrine in India. Standing inside a cloistered courtyard was a little hall on a raised stone plinth surrounded by a portico of polished black stone columns. Its roof was covered with thousands of gilded tiles, bowed in shape like the traditional thatched roof of peasant houses and shrines we had seen from the train all along the Cavery valley. The front of this structure was closed by folding doors of grimy beaten silver behind which the priests prepared their rituals. Further back was an inner chamber, but all we could glimpse of this was the glint of bronze and gold in the fire of puja lamps. Below the hall at the front of the crowd stood a chubby, bare-chested man in a long loincloth and with a briefcase under his arm. He was singing, not in Sanskrit as you would expect in any Brahminical temple in India, but in Tamil: quietly, almost as if to himself, more Quaker introspection than Roman chant. Around him everyone stood or sat rapt, listening to his soft quavering baritone – a honeyed voice, as the Tamils say (the very name of their language is said to mean 'sweet, proper, speech').

When the puja started, the congregation faced this tiny chamber. Two huge bells were rung; one was cracked and began to emit a continuous high-pitched howl as the noise grew. Behind us two drummers and a trumpeter worked up to a frenzy. Craning above the crowd from the back we could just make out the puja lamps but little else. I had been in Tamil temples before, but it was hard to see what was going on, so I edged through the crowd to the front of the platform near the singer. It was then that Mala detached herself from her women friends and came down to touch my arm. 'This is the Chit Sabha, the golden hall of Nataraja, the place of his sacred dance. Lord Nataraja is here; he is very beautiful,' she said.

She was small, quiet, dark. (How large, white and noisy I felt.) I had to bend to speak or to listen to her. In the end we sat together under one of the columns. She had black hair severely parted and brushed back in a long plait twined with white jasmine. She had the kindest smile, lovely eyes and an open oval face which would cheerily crease into a laugh. She wore a light blue bodice which left her stomach bare and a thin, patterned sari striped in lilac which draped over her left shoulder and was gathered at the waist.

She was quietly spoken, frail seemingly, but resolute. She spoke some English, and understood a lot more. This was unusual for her caste, but we soon discovered she was an unusual woman altogether. What stood out immediately was her shining enthusiasm for her own tradition, an absolute belief in its beauty, richness and enduring value. And her desire to share it with us.

When the puja was over I asked her about the man with the briefcase; he turned out to be her neighbour and she introduced us to him: 'He is an *oduvar*, one of the traditional poets of Tamilian lands. The name means "he who sings". These are secular people, non-Brahmins from the lower class of people. In them there is an unbroken line back to the saints. It is they alone who sing the saints' songs in the temples, songs from over a thousand years ago. They sing in Tamilian, here, and in other places, such as Sirkali, and Mylapore in Madras, where they still flourish.'

He was sweet-mannered and self-effacing, still clutching his briefcase. (During the day he was a clerk in a local government office.) He explained that the hereditary reciters of the Tamil hymns have handed down the saints' songs, usually within the family, in living chains of transmission from ancient times, an oral tradition which is specifically not Brahminical but Tamil. After a short while he excused himself – his dinner would be ready – and touching his palms lightly together, he bowed his head, turned and departed.

Eventually the crowd cleared, then Mala motioned us to follow her up the steps into the sanctum. Unlike many Hindu temples, this was open to all, of whatever caste or creed. Inside, a little knot of people quietly leaned on the rail, meditating or simply staring into space.

There in the heart of the mysterious little hall, framed by shimmering oil-lamps, was displayed the chief image of the temple. Not, as is the case in most other Siva temples, the linga, the phallic stone of the god, but a large ancient bronze of Siva in his ring of fire as Nataraja, 'Lord of the Dance'. His smiling features were almost invisible beneath the garlands of fresh flowers he receives every day and the strings of precious jewels given by wealthy devotees. But we could see it was the classic image, the four arms holding the fire and the drum, pointing to the demon of ignorance crushed beneath his feet and making the gesture of 'fear not'. These symbolize his attributes, Mala explained: creation in the rhythm of the drum and destruction in the fire; the inevitable nature of existence; the meaning of creation. His smile reassures the devotee; even when he excites fear, Siva is never far from playfulness. Here the central metaphor of spiritual experience is not crucifixion, but a dance. A quintessentially Tamilian idea;

around it, over the last thousand years or so, their culture has spun a marvellously intricate web of poetry, art and philosophy which has given endless solace and delight.

We peered through a lattice of silverwork into the inner room where none but the officiating priests may go, the 'little hall' sung by the saints over many centuries; a place already celebrated when the poet saint Appar came here and sang its fame in about AD 650. By then its legend was fixed: the primeval forest of *tillai* trees, abode of tigers, where a weird *rishi* (ascetic) was granted the boon of seeing the Dance of Siva. This ancient and venerated core was not demolished; in the twelfth century the vast halls of the Cholan age were built around it. On this spot, according to Tamil tradition, Siva's dance took place – and takes place forever, to those who can see it.

At the side of the statue of Nataraja was a curtain sewn with golden *vilva* leaves.

'What is behind?' I asked.

'Nothing,' she said. 'It is empty.'

'Why?'

'They say this is the secret of Chidambaram. It means that god is nowhere. Only in the human heart.' She smiled.

We left the shrine together. At the gate, as we put on our shoes, Mala stopped. Next day, she said, was Diwali, a great festival, and there would be many important pujas to see, many beautiful and significant rituals. She would show us. 'Come to my house for tiffin at 7a.m. No later,' she said firmly.

First meetings often fix relationships, and this felt like a momentous meeting: a door opening. She was the kind of person you meet in Tamil stories, the holy stranger, the wandering mendicant, the kindly householder who appears out of nowhere to point you in on a new road. It was Mala who initiated us into the traditions of Chidambaram and encouraged our adventures on the Tamil way.

★

Early the following morning, as the rain fell, we went to her home for the first time. We took her the traditional Diwali gift of sweets, a sixteen-rupee box from the vendor in VGP Street near the bus stand. When she untied the ribbon she was horrified. 'It is too costly,' she said. It was all we could do to stop her taking them back there and then. She was, we soon learned, not a person who spent unwisely or precipitately; she could afford no frills and she cut her cloth accordingly.

At that time her two sons were living in her father's house, but her four daughters were at home for Diwali, and over breakfast we met them (all of us crammed into that little room). They were handsome, intelligent young women. The youngest, Jaya, was fourteen, bold and spirited, with wonderful eyes; she was learning English at school. Bharati, who was more reflective and serious, was at technical college on the coast at Nagapattinam. Sarasu was doing a degree by correspondence at Annamalai University, a self-assured beauty in a crimson sari. The oldest, Punnidah, who was twenty-three, was more withdrawn and, unlike her sisters, spoke little English. (We had only a few words of Tamil, so we never got to know her so well.) She hovered in the background as we chatted. Mala had raised independent, capable and loving daughters.

All the while her husband sat in the corner on the bed, shoulders hunched. He was a dignified and gentle man, quietly spoken. The loss of his sight must have been a bitter blow for all the family. He had been forced to retire on a small pension; we learned later that Mala had spent 20,000 rupees on an eye specialist in Madras before receiving a definitive no to her hopes of a reprieve. To pay for it she had sold some parcels of inherited land. But we could see that his disaster had left her in a real sense as head of family, taking over the male duties of householder (and this in a society where women – Tamil women – are in any case seen as the driving force, pillars of the house, preservers of tradition). Indeed, although she would never have wished it this way, I wondered whether her husband's loss had in a sense liberated her. For she appeared to be freer than are many westernized women in Madras. If she wished to go travelling, for example, then she would ask family or neighbours to look after him, and she would just go. If she wished to travel alone with a Western man, then she would and, as it happened, no one batted an eyelid.

It was not long before we embarked on our first journeys with her through Tamil Nadu. Usually travelling on local buses, we touched on a pattern of life which is invisible in the tourist guidebooks. As we got to know the family better, I became 'uncle' to the girls (a catch-all honorific for any adult male who is neither immediate blood kin nor a marriage prospect). We followed Jaya's progress in Bharata Natyam, dancing in their bare room, ducking under the washing line as she fiercely stamped out the measures with bangled feet. We sat in Brahmins' houses in Tiruvengadu as they dispensed nostrums for her younger son's 'problems'. We were with her at the time of the death of her 'cousin brother' (Tamils marry within the family), aged thirty-five. 'He was the best car mechanic in Chidambaram,' said a neighbour as we sat comforting the dead man's mother. 'A very generous man who never overcharged.'

Looking back, I realize that we understood very little of what we saw. For quite a while, for example, we never even knew her husband's name, and we eventually noticed that Mala never used it, under any circumstances. Finally Bharati explained: 'In traditional Tamil society you will never hear a wife call her husband by name. Only a westernized woman in Madras will say "my husband" but even she will not call him by his name. Mala refers to her husband simply as "he", in the respectful form. This is the ancient Tamil custom; it is to protect him, for to name him would be inauspicious.'

At the time I did not understand this wariness (which amounts to a taboo) among Tamils against expression of the emotions. It is not that they don't believe in love. On the contrary, almost every aspect of their culture testifies to the overwhelming value they assign to it. But that is precisely the point. It is for just that reason that you will never hear a wife call her man by name, or see a husband and wife indulge in overt affection in public, still less praise each other. That would be to court bad luck. Children, too, need to be protected from the inauspicious, and not only from the evil eye but from the eye of love. New babies, for example, must not be looked at with 'too much love', or overpraised. Bharati said, 'A mother's love is so strong that it must be kept in check; too much can harm a child and too much love tempts fate.' Love is most powerful and can be most cruel – 'even for a demon parting is pain,' it is said. So control of the emotions is a deep cultural trait in a land where auspiciousness is a most fervently sought after, yet a most fragile gift. Never tempt fate. It was another world, which I only very slowly came to understand, even at the simplest level.

2

The Astrologer

One winter we went to stay in Chidambaram for a few weeks. It was the time of the December festival which takes place in hundreds of temples across the south. It is the annual celebration which marks the end of the dark half of the year and the coming of light; the inauspicious time is over. This is the heart of the cool season when mornings are clear and fresh, and the fields soft lilac in the early light. It is a time when outsiders flock into town. Temporary stalls line the streets around the temple; merchants from Maharashtra roll out their bales of cloth, towels, tools, tea sets, toys and trinkets. This is the ancient round of commercial life in rural India with its small-town entertainments. In the temple courtyard you will see hucksters and fortune-tellers; readers of palms, interpreters of the chirping of lizards; wizards with green parakeets which pick out the cards telling your future; traditional medicine men with dried snakes and mummified bits in bottles, and gruesome phials of oily goo. In Bazaar Street an elephant wandered up and down, batting passers-by on the head and collecting rupees for his skinny young keeper. There was even a snake charmer in the fruit market, prodding an old and bored cobra into a semblance of a show.

In East Car Street the marriage hall was given over to commerce for the whole month (there being no marriages during the inauspicious time). It was hung with the wares of travelling cloth traders, ladies' underwear dealers from Lucknow and Bombay, sari salesmen from all over the south, from Kanchi to Trivandrum. Most of them were outsiders, 'I am the only native of Chidambaram selling in all of East Car Street,' said a man standing in front of an Aladdin's cave of shining steel tiffin boxes, *iddly* steamers and *dosa* plates.

The temple priests, the Dikshithars, reckon as many as a quarter of a million people come through the town over the whole month – forty thousand on the big nights – so there is good business to be done. For the priests themselves, festival is a bonanza time. They are unique in India, a hereditary clan who marry endogamously, that is, only within their own kin. One of the last of the independent priesthoods to survive, they have always done things their way. Tenaciously hanging on to their patrimony here, they still administer the great temple by the old rules, even refusing to keep accounts, to the chagrin of the local tax inspector.

They trace their right to administer Nataraja's shrine back to the sixth century AD. Since the sixties they have come under increasing fire from the state's Dravidian nationalist parties with their atheistic, anti-temple and anti-Brahmin manifesto. Many temples have had land and endowments confiscated. But not the Dikshithars. Not long ago they defended their case vigorously in the High Court in Delhi, hiring the best lawyer in India to resist being 'nationalized' under the umbrella of the Hindu Board of Charitable Endowments. Citing their sixth-century foundation legend as the basis to their claim, they won.

They were said to be three thousand strong in ancient times, but today they number about seven hundred, of whom maybe three hundred are working priests who run the temple on a monthly rota. They are famed across the south for their meticulous orthodoxy in the performance of the old rituals; for the special care and sensitivity with which they handle the pujas. For this reason, along with its unique sanctity, the temple is revered across Tamil Nadu, and is still chosen by many Tamils for family rites of passage; indeed even today the visitor may come across an author dedicating the first copy of a new book at Nataraja's feet. For such people, as for Mala, the Lord of the Dance is still the family deity.

Maintaining such a vast and ancient place has become more and more expensive. These days, it is rumoured, the Dikshithars are finding it difficult to make ends meet, and many are starting to supplement their income outside; some, it is said, have left altogether. Their changing fortunes have even been the subject of a gloomy feature in one of the big glossy national magazines. In the New Year festival, however, they earn enough for a good many rainy days. It is a round of grand pujas, with gilded palanquins and flurries of trumpets, a blaze of camphor and gusts of incense on the dawn air. There are processions round the town streets with crowds craning on the rooftops; there are recitals of Carnatic music and religious songs; virtuoso *nagaswaram* – trumpet – and drum duels in the temple courtyard under the night sky.

The stars of the show, the Dikshithars, are even more punctilious than usual over ritual propriety. Basking in their portable neon spotlights, they turn out resplendent in holy ash, every bob and stripe in place, immaculate in fresh white dhotis, their ritual expertise on view for all to see. In the Golden Hall itself they perform every gesture of the flame with more than usual relish, cosseting and primping their divine patron with mirror, brush and fan like androgynous waiters in a celestial hotel. And outside, though the local bus drivers hoot impatiently half the night in streets blocked by silver carriages, the whole town comes together once more as people of all faiths ring in the new in the time-honoured way.

That Christmas we often went round to Mala's house to eat and talk, and to stretch out on the floor with the whole family and snooze when the early afternoon heat was too much to bear. At that time she was trying to finalize the marriage of her oldest daughter Punnidah. By now, as Mala had known us for some years, she treated us a little like family, and she was concerned that we too should do what all good Indian couples did: marry, settle down and have children. It had become a bit of an issue with her: why were we not having children? Especially at our age.

One afternoon she was sitting with Rebecca sifting applications from Punnidah's suitors, solemn-faced engineers from Cuddalore, unsmiling clerks from Mayavaram, all of whom had replied to Mala's advertisement in her caste marriage magazine. Spread out on the floor were their letters, with photo and curriculum vitae attached. Also enclosed were the horoscopes. These, it transpired, were of crucial importance. Mala would never dream of undertaking any important venture, let alone arranging her children's marriages, without consulting an astrologer. She obeys the almanac for all her children's rites of passage, for illness, jobs, even journeys. (Nor is such astrological fatalism confined to traditional people, or to the lower classes. In fact, I know highly educated professional people in Madras who regularly do the same, even for business decisions.)

So the likely son-in-law would immediately have his stars taken to the temple astrologer to be matched with Punnidah's in an exhaustive search of his character and antecedents; any major incompatibility of the horoscopes would be enough to bring the investigation to a halt. The point, Mala explained, was to find a person compatible not only in birth chart, but in temperament and family background, someone kind and good who would have sufficiently assured career prospects to ensure a stable home for the children. Love was not the first priority; love would grow later if the couple recognized the right spark in each other.

The dowry system was still firmly followed in all castes. A 'good' marriage with an engineer or doctor would cost at least a hundred thousand rupees, maybe several hundred thousand. With four daughters it seemed to me a burdensome way of going about things for someone in Mala's position, leaving aside the feelings of her daughters. But she disagrees: 'In your country every other marriage is ending in divorce; this is because of your attitude to love. We do things other way round; here we marry, then get to know and only then fall in love.'

Then, out of the blue, Rebecca asked Mala whether she could

get our horoscopes done too. Would it be possible for her to give our birth dates and times to the astrologer at the temple, in order to see how the Tamils would read our charts? Mala looked across at me, doubtfully. I shrugged my shoulders. It was fine by me. At the time, if you had asked me why, I would have said it was partly just playfulness, partly because we wanted to know more about the way these things are done in Tamil Nadu. I was fascinated by all this, although I had no interest in, or knowledge of, astrology.

Perhaps, though, there was more to the request than that. For don't we all sometimes seek some outside validation for our choice of one action over another? Indeed, liberated as we like to think ourselves, do we not yet in some corner of our sceptical minds invest meaning in imaginal worlds which are beyond the reductions of modern science? Even if it goes against our rationally held beliefs? Irrational, I know, but there it is. At any rate, the readings were done, the astrologer was engaged and we went to Mala's house to meet the Brahmin whom she had asked to interpret our birth charts.

Earlier in the evening there had been a power cut, and Chidambaram was still blacked out. We picked our way down the darkened lane, and were startled by an invisible but very solid cow outside her door. Mala was sitting by oil-lamp light, the priest next to her, mopping his brow. It was stifling hot in the room and the mosquitoes were having a field day. The priest stood up and smiled, pressing the tips of his fingers lightly together in the gesture of greeting. The charts had been drawn up by the temple astrologer in little booklets of thick, creamy-coloured fibrous paper like the school notebooks you buy in the bazaar, with sewn spines and yellow seal impressions in the corners of the cover. Inside were pages of flowery Tamil script written in light blue ink, with square boxes showing the planetary aspects. It soon became clear that we were to be treated as seriously as any Tamil couple contemplating marriage. Mala, though, was concerned that it was all rather late in the day. After all, the horoscopes could reveal some unforeseen incompatibility which might blight the whole thing. This was something you did at the start, not after some years together. Were we having second thoughts?

'Why do this now?' she said: 'You have already been blessed by Lord Nataraja. Look, I just prayed to God and did it, and I've been married for thirty years. Leave it too late and you'll be too old.'

Her husband muttered in Tamil under his breath. They clearly thought something was amiss.

We sat down, and at that moment the power came back on and the fan slowly began to turn a few inches above our heads.

'A good omen!' said the priest with a humorous wink of his eye, waggling his eyebrows. He mopped his glistening brow before beginning. Rajdurai Dikshithar was in early middle age. He had an intelligent and refined face, with a high forehead and neat short hair; he wore a clean white lungi with a purple hem. He spoke good English, but with a rather nervous, rushed delivery which at first made him a little difficult to follow. Brahmins are tolerated rather than loved by the Tamil masses, and as a group the Dikshithars are not universally liked in the town – arrogance and money-grabbing being cited as their main failings – but there were many exceptions, and Rajdurai was one of them.

His story was a rather sad one. Ten or twelve years ago, his wife had died in childbirth. The little girl survived and now lived with her mother's parents; but for Rajdurai, the death of his wife meant he could no longer do puja in the Nataraja temple, for in order to perform the rituals, the priests must be married; the death of one's spouse meant one was no longer auspicious, no longer ritually pure, and these old rules were still zealously maintained by the Dikshithar community. The major source of Rajdurai's earnings had gone. He now lived in his father's house on East Car Street, and those of his parishioners who were fond of him made a point of putting other work his way. He was considered to be a reliable interpreter of horoscopes, and a sympathetic one too, which was no small matter in an interpretative art so finely shaded in its nuances. Mala at any rate trusted and liked him, and usually consulted him on family matters; he was to be her guide over the impending marriage of her daughters. Mala plied us with tea and vegetables fried in batter, and Rajdurai began by perusing the charts for a few moments in silence. Then in Tamil he asked Mala a question about our religion. She replied, 'Christian.' (There was nothing strange in that – Rajdurai's clients include Hindus, Christians and Muslims.)

He started by running down some basics.

'In Tamil Nadu, horoscope is essential for life. Birth, marriage, building a house, buying a wedding sari, starting a new job: for all we make a horoscope. All politicians will consult astrologer before elections. You see, we believe planets are major influence on life. Now, in personal horoscope everyone has natal star. In Tamil astrology the star under which you were born is very important. You both share the same star: Arbitam, the twenty-seventh and last of the important stars to the Tamil astrology.'

He ran through some of the main features of our charts: my sun was very good, Rebecca's moon the same; and our suns and moons were conjunct, which apparently was both extraordinary and very auspicious.

Mala beamed as she scooped rice on to my plate: 'Eat, eat.' (My protestations would invariably be met with: 'You are too thin.')

Rajdurai continued. 'My Mars, and Rebecca's Venus were strong; my Jupiter particularly important. (As in Western astrology, the Tamils see Jupiter as to do with religion, love of knowledge, travel, philosophy, exaltedness, spiritual gnosis.) But most prominent was Rebecca's Saturn, and this was of great concern to Rajdurai.

'Saturn is a great malefic to the Tamils: by nature he is arrogant and ill-omened. His blessings are overwhelming but his wrath can create untold misery. Consequently he is universally worshipped,

though more out of fear than reverence, and he has to be propitiated before all others. At Tirunallar near Karaikkal there is an
ancient Saturn temple which is visited by people from all over
Tamil Nadu, indeed by Tamils from all over south Asia; the
temple is dedicated to Lord Siva but Saturn has a place inside the
outer wall of the temple. Here, the legend says, Saturn was made
powerless when King Nala took refuge with Siva when Saturn
wanted to destroy him. It will be necessary for you to go to him
to make the appropriate offerings.'

Saturn is about hard lessons, hard grind, hard work, obsessive
even; there is a sense with people touched by Saturn that things
can never be relied on to remain good, that happiness is transitory
and that things may always turn against you. All of this was over
my head, but Rebecca, who is a psychologist, follows Carl Jung
in thinking that the symbols of astrology – the sun for example,
the moon, Saturn, the Lion – are so ingrained in us that they have
a meaning which resonates in the unconscious even when formal
religious belief is no more. And of course they are woven into the
archetypal patterns which inform our art and poetry as well as our
religion, whether in the hands of the Tamil Kampan or the
English Shakespeare – and so they are still a means to enchantment,
even if you believe that the fault lies not in our stars but ourselves.

Which is all well and good, of course, but to Mala these are
tangible forces for good and ill that can wreck your life, and
have to be acted on or disregarded at your peril. This is one
dimension of the unseen powers for which she marks out the *kolam*
on her doorstep every morning. And when you have four daughters with back-breaking dowries to pay, and intractable astrological
injunctions to obey, it is easy to see how such invisible forces can
become all too concrete and may conspire against you. For her,
Saturn is nothing if not a real presence.

My lack of earth then became a subject for comment and
amusement.

'Mm. You are all wind,' said Rajdurai, furrowing his brow as a smile hovered on the corner of his lips (the joke is the same in Tamil). 'And fire too. Some water. But no earth.'

'Yes, it's lucky you've got an earthy ascendant: otherwise you'd be completely unrealistic,' Rebecca added.

I had to admit that this sounded not too far from the mark.

'Still, you are a good combination,' Rajdurai continued. 'Very nice. One thing, Michael: in consulting with your wife you must defer to her in everything for final decisions on important matters.' Then he paused. 'You will be having two children.'

'Boys or girls?'

'Both female.'

'You will do much travelling. God will do this for you. Though you may wish to stay in one place. One important warning. Do not take up other people's problems; if you do, the problems will come to you and you may end up in prison. Also, Michael, beware wheeled traffic during this next year.'

He looked up. 'Rebecca, your long-lasting stomach pain – is this now gone?' It was. She had got rid of her ulcer after ten years. (Her sign, Cancer, is held to rule the stomach in Western astrology too.)

'You have government jobs?' (To an Indian this means salaried employment.)

'Not exactly,' I replied, 'though I did once work for the BBC.'

'Whatever, you will be millionaires in ten years' time.'

By now, Mala was getting visibly excited at such positive predictions.

'You are a good combination. Now, there are some things you must do. Michael, for the good of your soul, it would be better if you fasted on Tuesdays and pray to Mars. Take only small food before dawn.'

I decided to take that as optional.

Rajdurai continued, still addressing me: 'But this is the most important thing you will do. Some time in the future you will come back here to Chidambaram to Lord Nataraja and you will make a pilgrimage. Now, there are thousands of holy places in Tamil Nadu. Among them the most famous are 274 temples of Lord Siva which were sung in the hymns of the saints in ancient times. Also there are 108 especially holy places of Lord Vishnu. They are joined by living paths of pilgrimage. Even today there are ordinary people who take a vow to visit all of them. In addition there are many others. For example there are five temples dedicated to the elements of Earth, Wind, Fire, Water and the aetheric. There are eight shrines to the planets and eight holy places where Siva performed his great deeds; there are twenty-two temples in Chola Nadu specially sacred to Siva and seven places where the Lord performed his dance of bliss.' He relished each number like a cricket enthusiast turning in his memory through the almanac of great innings. 'There are also many places sacred to the goddess, who is revered by Tamilians. This is not to mention holy places of the Muslims and Christians which also confer spiritual benefit. Unlike in north India, in Tamil country we do not discriminate against one religion at the expense of another, and members of one religion find benefit in pilgrimage to those of the others.'

Mala interjected to agree. She herself goes with Hindu friends to the Muslim pilgrimage centre at Nagore, where a famous holy man is buried; the Christian shrine of Our Lady at Velankanni is another favourite. She has a Muslim friend and neighbour who takes off her veil and attends the 6.30 puja in the Nataraja temple every day because she finds it beautiful and uplifting, and a nice social event after work. Down here communal relations are not the gloom and doom you might think from the news bulletins.

'A lifetime would not suffice to see all of these places. But in everyone's birth there is a particular journey revealed which one day they must make. A journey special to their own astrological chart. This is the one which you must undertake. Indeed you will undertake.'

I had been nodding off in the soporific heat, baffled by incomprehensible star signs and conjunctions, my mind reeling with aspects I never knew I had, and others I had hoped to keep to myself. Now I found myself craning forward attentively, pen and paper in hand, anxious not to miss a word.

'One day you will come back to Chidambaram to visit Lord Nataraja. Then you will go to a place named Vaithisvarancoil. This is a very beautiful and ancient temple near to Sirkali. Only an hour or so south of here by bus. It is a temple of Lord Siva as God of Healing. It was sung by the Tamil saints of thirteen hundred years ago. Many people resort to this place to be cured of illness or disease. It is very famous among Tamil people. In the summer months people perform their vows by walking there barefoot from hundreds of miles away. There is a sacred tank for bathing, and a holy *neem* tree. Now here at Vaithisvarancoil, near to the sanctum of the Lord, there is also a shrine to Mars. You will do puja there.

'Next you will journey to the sea coast, to Karaikkal, which was formerly, like Pondicherry, a French possession in India. Here there is the temple to Lord Siva at Tirunallar which I have mentioned. Before you go into the sanctum, on the right-hand side, there is the famous shrine to Saturn. This is very important for you to visit. It is the most celebrated shrine to Saturn in India. Very many people go to this place, even Indian people from abroad. The lord here is very powerful and not to be disregarded.

'There are many other places which might be beneficial on your journey. On the way by bus from Sirkali to Karaikkal is a famous shrine at Tirukkadiyur. This is where Lord Siva overcame Yama Dharmaraja, the god of death, the keeper of the life span of each human being. Tamils consider it must be visited by every pilgrim in his lifetime. It is a huge place, and probably one of the best in the south for artistic and sculptural beauty. The goddess here too is very popular among the Tamil people.

'Then go inland from the sea coast up the Cavery river to Suryanarcoil near Kumbakonam. This is the only temple to the sun in south India – very popular. Here all the planets can be worshipped together; and you will see Jupiter is standing opposite the sun as his guru. This is a small temple but very beautiful, deep in the forests close to the river, and many of the most famous places in Chola Nadu are close by: Tiruvalanjuli, Saktimuttam, Tiruvidaimarudur, Tiruvavaduturai, Tiruvilimilalai. Very lovely places.'

Lovely-sounding places too. Their names rolled off his tongue like a magical incantation. I was already dreaming of Tiruvidai-marudur.

'Several days might be profitably spent there. Then you should journey south – there are many convenient buses. Visit the goddess Minakshi at Madurai. She is most beneficial to couples desirous of children, and she will bless your marriage and your forthcoming daughters. Her temple is one of the most magnificent in all India. Going southwards still you will come to the mountains bordering Kerala. Here there are also many famous places. One is called Courtallam, which is also sacred to Nataraja, close by five sacred waterfalls. In July these waters are at their most delightful; but also in this present season of the monsoon in October and November. Bathing here is most beneficial to the mind and the body. Indeed this place was a very popular health resort among English types during the British times.

'From there you should go to Cape Comorin, which is the very tip of India. Here the three oceans meet, and the sunrise and moon set can be seen together simultaneously over the same sea. Here is the ancient temple of the virgin goddess, and you should bathe there, taking a dip in the ocean. But your journey should conclude by going to Tiruchendur. This you have to do. For Jupiter. It is in your birth signs and you will return to do this. Others may be optional, but these you will do: Chidambaram, Vaithisvarancoil, Tirunallar, Suryanarcoil, Madurai and Tiruchendur. This is your journey.'

He paused to sip tea from a small metal cup. I pulled a map

from my bag. At a guess it was a round trip of nearly a thousand miles: off the beaten track as far as the tourist trail was concerned, but most of it on well-frequented bus routes – not surprisingly, as all the places were on religious itineraries which must be travelled by thousands of pilgrims every day, although invisible to Western tourist guidebooks. It seemed a wonderful idea. To be given a journey special to oneself, which one had to do. From that moment, the journey to Tiruchendur took on a life of its own in my imagination, and I resolved there and then that, fortune permitting, I would return one day to Tamil Nadu and do it.

'What is there at Tiruchendur?

'It is a most beautiful temple far to the south of here, standing right on the seashore on the coast opposite Sri Lanka. It is one of the six abodes of Lord Murugan, the son of Lord Siva, who is most beloved of Tamil people. It is run by an ancient community of Brahmin priests, who resemble the Dikshithars who serve Lord Nataraja here in Chidambaram. There is a shrine to Jupiter, where you should pray after bathing in the sea and having *darshan* of Lord Murugan. There you will find what you are looking for.'

(What was I looking for?)

'It is a most happy and blessed thing to do, and many good things will come of it, especially if you practise some kind of fasting or austerity while you do it. Many good things will come of it, even if you do not know them at the time. The full benefits of such pilgrimages often only become clear later. Whether Hindu, Christian or Muslim, this is the same I think.'

I said I wasn't really sure at this point in my life that I came into any of those categories.

He smiled and smoothed his lungi down over his knees.

'No matter. It is important to be open-minded, that is all. A good atheist will also draw nourishment from such a trip! The point, as the saints say, is not temples or idols or holy baths, but what you carry with you in your heart.'

Mala came out of the kitchen and spoke with him in Tamil for a moment. For her it was still important that the whole thing be done in the right way, that the rituals be performed 'correctly', a word she emphasized with a vigorous shake of the head. The doing was all. It didn't matter that I wasn't a caste Hindu. But it would be pointless if I didn't do it right. And for traditional Tamils, like her caste, doing it right was some task, for literally every action was loaded with significance. Even the timing of a journey must be auspicious, and even a Christian was not advised to take the Dakshinapath – the route south – in the wrong season or on the wrong day. And of course Mala believed absolutely in the efficacy of the bathing and the pujas. I saw that this adventure could get very complicated.

Rajdurai turned back to us: 'But returning to the purpose of our meeting, please be assured you are a fine combination, a good pair, and the signs for your marriage are auspicious. As for children, as it says in the *Kural*, the ancient Tamil book of wisdom: "Of all the good things on this earth, there is no finer gift than to have children who are able to learn the lessons needful for life." '

He smiled. 'Any questions?'

'Any doubts?' I said.

'You must always remember Saturn.'

We sat on the floor to eat our plates of rice and *sambhar* while he talked to Mala about other matters; her continuing worries about her youngest son, the planned marriage of her oldest daughter. At last he rose to go. We stayed for a little longer while Rebecca tried on a skirt which had been sewn by Mala's oldest daughter Punnidah. Punnidah hovered in the shadows and said nothing, only a shy smile, Cinderella-like. Then towards midnight we walked back down the lane in the fitful glow of the street lamps as dogs barked and scuffled, and the neighbour's cow still patiently turned over the rubbish in the drainage ditch hoping to find some scrap of food. At the corner of the lane, behind the locked grille of the shrine to Ganesh, an oil-lamp flickered on the broken tusk and the jolly smile which brings good luck at the start of all adventures.

Part Two

THE SEASON OF RAINS

It was four years before I returned to India. Our two children duly arrived, both daughters, just as Rajdurai Dikshithar had said, and inevitably other priorities took over. I continued to write to Mala and her family, exchanging news at Christmas and Diwali. In the interim, Punnidah finally got married to a young engineer from Tirukaddiyur, and they moved to the industrial city of Coimbatore in the north of Tamil Nadu. For us for the moment there seemed little prospect of an early return to the south. We felt our children were too young to be subjected to the vagaries of Chidambaram's water supply and the cooking at the Hotel Tamil Nadu, let alone the danger of mosquito-borne diseases out in the countryside.

Not long before our firstborn's first birthday, Mala wrote asking us to go to celebrate the occasion in her house. 'I have prayed to Lord Nataraja for her long life and happiness,' she wrote. 'I would like to have her first birthday celebrations in India in my house. We will do ceremony of putting on her earring at Vaithisvarancoil temple.'

Life is constantly fraught with dangers in traditional Tamil society. On any station bookstall or bus stand you can pick up booklets which enumerate the dangerous times and psychic perils for the first sixteen years of life, starting with day one and going month by month and year by year right up to maturity. But passing the first year is the major hurdle – perhaps because in the old days so many poor children never made it that far. Tamil families still make much of it. It is not just a matter, as with us, of the naming. There is also the first cutting of the hair, the first feeding with cow's milk, the first seeing of the sun and moon, the seeing of the first cow, the first giving of solid food (rice): all these are accompanied by special rituals. Then, on the first birthday (or more precisely on an auspicious day under her natal star around the time of the first anniversary), the child is ceremonially bathed, given new clothes and an earring; the proper ceremonies are performed for long life, good health and success.

'So when she is one year old, you must come!' Mala's letter ended. 'I hope very much to see her very soon, to watch her play in my house and hear her speak and sing. She is my first grand-daughter! We are awaiting news of your arrival anxiously. Please write to me the date and I will come to the airport in Madras. Yours affectionately.'

I was touched more than I can say by her open-hearted efforts to coopt us into her world, but we declined her invitation; we were unduly cautious, I see now, but we feared our unruly one-year-old could only get into trouble in Chidambaram's dusty streets.

Then, a year later, Mala wrote saying that Sarasu was hoping to marry before the end of the year, if a suitable match could be made. The marriage was provisionally set for November. I took the chance of a short break and flew to India with wedding presents, photographs and letters, intending only to stay in Chidambaram for two or three weeks. After an overnight stop in Bombay, I reached Madras on a mid-October afternoon. It was a balmy end-of-summer day and the city was bathed in golden sunlight and saturating heat as I took a taxi from the airport to the city centre. On the hot leather back seat of the Ambassador, the sweat ran down my arms and my shirt was soon as wet as a dishcloth. 'The monsoon will be coming shortly,' said the driver. 'There have been water shortages everywhere this summer. Everywhere is so dry, tanks are empty and people are becoming desperate: everyone now is waiting for the first signs of rain.'

3

Madras

There had been big changes even in four years. After Rajiv Gandhi's assassination here in Tamil Nadu, in 1991, the new government had set out to put an end to more than forty years of Nehru's socialism, the creed on which independent India had been founded. Ironically the prime minister, Rao, was himself of the Nehru generation: an old literary figure, translator of Telugu poetry; a godman who had no qualms about being seen in the press worshipping at Tirupati before a political campaign in the south. At first tentatively, now with growing speed, this unlikely figure had inaugurated massive changes, loosening the bonds of protectionism which had been in place in the economy since Independence. And with that there had come a dramatic and perceptible acceleration in the erosion of traditional culture in India. Everywhere the élites and the growing middle class were consciously rejecting the old ways which had sustained – and oppressed – society since long before there was such a thing as India.

You could see the signs everywhere. Once a city of gardens and low rise, Madras was booming. Huge new buildings were being thrown up along Mount Road; tower blocks, offices, car showrooms, even fast-food restaurants. At the junction with Harris Road a massive new emblem of the city, Tarapore Towers, stood over the choking traffic, the pavements lined with huge, hand-painted movie hoardings. Old landmarks were going; a new concrete-and-glass Spencer Plaza was rising next to the red-brick fragment of Victorian Gothic which was all that remained of the famous store. It was comforting to see the pretty arcade of Higginbotham's Bookshop, founded in 1844 and still going strong.

I stayed in a lane round the back of Ellis Road, a bustling down-at-heel neighbourhood, in an old courtyard house which had once belonged to a wealthy Muslim merchant. 'His harem place,' said the desk boy; if so, he was a man of regal energy, for there were dozens of rooms clustered round three delightful courtyards full of potted plants and luxuriant banana trees; mine was a bare loggia on the roof terrace which overlooked a bone-dry water tank.

It felt like the same civilized place, though. Madrasis proudly and rightly see themselves as guardians of their southern culture. An easy place too; although deep in the tropics, the city is never hit by the ferocious heat you get in the northern plains. For much of the year it basks in sunshine, but it is always cooled by the sea breezes from the long town beach, the Marina. There in the evening Madrasis take a stroll in the golden hour, stopping at little wheeled carts selling spicy peas, roasted nuts and other delights cooked over charcoal. They stand dipping their toes or just watching the rollers as the wind whips up the edges of their saris. Thousands of people of all ages, and a good few ribby, long-horned cows too, simply sitting or standing as the waves crash and the sun goes down. On the shore there is a monument to Anna-durai, the Dravidian nationalist who delivered Tamil Nadu its first DMK government when Nehru's Congress Party was kicked out in 1967; this was the beginning of the state's proletarian revolution. Here too is the memorial to MGR, the film-star chief minister who died in 1987: 'People here have now given their verdict on behalf of MGR's co-star Miss Jayalalitha as the new chief minister,' said my Tamil friend. 'She will be another Iron Lady.' He smiled. 'If they cannot be gods, the Tamils at least like their leaders to be stars.'

★

Around six I took an auto-rickshaw to book a ticket for my journey at Egmore Station, the terminus for trains to the deep south. It is a little ritual I always like to do the night before setting off south. Egmore is a crowded quarter of cheap hotels and all-night food stands, huddles of shanties along the line. Across the tracks is the unkempt graveyard of St Andrew's Kirk, whose spire rises over the station. When it was built in 1820 this was the 'Queen of Scottish churches in the east', 'the most magnificent edifice in Hindustan'. It is still a lovely building, made, like the temples, from Madras *chunam*, a hard white lime stucco which gives a polish of finest marble. Inside, supported by a ring of white Doric columns, is a sky-blue dome painted with the constellations which can be viewed over Scotland, 'so the devout kneeling in prayer could imagine themselves under their native skies'.

It was a typical early evening at Egmore, a good place to savour the beginning of a journey. My shirt was still damp with the lingering heat of the day. Thousands of people were sitting every-where on the platforms, surrounded by their belongings, bedrolls and cooking gear, waiting for the night trains, the women in brightly coloured saris, kids asleep across their laps, men in cotton shirts and lungis. On the TV monitors above them old film musicals jangled away. Picking their way through the crowds food vendors were calling out '*vadai, vadai*'. Alongside the car-riages, stalls were selling fruit, nuts, biscuits and water for the journey. An old woman, still athletic and willowy, walked lightly past me on bare feet, wearing a wide-brimmed straw hat and carrying a big basket overflowing with jasmine, which women buy to tie in their hair. It is said that no culture loves flowers as much as the Tamils. (You can see it in their poetry too: in the Tamil Odes, one poet manages a minor botanical *tour de force*, naming ninety-nine different kinds of flowers in a single poem.) After the woman had passed, the platform was left for a while with the lingering fragrance of jasmine.

The station's big gloomy interior is held up by rows of cast-iron columns rather like St Pancras in London, but on reflection more like the hall of a southern temple – an impression heightened by the smell of incense and flowers. Through an open doorway in the line inspector's office is a huge old framed print of the god Venkateshwara, festooned with shrivelled braids of the morning's marigolds. (Venkateshwara is the bringer of money: his is reputedly the single richest shrine in the world.) The inspector puts down the phone, rises and comes out, clipboard in hand; on his forehead are three vertical stripes of sandalwood paste and vermilion. Here in the south, even in a station, you never quite lose the sense of the presence of the divine.

On the departures board are the the Quilon Mail and the Lalgudi Passenger. The Rock Fort Express is leaving for Trichy at nine. The Rameshwaram Express has just gone, and will arrive at the island tomorrow afternoon, but there's still the slow train if you have the time – twenty-four hours and 118 stations! Travel here has a different rhythm and different pace. I picked up a timetable from the ticket office, a two-hundred-page book for 7 rupees. There are sections telling you how to order bedrolls and 'non-veg food' up the line. (Vegetarianism is strong in Tamil Nadu; places serving meat usually specify. They are often still called 'military', a hangover from British days.) The timetable is a complete travel guide: it carries adverts for Ayurvedic doctors ('handy for Tirur station'); bookshops ('Public depend on Higginbothams Ltd') and pilgrim hotels, pages of them ('World-famous A/c restaurant . . . homely food and princely treatment . . . close to holy Mahamaham tank'). There's even a form 'for lodging complaint in case of robbery or dacoity in running trains'. And there, on page 128, is what the timetable in an uncharacteristic moment of restraint calls Paradise on Earth, 'the seat of the grand conception of the Cosmic Dance, the noblest image of God and the peak of Hindu art': Chidambaram.

Clutching my precious ticket I walked back to Ellis Road along the canal, past the sleepers on the street submerging in the rumbustious street life as night came on. Along Mount Road the street sellers were out with the evening crowds, spreading their wares on cloths along the pavement: antiquated clockwork parts, medieval-looking door locks, coloured apothecary's bottles, pornographic pictures, cheap watches from Hong Kong, city maps, magazines, shoes made out of strips of tyre rubber. At little wooden cubicles with drop-down fronts the owners sit, preparing pan, selling biscuits and matches, or offering to repair anything mechanical ('We undertake tinkering'). At the entrance to an alley, in a ring of oil-lamps, a mongoose straining on a leash prepared to fight a drugged cobra, while his owner took five-rupee bets. Further on, the crowds poured into a cinema to see the latest hit by the Tamil star Ragini Kanth. (Madras is now the hub of the biggest film industry in the world.)

Outside Higginbotham's Bookshop are some of the permanent denizens of this part of Mount Road: two beggers, a mother and her daughter. The mother has lost the fingers of one hand through leprosy and has plied this broken bit of pavement for years. And close by, outside the latest fast-food house, with its uniformed door-keepers and rows of Ambassador cars, there is a Saiva holy man who has also been here for years in between his journeys north and south. He is almost bald now, with an ash-striped forehead, his beard white. He has a saffron wrap, a cloth bag, an old umbrella, an iron trident and a bowl. A figure from a different age, from another history, he sits murmuring an old song over and over again: 'He is always hard to find ... but you will find him in a good heart.' Above him is a thirty-feet-high, hand-painted cut-out of Arnold Schwarzenegger as The Terminator. 'Non-stop excitement!' says the caption. 'He's here. The screen's greatest action hero.'

That evening I took a taxi down Radakrishnan Road to Mylapore for a meal with friends. Prithvi is a journalist; Ashvin a business-man; they have a nice unpretentious house in a leafy suburb bristling with wrought-iron gates, security guards and imported

Maruti cars. It is so pleasant, in fact, so leafy, ordered, and clean, so far removed from the shanties along the city's stinking central canal, that if you narrow your eyes you could almost be in retirement land in Brighton. Until, that is, you notice the long-horned white cow on the corner or the old sadhu with his trident walking doggedly along some ancient Tamil songline through what is for him invisible modernity.

Their big main room is sparsely furnished with divans and steel-framed chairs; there is modern abstract art on the walls, a tribal rug under a glass coffee table. On the sideboard a little Nataraja. A fan turns in the ceiling. Ashvin and Prithvi have two children, a boy aged fourteen and a girl of nine. They also have a cook cum housekeeper. Prithvi is beautiful; she wears winter worsteds at the moment, in autumnal browns and reds, and the finest Kanchi silk in the summer. She has long loose black hair and a pale face. She can be frosty – she is an intimidating intelligence – but she has devastating charm when she wishes. A dark languid beauty with an alluring hint of melancholy, she floats across the room tall and erect. When she looks at you with her big eyes over the table she resembles no one more than those airbrushed faces of goddesses you see on the pilgrim stalls. It is hard not to be in her thrall; especially, one imagines, for Ashvin, who is a gentle and good-natured man, and comes over as reasonableness personified.

When I arrived, the conversation was on the usual Madras hassles: the long drought and the vanishing water lorry, the unpredictable electricity supply.

'Current is so variable; bulbs keep exploding. Oh, Ash, I do wish you would sort it out with the Electricity Board. They need to come and check it all out; I told you to do it last week.'

The lights wavered again and we all waited with bated breath until the bulb did indeed explode, showering the polished tile floor with shards of glass. Roused to action, Prithvi humphed, seized the phone and laid into a trembling minion at customer complaints. Letting it all wash over him, Ash continued serving beers. Everyone, he said, was excited about the changes which had already come about within two years of Rajiv Gandhi's death; in particular, Rao's government's loosening of the restrictions of forty years of protectionism.

'The free market is coming to India now – the only way forward – advance the life of the people. We are potentially the biggest market in Asia.'

Their friend Bhima, who is an old-style lefty, was unconvinced. 'Congress government had great achievements: a dramatic fall in infant mortality, nationwide provision of electricity, the huge rise in the middle class – nearly 40 per cent of the population. But what bothers me now is the fear that unfettered capitalism will ride roughshod over the five hundred million poor who live in dire poverty. They will not share in this improvement once we abandon the socialist ethic. I fear the gap between them and the rich will grow only wider.'

Still hanging on for the local manager, Prithvi shook her head. 'Key is economic advancement. The free market is the only way to lift people.' She put down the phone. 'I just wish he would go further and faster.'

'Frankly,' said Ashvin, 'I think the biggest worry at the moment is the Muslim–Hindu question: there is a distinct smell of burning in the air.'

This was the time when the Hindu fundamentalist party, the BJP, was threatening to 'reclaim' the sites of Hindu temples allegedly replaced by mosques in the Middle Ages; in north India the Ayodhya mosque, the legendary birthplace of Rama, was already a battleground.

'I fear for the future: there is trouble brewing and the prime minister is not handling it. These communal issues are being exploited by unscrupulous politicians just for political gain. We brought up our kids not to be aware of it. The success of the BJP is to bring it to the fore. Thankfully this is not such an issue down here, where Hindu–Muslim relations have always been peaceful.

'That said,' he added, 'it seems to me that the India we grew up with, the secular India of Nehru and Gandhi, is now over. And a different India is emerging. Less likeable, sure; more Indian maybe.'

Tamil Nadu has had its own conflicts over myth and history. Not as explosive perhaps as in the north, but still tumultuous. The great issue here has been the Tamil nationalist or Dravidian movement which has dominated the state since Independence. It started back in the twenties as the Self Respect Movement: asserting that caste and Brahmins and Sanskrit were alien elements in the south, and that northerners had discriminated against the dark-skinned southerners. There was a pure 'Tamil' culture, it was claimed, which could still be recovered by rejecting these intrusions from the north.

At one period Dravidian political independence was seriously mooted among the reformers. Most prominent of these was E.V. Ramaswami Naicker, or 'Periyar' (the great prophet), a rotund iconoclast, who died in 1973 aged nearly one hundred. In 1947, as Indian Independence loomed, Naicker wrote in the *Hindu* newspaper warning the south 'not to replace the domination of the British by the Aryans in Delhi', and calling for an independent Dravidistan. That never came about; nor in the eyes of most Tamils was it ever likely. But the reformers did not let up in their fierce agitation against traditional Brahminical culture in the south. Naicker even publicly burned the *Ramayana* on the Marina beach, saying that the story of Rama's conquest of Sri Lanka was merely a parable of the Aryan domination of the south.

Naicker was above all unremitting in his railings against the privileges enjoyed by Brahmins – not only temple priests like the Dikshithars, but Brahmins like Ashvin and Prithvi. In his most vitriolic speeches he even called for the killing of Brahmins. Historically, of course, the Brahmins had been top of the caste system. Though not necessarily the best off economically, they were supported by great tracts of land across the south in the form of temple endowments. Also, they were the specialists in literacy. Hence, not surprisingly, they had done well under the British, who needed their skills to administer the empire. But in the south the tide turned against them long before Independence. Later, when Congress was voted out in 1967, a wind of change blew through Tamil Nadu as the lower castes began to exert themselves: a revolt against a millennium or two of history. Suddenly Brahmins found the boot was on the other foot: discrimination against them, including wholesale seizure of temple lands and treasures. In a few decades the old world which been inherited from ancient times had been turned upside down.

'We've now had forty years of anti-Brahmin politics by the DMK parties down here,' said Ashvin. 'Especially since DMK won in 1967. We've had university and employment quotas since then. The crazy thing is, we have brought the children up not to consider themselves Brahmins. Now the quota system which guarantees places for the lower castes has put terrible pressure on them – only the very top marks can get them a place in university. And, to cap it all, with the fundamentalists on the march, our kids come back from school saying, 'I'm a Brahmin, after all. Why can't I say I am proud to be a Brahmin?'

They were amused by my return to Chidambaram; by my affection for its small-town atmosphere; by my attachment to its traditions. Though Brahmins, Prithvi and Ashvin simply do not identify with this world. They are secular, modern people, the product of Nehru's India. Their friend Bhima took a gentle dig at me: 'Western people are very naïve about Indian religion. Most of these sadhus are fakes; they represent a dying culture which has long ceased to be creative. It can only imitate its own past in a debased form. When the TV revolution hits the villages, communications will transform and democratize the country. This has been the biggest bar to progress; we are an ancient land, but we are still a juvenile nation.'

He bearded me with a twinkle: 'Mark my words, Michael, all this religious mumbo-jumbo, myths and epics – India will be the least religious country in the world ten years or so from now!'

'Oh, come off it,' said the other guest, Kamala, a classical dancer. 'You're just pulling his leg now.'

'Not at all. I believe it; and the sooner the better.'

'But surely not in the south?' Kamala said.

'Well, maybe not the south,' he conceded.

Kamala went on, 'We Tamilians have always been more success- ful at preserving our culture. There is no reason why the best of traditional cultures cannot coexist in the modern world. India has always been good at taking what she wants of the outside and discarding the rest. Look at Prithvi, she's the model of a modern Indian career woman. Flies off to Washington at the drop of a hat. But she is still a traditional Tamil in some aspects of her life. She still sees her astrologer for major decisions, don't you?'

'Well, it's partly just a bit of fun,' said Prithvi, pulling a face. 'Though Ashvin did not change his job this October because the astrologer said not.'

'More beer?' said Ashvin, coming in with a tray from the kitchen.

Kamala continued, 'And take Ashvin here. Here he is, born a Brahmin but he brings his children up as good secular Indians, don't you, Ash? Years ago he put his Brahmin's thread in a drawer.' The six-string thread is supposed to be worn from puberty to death by Brahmin men.) 'Look at him, he drinks beer. You eat meat too, don't you, Ash?'

He spluttered.

'He's never been down south, have you, Ash?'

'No. Look, you are either modern or traditional. We are secular Indians; we are Salman Rushdie's *Midnight's Children*. We have tasted the fruit. We cannot go back. Sad, but there it is.'

Kamala disagreed. 'Where's the poetry in your soul, Ashvin? Discover your past. Go down and spend a few days by the Cavery.'

Everyone laughed – Kamala was on her hobby-horse.

'No, no, really,' she went on. One day you should take a trip down there; take a trip to Tiruvidaimarudur.'

'Actually,' said Prithvi, 'it's funny, but Ashvin said something about all this recently. He found his Brahmin's string in the drawer the other day. Tell them what you said, Ash.'

'It's true,' said Ashvin.' I was thinking again about my Brahmin's thread and the rituals of the twice born. It made me think of the festivals at Mylapore when I was a child: the celebration of the saints, the great processions when all their statues are taken round the streets. These shadowy things have made us. I did think that I might one day go down south off the beaten track and see what you have seen.'

'Yes, Ash, you must go and spend a few days by the Cavery river. Go to see the temples and listen to the songs of the *oduvars*. Go to Tiruvidaimarudur.'

'OK, I will. I promise.' He laughed. 'One day.'

4

To the South

The day was already hot when the train emerged from the dark
canopy of Egmore into the blinding sunlight and rumbled slowly
out through the suburbs. Over the Coum canal and the Adyar
river, and past St Thomas Mount. The rains had not yet come, and
the air was stifling despite the overhead fans in the carriage. In
between gardens of coco palms, new buildings were sprouting
everywhere. Further on, the lakes at Chingleput looked magnificent: a shimmering expanse covered with birds. A big kite wheeled
and fell out of the sun to take a fish from the water. The crystalline
blue water reflected the fringe of rocky red hills and the pointed
spire of Tirukalikundran, where it would soon be lunchtime for
the eagles.

I had a conversation with an advocate from Gwalior, on the
way to Pondi with his wife, who was also an advocate. He wore
traditional clothes, a white kurta, *tilak* mark on his forehead, tiffin
box by his side.

'Don't be idealistic about India; 95 per cent of people here don't
believe in God either! Open your papers any day: how many
women are brutalized, even burned, by their husbands' families. It
is another view of India from the bench of the law, my dear
fellow. But all is changing: there is TV and video, even in the
villages now. This will inevitably advance the cause of democracy.
Change is always, but it is more rapid now, and ideas are the
motor of change. Now – or soon – all will have acess to them.
Look, not so long ago as a Brahmin I would have been outcast for

travelling abroad, as we have done; we would have lost our Brahminical purity. Few adhere to such outdated taboos now. Even mixing with you foreigners was not so long ago impossible.'

His wife shifted the tiffin box to her side and began to spread out lunch. 'Now, would you like to share our *jaggery* rice?'

In fact I had already placed my lunch order. They have a great system on the southern railways: after Chingleput a boy comes round with little coffee flasks and takes your order, which they telegraph down the line from Tindivanam. When the train arrives at Villapuram Junction, usually around 1.30, the chap with the catering concession races across the platform with his kitchen assistants, holding towers of teetering metal lunch plates like circus jugglers. Vegetarian or 'non-veg' dishes – *sambhar*, dhal, curried vegetables, juniper berries, curd, pickle, a twist of salt – these you consume at your seat in the fifteen-minute stop at Villapuram. It is a simple and usually foolproof system, but today there had been a snag: after all the meals had been served, there was no food for me or a man across the aisle. The chap in the seat behind immediately insisted I take his: 'You are our guest in our country. Besides my wife has brought us a picnic already.'

He lifted the cloth from their basket to reveal a pre-prepared feast, including chicken legs. 'We are non-veg, you see. We ordered extra vegetables just in case.'

When we set off again, the kitchen manager was still arguing with the one irate passenger who had missed out. As the train pulled into Cuddalore the concessionaire was still scratching his head as his figures failed to add up one more time. Around him a mountain of used plates stood by the door ready for the journey back to his kitchen at Villapuram.

Through the drowsy heat of the afternoon we travelled slowly down the coastal plain, rumbling over long bridges across the dried-up courses of rivers where only the odd green pond was left in immense tracts of wind-blown sand and camel thorn. In places the sandbanks were covered with brightly coloured clothes, sari cloths and bedspreads where the dhobis had found enough water to do their washing. I kicked off my shoes and spread the map out on the seat.

This plain is the heartland of Tamil civilization. It is framed by the sea, the long chain of mountains and the high plateau of central India: the Deccan, an ancient fissured red land, arid and austere, burned by the sun for ten months of the year. Here in the south-eastern corner of the subcontinent is a fertile flatland cut by the rivers Pennar, Vellar, Vaigai and above all the sacred Cavery: these rivers made the civilization.

The southland – Ten Nadu as the Tamils call it – is different from the north in culture and language. The dark-skinned south-erner going to Delhi feels himself to be in a foreign culture, and may even find himself subject to racial jokes and stereotypes.

'It's a foreign land to us up there,' said the dapper young Tamil man whose family were sitting across the aisle. 'I am working in Indore, inland from Bombay. It is really another world for a Tamil; without English I would be lost there.' His two little daughters spoke and wrote Hindi, and were already losing their Tamil.

'The English language has helped give unity to India. I could not work up north without it as I don't speak Hindi.' He's working for a Japanese multinational tractor company. They are going back for a holiday to his home town, Kumbakonum, a lovely place on the Cavery river.

'My dad was a schoolteacher there; he's a traditional Tamil, you know, he still wears his dhoti and goes to the temple every day. I did an engineering degree; I escaped from that small world.'

Exactly when the Tamils came into the south is a difficult question. They like to describe themselves as the original Indians. But the tribal peoples and aboriginals who still inhabit the forests of the Deccan and the Nilgiris obviously preceded them. The

Tamils themselves are first mentioned in the inscriptions of the northern emperor Ashoka in the third century BC. But in the south they go back much further. Their language group, which we call Dravidian, is the fifth largest in the world: it includes Telugu Kannada and Malayalam, the other main languages of southern India, each of which has a long history and a great literature. But where Dravidian speakers originated is still a mystery. Clues to their origins are lost, perhaps for ever, in prehistory (though it is possible they may yet be recovered in the undeciphered script of the Indus Valley civilization). Their language has affinities with Elamite, the archaic and long-dead language of Persia. Mysteriously, it may also be linked through the Altaic speech of central Asia with Japanese, of all languages – but that connection is so controversial and in any case so far back in prehistory that for the moment it must be set aside. The northwest Indian–Iranian root is the one which at present looks most promising; indeed an outpost of Dravidian, Brahui, is still spoken by transhumant people in the uplands of Baluchistan on the Iranian border with Pakistan. Dravidian speakers almost certainly came into south India from this area some time during the last few millennia BC.

Meanwhile the 'Aryans', Sanskrit speakers, migrated through the Hindu Kush into north-west India in the middle part of the second millennium BC, settling first in the north-west frontier, the Indus valley and the Punjab, and then, in the first millennium, in the Ganges–Jumna plain. Their language is Indo-European, distantly related to Latin and Greek and the western European languages. It is the language of classical Indian civilization, of the Vedas, the Upanishads, the *Mahabarata* and the *Ramayana*. The modern northern Indian dialects, Punjabi, for example, Marathi, Bengali and Hindi, are all derived from Sanskrit. The southern languages, on the other hand, are all from the completely unrelated Dravidian root.

It used to be thought that the Aryans were the only begetters of Indian civilization. A century ago, as European imperialists sought validation of their domination of far older cultures, they lighted on the Aryans as their progenitors. As the authors of the oldest scriptures in world, in some sense the Indian Brahminical sages could be seen as standing at the root of Indo-European as well as Indian culture. Out of all this German Indologists in particular extracted crackpot ideas about the core values of Teutonic society, and weird racialist theories about the supremacy of the Aryan over the Semitic and the African; it was the ideological foundation of the Aryan ideas used by the Nazis.

But of course the real history was much more rich, complex and elusive. Already in the 1920s the discovery of a great literate urban civilization in the Indus Valley in the Bronze Age – long before the 'Aryan' arrival in India – had thrown into question the relative contributions of the 'Aryan' and the Dravidian to India's cultural make-up. Even today the significance of these sensational discoveries is the subject of passionate debate, and not just among scholars.

Many now believe, surely rightly, that some of the oldest conceptions (perhaps we should say obsessions?) of Indian civilization, are pre-Aryan: yoga, tantra, the worship of the goddess – and perhaps, too, one of the most characteristic Hindu ideas, ahimsa, non-violence. Transmitted through Buddhism to medieval Hinduism and on to the likes of Gandhi, it is still alive today. Some ideas are probably even earlier. The Great God Siva, who has long been suspected as being pre-Aryan, may be pre-Dravidian too, if the Mesolithic dancing shaman in the caves of Bhimbetka is anything to go by, with his trident, horns and bangles. The elephant-headed Ganesh and the monkey-faced Hanuman are presumably far older than Indo-European religion in India. Indeed the more archaeologists discover, the more the bounds can be pushed back.

So it was from these prehistoric substrates, along with their own particular genius, that the Tamils built their civilization, later assimilating Sanskritic culture to their own. And whatever profound influences the Sanskritic, Islamic and Christian may have exerted – and however much we discount the nationalist myths of today's Dravidian politicians – it is still true to say that there has been a continuous and relatively unbroken development of civilization in the south from prehistory to the present day.

The distinctive qualities of a civilization are often as much the product of landscape and climate as of history. Tamil civilization arose in a climate of fierce extremes, in particular the enervating annual cycle of autumn monsoons and scorching summer heat. The blessings of nature here are superabundant, but they are also unpredictable and can be taken away with terrifying violence, especially in the years of cyclones, which can be absolutely devastating. The effect of living with such extremes is everywhere to be seen in the Tamil thought world; in their myths and beliefs, in their attitudes to love and sex, nature and society. There is a deep-rooted preoccupation with extremes, and the need to control them. So theirs is a culture which values restraint, both in its psychological and its material life. A central practical concern, for example, is the control of water, and for this reason Tamil Nadu is pre-eminently a land of tanks and irrigation.

By the end of summer here the rivers are mostly dry and one may walk across the bed of the Vaigai in the middle of Madurai. Even the main flood of the Cavery, the Coleroon, is reduced to a shallow flow and intermittent pools; the paddy-fields are burned up, bone-hard, brown, the rutted tracks hard as iron on bare feet. Then, when the tremendous rains come at monsoon time, 'when the rains fall on the red earth', as the Tamil poets say, the rivers rise and fill up the tanks everywhere. Every village, every temple, has a tank, an artificial reservoir, a brick- or stone-lined pool with steps, and a covered *mandapa* to give shade. These are a source of water throughout the rest of the year, where people drink, wash and bathe, and where the children swim and play. You pass them

all the way down on the train: there are thirty thousand registered
by the state government in Tamil Nadu, leaving aside uncountable
numbers of smaller ponds and pools. Virtually all are pre eighteenth
century, and some still in use go back as far as the seventh century,
still carrying their weathered inscriptions which testify to the civic
spirit of thousand-year-old management committees. The tank
which feeds Chidambaram, for example, was built in the eleventh
century and will continue to be the biggest man-made lake in
India until the Narmada dam is finished.

Not surprisingly, water has long been viewed here as sacred; the
act of purification by washing is the central ritual act of Hindus'
daily worship, which no Indian omits to do. Unlike most cultures
they never lost this idea of the sacrality, the life-giving force of
water. The Tamil lands are ringed by sacred bathing places,
streams, shores, waterfalls, rivers and tanks. Rivers in particular
were and are viewed as sacred; and the Cavery above all is revered
by Tamils as Ponni, 'the Lady of Gold', a form of 'liquid Sakti', or
divine energy, which nurtures the people. It was praised in poetry
as far back as the time of the Roman empire, and still today, on the
eighteenth day of the solar month Adi, in the middle of the heat
(in late July), Tamils celebrate the rising of the Cavery, which is
considered to happen punctually on this day every year. 'To be on
the banks of the Cavery listening to the strains of southern music,'
says a Tamil proverb, 'is to have a taste of eternal bliss.'

So in this climate and landscape, with its natural boundaries of sea
and mountain, and the austere plateau of the Deccan, Tamil
civilization arose. It was made by a people with deep roots in their
landscape, possessed of an ancient, copious and versatile language
and a profound sense of beauty. Its first flowering is known
through a remarkable body of classical poetry which was largely
rediscovered in the nineteenth century, the so-called Sangam
poems, which fertilized all that followed. And what followed was
remarkable. From then on until today there has been a continuous

flood of great literature in Tamil, poetry, epics, grammars, drama and philosophy, including a rich Muslim Tamil literature.

The greatest era of the south is generally agreed to have been the Chola dynasty between the ninth and thirteenth centuries; an era which has been compared (not entirely unjustly) to Renaissance Italy and classical Greece, both for the range of its creations and the astonishing fertility of its imagination. The Chola period is still alive in the minds of traditional Tamils. Its kings and saints are still real people in a way found in few other societies now. The oral poetry of the saints, which was strongly rooted in classical poetry, is a still-living tradition, not only in temples and religious houses, but also in popular culture. In the fifties and sixties, for example, many hit movies were based on its stories, and Sivaji Ganeshan, the greatest character actor of southern cinema, played wandering saints like Sundaramurti in his days as a juvenile lead. The greatest of all Tamil literary works, the twelfth-century epic of Kamban, is also still recited in folk plays; it receives earthy but careful exegesis from the actors, incorporating what appear to be genuine oral traditions of the author or himself and of the circumstances of its composition.

The riches of southern culture were virtually unknown to the outside world until the nineteenth century. From then on, as more of the ancient texts became available (and they are still being recovered), the extent of the achievement of Tamil civilization became apparent. Tamil Nadu now appears to be one of the great classical cultures – perhaps, indeed, the last one. The fact that these traditions are still alive in the late twentieth century makes a journey to Tamil Nadu all the more charged with expectation for the interested outsider. The train journey south to Chidambaram and the Cavery takes you into its heartland.

THE CITY OF THE COSMIC DANCE

Late in the afternoon we crossed the Vellar river, and entered the

THE SEASON OF RAINS

northern edge of the Cavery delta; here you meet the landscape of rice paddies and palm forests, but the soil was parched and dry after a summer of no rain. Long lines of acacia palms stretched as far as the eye could see, lining the horizon. Brilliant white egrets in the brown fields; a pair of yoked bullocks with bright blue painted horns swaying across parched red earth; brightly painted plaster shrines – to horse deities and red-skinned moustachioed demigods – sitting in little thatched compounds among the trees. Then at last, still several miles off, we glimpsed the temple towers over the darkening palm forests.

It was dusk when we reached Chidambaram. An elderly couple got off, assisted by a wiry and even older porter in an orange turban, who helped them to the cycle rickshaws outside. On the platform, by the door to the station master's office, is a glittering weighing machine with mirrors and whirring coloured wheels which tells your fortune on a printed card. ('You will find the joy of reciprocated love.' On the reverse: 'Remember to flush the lavatory: antisocial behaviour costs us all.') Above it is a glass case containing a brightly painted statue of Nataraja performing his dance of bliss: 'Welcome to the city of the Cosmic Dance'. Around the station you will also find Vishnu and Kali, and the symbols of other faiths, including Islam and Christianity: Southern Railways is nothing if not eclectic. But Siva is the great god of Chidambaram and, as if to emphasize it, Nataraja surmounts the roof outside beneath a little *gopura* where the station name glows in neon in English and Tamil. Facing him, his faithful bull Nandi sits in a roundabout across a dusty forecourt, where the cycle rickshaws queue patiently for the infrequent trains, ringing their bells in hopeful unison when any passer-by emerges from the booking-hall.

The dusty station road led along a fence draped with bougainvillea, past darkened pilgrims' hostels, all empty at this time of year. Only a century ago there used to be nearly seventy such establishments in Chidambaram; only about a dozen are still functioning.

Not that the number of people on pilgrimage has lessened – far from it. With mass transport, pilgrimage is booming; it is just that it is quicker now, and few need or wish to stay in places like Chidambaram for more than a few hours. But at festival time in these places Hindu charitable organizations still feed and shelter the holy men and women who constantly wander the roads of India in their millions. I booked a room with a roof fan in the Hotel Tamil Nadu and strolled over the canal bridge into town. In the main street the sweet shops and flower stalls glowed in pools of lamplight: stacks of marigold, jasmine, roses, and slabs of sweets, bright yellow, white, orange and green. At the almond milk stall, the chubby-faced proprietor was preparing the first bowl of the evening, stirring the crumbled nuts into steaming creamy froth, a small-town Vishnu stirring his sea of milk.

I had a *dosa*, a rice pancake, on a banana-leaf plate at the New Carner Tiffin Centre (so called because it stands on the corner by Gandhi's statue). Under a corrugated sheet, an ailing neon strip sputtered fitfully as a family of albino lizards scampered down the wall to eye the clientele. At the back, through a curtain of plastic strips, was the interior of the kitchen: a dark hovel bathed in firelight from a big clay kiln, where a grizzled old man, bare-chested and glistening with sweat, expertly tossed wafer thin *dosa*s on to a flat steel griddle. Across the road, distorted film music swelled and crashed at the Lena cinema as the early evening show churned out the latest *iddly* western. Around the statue of Gandhi auto-rickshaws did battle, horns blaring, like a scene from the TV 'Mahabharata'. Clouds of dust were rising in the last pink light behind the cinema. Meanwhile, ignored by all, the Mahatma strode forward confidently into an uncertain future, faded circlets of flowers still hung round his neck from his birthday celebrations.

Soon the great mass of the east tower of the temple reared up black against the starry sky, gilded finials glinting. Inside, the wide courtyard was open to the sky. To the right the hall with a thousand pillars, and beyond it the huge tank, glinting in the moonlight; in the interior, granite corridors stretched off into the darkness, peopled by beardless androgynes, dressed in white loin-cloths with shaved foreheads, their long shiny black hair worn in a tight bun to one side, half-man, half-woman. As one old British administrator remembered them: 'sleek well-grown fellows . . . the boys pretty neophytes in white clothing, their sallow shapeliness especially charming. The younger ones reminded me of Italian angels.'

Mr Velu, Mala's neighbour, came up and joined us. He wore a short-sleeved cotton shirt with a row of biros in his top pocket, and a *vesti*, the long wrap worn by Tamil men which they lift up and tuck into their front waistband. He used to work in an agricultural office in the north of the state.

'I have retired now since you were last here: I came back here because my daughter works in the Indian bank here – 2200 rupees a month.'

Like most Indians he was quite unembarrassed about discussing his financial affairs in the greatest detail. 'I am receiving 1600 rupees pension monthly,' he volunteered. 'But food is so much cheaper here in Chidambaram and in the countryside than in Madras – we can feed a household of five for 2000 a month. So here I can save a thousand a month to go towards my daughter's marriage. Really I came here to live with them. My son is at Annamalai University, my daughter working here; I lost my wife four years ago, you see. I come here every day to the temple. Also I go to read in the university library through the middle of the day when it is hot. What better way to spend the time than to worship god and to read in the library?'

Behind us the drummer wrapped up his instrument in an old figured cloth, put it in the chest and closed the lid. Then Mala appeared: her oval smiling face, her black hair showing streaks of grey now, but still centre-parted and tightly brushed and plaited with white jasmine at the back. She gave me a slightly bashful smile, hands together, fingertips touching in greeting.

'I received your letter yesterday. Come home for tiffin.'

We exchanged family news. Jaya was working in Madras now, in a clerical job for a company making coated ribbons for computers. She and Bharati and Sarasu were all sharing a little house out in the suburbs. Kumar had been in Saudi Arabia for three years, but he had not had a happy time; he had been cheated of his rightful money either by his employers or by the agent in Madras – it was a common story. Balu, the black sheep of the family, was still living at home. He was doing a bit of dogsbodying at a video studio which had opened up in Chidambaram and hanging out with wealthier friends who could afford to lounge about all day in Hawaian shirts, quiffing their hair like the latest Tamil movie stars. But he really wanted to get into driving for a living; maybe start with a secondhand auto-rickshaw and move on to his own taxi. As for Mala's husband Mani, he still sat in the same place near the door, still listening to the main news on All India Radio, keeping up with the world. His sight was gone now but for a blur of light; his main pleasure was going for walks with their neighbour, Mr Velu, who would sit and talk with him in the passageway, and take him by the hand to the temple for the evening puja.

Mala pored over the pictures of our babies. Was I troubled to have only girls? In Tamil Nadu this was a big problem because of raising the money for dowries – as she was all too well aware. I told her I was delighted. She walked into the kitchen end of the room to make some tea. There was no power, the fan was motionless and the hot stillness of the air was broken only by the distant sound of children playing in the street outside. Mani stared into space. Looking around the bare walls of the room, nothing seemed to have changed since I had first sat here six years before: the wooden bed opposite the door; the Usha sewing-machine with its foot pedal; on the floor the old padlocked metal chest where Mala kept her treasures and secret things. On the walls were still the same old religious calendars; over the bed on a nail was a plastic pilgrim souvenir of Somaskanda – the Saivite Holy Family; lastly a faded black and white picture of the Mother, the strange French woman who had established her ashram at Pondicherry in the 1920s with the Bengali guru Aurobindo. (Mala had stayed there and prayed at his tomb when Mani's sight failed and she had travelled the length and breadth of Tamil country looking for a reprieve.) Hanging down on a string over the sewing-machine was Mala's well-thumbed copy of the *Panchang*, the religious almanac which all traditional Tamils live by, where you will find every eclipse and conjunction, every auspicious and inauspicious day, every religious festival and special puja – the world as seen through Tamil time.

As we sat there I could feel the heat already soaking into my bones, and that light-headedness which comes with such a sudden and abrupt change in the pace and focus of one's life. Mala came back with the tea in little stainless steel cups. Then, in a perfectly matter-of-fact tone, she announced: 'Goddess Sivakami appeared to me in a dream.'

Sivakami is the name of the Great Goddess, Siva's consort, here in Chidambaram. Like all such manifestations of divinity in India, she has many guises. She is most famous for her terrifying aspects, like the omnipresent Kali whose chthonic powers must always be propitiated, especially by men, who from time immemorial in India have both feared and worshipped the primal female power. At Cape Comorin the goddess is enshrined as the ever-auspicious virgin, the Devi; she is the 'love-eyed' at Kanchi, the 'one who cools' disease at Samayapuram, and the giver of children at Madurai. Nowhere on earth as in India, and nowhere in India as in the south, are the powers of the Great Mother still accorded such wide reverence: and this, paradoxically, despite the pervasive discrimination and violence here against women, and especially female children. Here in Chidambaram, Mala's favourite incarnation of the goddess, Sivakami, is 'she who is beloved of Siva', mother, wife and lover; the embodiment of benign, auspicious and healthy female power. She has her own shrine within the temple, an exquisite and unspoiled twelfth-century building in honey-coloured stone. Sivakami is like an inner voice to Mala, a guardian angel; and she never omits to pray to the goddess every day.

'Sivakami came two weeks ago. She spoke to me and told me I must go to Tiruchendur for Skanda Shashti. This time of the year is the main festival at Tiruchendur. The whole thing lasts twelve days: sixth day symbolizes triumph of good over evil. On this day, called Soora Samharam, there is very big puja there for Lord Murugan. Also there is a very big festival on the beach. This is next Saturday. It is very beautiful, a very lucky time. There is a pilgrim bus tour going there from Chidambaram. You are coming?'

It did not sound like a question. Mala had not forgotten our meeting with Rajdurai Dikshithar four years ago, when my horoscope had been read. This was the very journey he had foreseen for me, written in the charts of the temple astrologer at Chidambaram; one day, he had said, I would return to go on pilgrimage to Tiruchendur. Rajdurai's words had been the last thing on my mind coming out from London for a short stay. I had just planned to sit still, meet friends and take stock of any life. I had not the slightest wish to go careering the length and breadth of Tamil Nadu on a bus tour. Tiruchendur, I had thought, I would visit one day in the future, at my leisure, preferably ensconced in the back of an Ambassador car with Rebecca and the girls, with a few nice hotels to look forward to. As far as Mala was concerned, though, the moment had arrived.

'We go in three days' time, on Friday night; come back early Tuesday. Visit twelve big temples, many pujas. Many holy baths in the sea and sacred waterfalls. Cost is 200 rupees. I have already asked the organizer to keep a seat for you, as the trip will be sold out. The bus will be leaving at nine from the Vinayaka shrine at the junction of North and East Car Street. Come to my house for tiffin at eight.'

I could hardly have refused.

THE LORD OF HEALING

We had three days free before the big journey. Mala is not the sort to let the time go by unfilled. The next morning she suggested we make a trip to the famous shrine at Vaithisvarancoil. We could go there to do a puja before the pilgrimage, and then meet Mala's daughter Punnidah and her husband and baby at Mayavaram at about 8.30. Vaithisvarancoil was the first place Rajdurai Dikshithar had told me to visit on my pilgrimage. It seemed a good way to start.

At about three in the afternoon, with the sun slanting over the flower stalls, we walked to the bus station. There are other shrines which Mala prefers, but she goes to Vaithisvarancoil every month to do puja and pray for her family. The bus takes you over the wide Kollidam branch of the Cavery river and into the delta: a fertile land of rice paddies fringed with forests of acacia and palmyra palms. At this time of day it is nothing short of gorgeous, when the heat fades and the sea breeze comes up. Then the landscape becomes suffused with a golden light and the colours stand out with dazzling intensity. You pass tanks carpeted with purple lilies, clumps of banana and bamboo, and little painted shrines in the fields; in the paddies the new rice sparkles in the sunlight. It is a time when everyone comes out into the village streets to enjoy the air and talk with friends.

I sat on the men's side of the bus. As far as the Kollidam bridge my companion was a rather serious young man doing a degree at Annamalai University: a BA in tourism. A sign of the times indeed, as Rao's government loosens the fetters of forty odd years of Nehru's socialism and lets in foreign companies and investment. Everyone is hot on tourism these days: potentially a big business here, as it has been up north on the Delhi–Agra–Rajasthan circuit.

'We have many excellent things for the foreign visitor in Tamil Nadu but facilities need to be upgraded,' he said, and proceeded to fire questions at me with a fierce look of concentration, as if this were a test interview and his course supervisor were breathing over his shoulder.

'So, first, what is your opinion of the touristic facilities here? Transport, hotels, communications, infrastructure? Starting with Chidambaram. Please enumerate.'

'Er . . .'

'Please be frank.'

'Well . . .'

'It is not five-star Taj type, am I right?'

Now it has to be said that the hotels in Chidambaram have not elicited uniform enthusiasm: 'the low point of our trip,' wrote one respondent in the latest trendy handbook; 'stay in another town,' said another, curtly. Western-style tourism here is a new phenomenon; as recently as 1977, an Indian guidebook recommended the visitor try, in descending order, the railway retiring room, the public works department inspection bungalow, or private lodgings and *choultries* for pilgrims: 'Nadar's *choultry*', it says, 'is neat and tidy; advance reservation can be made with the *choultry* manager. Provisions can be obtained in the bazaar.'

Not exactly the Hilton, then. But that was what appealed to me about it: you weren't stuck in the dreadful uniformity of international hotels. They ignored all that here; it was part of an older pattern of long-distance travel. And though a couple of modern hotels have been built since then, they have not yet really abandoned the old way of doing things. Take the Hotel Tamil Nadu in Railway Feeder Road. 'Five-star Taj type' it is not; I have seen the staff drive some guests (especially impatient north Indians) up the wall with their opaque smiles and their dedicated lack of purpose. But it is comfortable and clean, and works perfectly well. In fact (I confess) it is one of my favourite hotels in all India, but I could not begin to explain why. I could see I was beginning to disappoint my friend, who had clearly thought that, as far as Western tourism was concerned, I was the horse's mouth.

'Our new chief minister, Dr Jayalalitha, has big plans for the state. She has designated several new tourist zones in Tamil Nadu. Chidambaram is one of these, and Mahabalipuram too. At Tranquebar also there will be a new tourist hotel built by the Taj chain, converting the old Danish Fort on the seashore. Also plans are afoot to construct a highway from Madras down to Cape Comorin; a 500-mile dual-carriageway coastal road which will open up all of Tamil Nadu to tourism.'

My heart sank, though I did not say so. The times, after all, are there to be moved with, and I could think of no one in Chidambaram who would not welcome a new injection of investment into the town, and that included the temple priests. My companion was now in full flow.

'There are also many opportunities for touristic and folkloric performance here, such as they have with the Thrissur Pooram festival at Trichur in Kerala. Next year there will be one hundred elephants taking part in the changing of the multi-coloured parasols. It is a magnificent spectacle which draws people from far and wide; now there are many similar possibilities being mooted here. For example, a dance festival inside the Nataraja temple to bring international artists and tourists to Chidambaram, put the City of the Cosmic Dance on the world map. What is your opinion of the touristic potential of this?'

My heart sank again, though I tried to smile enthusiastically. The writing is on the wall; no doubt the packaging of culture for tourists will come here too. And all will welcome it. For a time, at least.

The future minister of tourism shook hands stiffly when he got down at the Kollidam bridge, a perplexed look on his face; I could see I had been a let-down. No sooner had he gone than another young man took his place; he was almost beside himself with glee.

'What is your native land?'

'England. London. And yours?'

'Here in Sirkali. What is your job in England?'

'I work for the BBC.' (It seemed the most convenient way to describe a life in TV.)

'What is your salary?' (Indians, as I have said already, are completely uninhibited about discussing the minutiae of their financial arrangements with total strangers, a habit which some might find excruciating. I was evasive.)

'You are working here?' I asked.

'Since Christmas I have been working in Saudi. I have just returned for a holiday for two weeks.'

'How did you find it in Saudi?'

A delighted smile enveloped his face. 'Very nice. I am working as a carpenter. BSc qualified. I am receiving two thousand rials per month, not including food, lodging and laundry, which my employers are also providing.'

That was over five hundred dollars. Over fifteen thousand rupees. For an ordinary Tamil it was a simply fabulous sum. He told me his story. He was not married, and he had already saved several thousand dollars in just ten months. As the story progressed he squealed with delight and squeezed my hand, refusing to let go till we reached Sirkali, chortling with happiness at his good fortune. He was plump, with the smoothest of skins; he had a little moustache in the style cultivated by the latest Tamil movie stars. He wore Nike sports shoes, neatly cut slacks, a T-shirt with a golf pro. logo on it, and on his wrist (as he did not neglect to show me) a gold watch, 'eighteen carat'.

At Sirkali he gave my hand one last squeeze and bounced off, light footed, giving me a cheery wave as he disappeared into the crowds around the bazaar. His delight at being a success in his own land was a pleasure to behold. What a contrast with Mala's son Kumar, who was working as a warehouse supervisor and storeman in a pharmacy in Buraidh; his promised income of 160 dollars had turned out to be only half that, after deductions made for food and washing. Judging by his last letter, he would be lucky to come back with any savings at all.

Beyond Sirkali the flat green landscape of paddies and palms stretches away eastwards to the sea and south across the delta. You can see the temple towers, the *gopura*s, of Vaithisvarancoil, from two or three miles away. The bus dropped us off at the side of the temple soon after four. A wide sandy lane surrounds the outer walls of the temple precinct where the huge wooden cars are pulled during the annual festivals. Along the lane are the priests' houses, with their pillared fronts, terracotta roofs and plastered walls, painted with the red and white stripes which always signify a Saivite temple. On the south side the lane was lined with stalls strung with streamers and flags. Mala marched up and down looking for the best price for coconuts and bananas for puja. While she bargained, I had a cup of tea in the Kumaran Vegetarian Hotel, a cavernous tea shop with an old pendulum clock and a big wooden dresser where a pan of incense wafted smoke under a row of deities and portraits of the Gandhi family. We left our shoes in the shop where Mala bought all the other bits and pieces necessary for puja – camphor, *vilva* leaves, and fruit. Then we turned into the wide approach which leads up to the temple gate.

The temple at Vaithisvarancoil is dedicated to Siva as Lord of Healing, literally 'The Lord who is our Physician' and is very popular among Tamils, especially those suffering from disease, sickness and mental trouble. It is widely believed that Siva will cure even incurable diseases here. People also come here to fulfil vows or perform the rituals for young children. (This was where Mala had wanted to bring our daughter for her first birthday, for the first giving of rice.) It is one of the famous shrines sung by the Tamil Saivite saints in the *Tevaram*, so it must have been in existence at least by the seventh century AD. Then Appar came here to hymn 'the Lord of a thousand names, Lord of mantras, tantras and healing potions, who by his grace cures our incurable disease' – the disease which Appar makes a metaphor for existence itself.

The shrine has a beautiful colonnaded tank whose waters are believed to have curative powers; it has an ancient and sacred *neem* tree whose leaves and bark have medicinal qualities; the food offerings prepared in the temple kitchens and given at puja are also thought to be beneficial to health. Off the beaten track as far as the tourist is concerned, you will find it in no Western guidebook, but to the Tamils it is a loved and famous spot.

Vaithisvarancoil is also a good place to get an idea of the classic layout of the Tamil temple. Past the pilgrim stalls you come to the main gate, a pyramidal tower whose weathered sculptures tower over the surrounding town and countryside. This is the *gopura*, one of the most characteristic features of the Tamil landscape, so well known that it has become the badge of the state government. The word simply means 'gateway'. In early southern architecture, the tower over the central shrine was the main feature and the gates were small. But in the tenth century, gate towers became more prominent and soon rose over 150 feet, fantastical pyramids teeming with brightly coloured statues of gods and spirits, as garishly coloured as the pediments of ancient Greek temples.

As in the Gothic cathedral boom (or the skyscraper craze in the thirties in the USA, for that matter) once the idea became the rage, it did not stop. These great constructions were thrown up in literally thousands of shrines all over the south between the eleventh and the seventeenth centuries. In some of the big temples, all the enclosures had their gate towers; at Sriringam, for example, on its forested island in the Cavery river, there are no fewer than twenty-one, the last of which was completed only in 1987. Some of them soar to well over 200 feet, and are covered with sculpture so strange and exotic, so unlike any other architectural tradition of the world, that when glimpsed for the first time above the palm forests it is easy to imagine one has found oneself by accident on another planet.

The *gopura*s mark out the rectangle of the sacred area. Walk under the gate at Vaithisvarancoil and you enter a long and gloomy pillared hall, painted a dark institutional green; here the temple carriages are stored, and there are stalls selling pilgrim literature and pictures. This hall lies along the axis of the temple, and once inside you can look all the way down the main nave and through the inner gate to the sanctum itself, where you can just make out a flickering circle of lamplight nearly a hundred yards away.

It is basically a very simple architecture, but the effect is intensely dramatic. On a larger or smaller scale this is the essential idea of Tamil temple architecture, an idea which in places like Madurai is elaborated in a stupendous manner and scale to create some of the greatest sacred buildings on earth.

The tall gate towers, like cathedral spires, are intended to be visible from far away across the landscape, but the principle is the opposite of Gothic architecture, for the Gothic cathedral encloses space. Once you are inside a Tamil shrine you find yourself in a vast rectangular area open to the sky, and then a dark labyrinth unlit by the sun, in which space becomes smaller and smaller as you go inwards. Finally you enter the sanctum, which in a Siva temple contains the linga, the simple black stone cylinder, phallic in origin, which represents the presence of the Great God. This place is called the *gharb griya*, literally the 'womb chamber', the warm and dark space where you encounter the divine. The act of worship itself is called 'puja', the whole encounter which takes place between deity and devotee is *darshan*, literally 'seeing'. (Television is *doordarshan*, 'long-distance seeing'.) The pilgrim comes for *darshan* of the Lord; the Lord gives *darshan*.

The encounter is lit only by lamplight; your senses are heightened by the sound of music, drums and cymbals, by the singing and chanting, by the sight and heat of the flame, and by the smell of incense, ghee and flowers – sometimes in fact it is the smell which is the strongest of the sensations during puja, for the air of the inner sanctum is often saturated with the sweetness of jasmine, by the pungency of aromatic incense and the cloying thickness of ghee.

The intention of all this is to take the devotee inwards, away from the bright sun and harsh shadows of the day, into a dark and magical world for a purely personal transaction. No matter how large the shrine in Tamil temples, the centre remains simply this small place where the divinity can be encountered directly. Srirangam, for example, covers 155 acres – it would take up a sizable part of the City of London – with seven concentric enclosures and twenty *gopuras*; but at its heart is a tiny round chamber where a black stucco Vishnu offers *darshan* to the faithful in the warm flickering darkness, reclining on his seven-headed serpent Ananta, 'Endless'.

We headed off to the right towards the tank to buy our ticket. At the counter we poured our offerings of natural salt on to the big pile, and took from it some salt and peppercorns, which the devotee eats before going in. By the pile was a basket full of little silver-foil pictures of human limbs, hands, feet, legs, arms, heads, eyes, male and female genitalia and babies, for pilgrims to leave with their prayers. Then we went off to the sanctum for the puja. It was floored with grey-white veined marble. The priest took our names and the *prasad* – coconuts, bananas, flowers – lit the lamp, recited the ritual in Sanskrit and blessed our offerings, which we received back with the ash from the lamp which Mala daubed across her forehead. We then walked round the shrine.

Temples like this are really huge campuses with dozens of separate shrines and myths: often the pilgrim can encounter stories from shrines all over India in one place, which thus becomes a mnemonic for all the pilgrimage places in India. The more of these gimmicks a shrine has, the more popular it will be and the more revenue it will earn. Conversely there are some magnificent shrines which do not have a special pulling point and which attract few pilgrims from outside their own locality. Vaithisvarancoil, however, is rich in this respect: the local legends connect the shrine with an incident in the Rama legend; there is an important image of Murugan here too. Like all Siva temples, they also keep the statues of the sixty-three Tamil saints, which are revered by all in Tamil lands, and whose poems are recited on the big festivals. The planets too are represented here, and the special shrine to the planet Mars which I was instructed to visit by Rajdurai Dikshithar. Mala took us to it. Very jolly, this Mars, not martial at all, his four arms bristling with weaponry, but his plump face without a trace of aggression: pudgy cheeks, jolly eyes, a red cloth veiling his pot belly, and a self-satisfied smile. Rather like the chap on the bus to Sirkali in fact. Mala waved me in front of the priest, who fired away.

'Star?'

'Arbitam.'

Mala told him my story. He did puja for us, and loaded me with packets of ash and *kun kum*. Thin face, bent, skin like a shrivelled mummy. His eyes were startled, as if he had seen a ghost, but he greeted my inquiry politely and seriously.

'Arbitam the star rules Mars.'

'Why is Mars important for me?'

'He remedies defects in horoscope.'

'Ah, good,' I said. (Starting with excessive wind, I thought to myself.) 'This is because I don't have enough earth?'

'Yes,' said Mala seriously. 'When we build a house we do puja to Mars for a good foundation; people are the same. You are always flying in the air, Michael, much imagining. Your children will give you a good foundation.'

'I thought it was supposed to be the other way round?' I said.

She laughed.

'Sometimes it is mother and father who need, and children provide.'

We walked to the tank, beautiful in the evening light, with a domed hall on an island in the middle. Some people were bathing on the steps, some sitting reading; a few children were doing their homework in a corner. Mala bathed her feet and washed. Exquisite light now, the sun setting over the palm trees in the outer enclosure sending long rays through the cloisters; the lovely warm coppery colour of the weathered brick of the towers, crumbling, sprouting grass and flowers, swallows swooping; the sound of temple music, drums and reedy trumpets, from deep in the interior.

Then we stumbled on a remarkable scene: a young woman with an absent face was being exorcized by an older woman. White-haired and vigorous, wearing a bright orange patterned sari, hair swept back in a bun: catechizing, cajoling, at times loudly, at times in a whisper. Quite a crowd gathered. At first the patient said nothing; she appeared depressed and was closely attended by anxious parents and friends. On the floor the older woman had a bowl of ash, a framed image of Mariamman with flowers and small pictures of several other goddesses. The girl looked as if she was fighting within herself, wringing her fingers. The woman was jocular, her eyes never ceased to smile. We watched as she blew sacred ash on the girl's left cheek and then slapped her right cheek; slapped again, blew ash right into her face, and held her face in both hands.

At first sight this could have been mistaken for the substance of her 'cure', but it soon became apparent that the business with the ash was merely a bit of religious showbiz, playing to the gallery to impress the crowd and the kin; the pictures and divining sticks, mystical squares and yantras, lent metaphysical respectability to the encounter. But the exorcist's real art seemed to be to talk like a good doctor, or more accurately, like a much-loved granny, who under a brusque, no-nonsense exterior had a heart of gold. She was in her sixties at a guess, strong, handsome, with a lovely clear skin; and she exuded good health – always an encouraging sign in a doctor.

She talked in a way to gain the girl's confidence, focusing on her absolutely, trying to bring her out of herself. At one point she told the father off for interfering, put her arms round the girl and engaged in a bit of good-natured banter with the crowd, clearly taking the girl's part against her family who had brought her there. She never acknowledged my presence; but then suddenly in the middle of all this, not looking my way, she called out loudly in English: 'Sir, where are you from?'

We talked while she massaged the girl strongly and kindly, whispering to her all the while; and strangely enough the patient seemed to become more animated as we all took an interest in her. The exorcist had come from Mayavaram at the request of the family. She told us about Mariamman, the 'cooling goddess' who is much sought after in matters of health where women are concerned: 'She's like your Virgin Mary, mother of Christ,' said the woman (a strange idea, this, but then the Tamil Mary whose shrine is on the coast at Velankanni is much more like a Hindu goddess in her cult and rituals, and popular among all communities). The exorcist ended her performance by blowing more holy ash into the girl's face. In her last prayer for the girl, she used Mary's name again.

By now, the girl had been loosened up and relaxed by the engaging personality of the healer. Eventually she nodded, replied briefly to some questions and took a drink of water. Progress had been made. The parents stood up; the exorcist spoke to me.

'I tell her to go and sleep. I'll see her tomorrow again. Half of the problem is always family. Family and society – these are the people who make people mad. Especially for women here in India life can be very difficult. Now we are between two worlds: they see all Western things, consumer products, romance, different kind of freedom – yet they live in Tamil Nadu. Sex is now a very big problem, cause of much mental unrest here.' She paused. 'What these people need is not drugs but to be treated like people. The best skill needed to help these people is simply to conduct the conversation honestly with the patient. Try to get them to accept certain things as true the way they see it. There is a kind of game, a playfulness. They are bogged down in a rut and you have to help them out. Some you cannot help, but most you can.'

'How did you come to do this job?'

She laughed. 'Well, my father was a healer. I learned from him sitting with people in our house. I don't have a degree at Annamalai University, if that is what you mean. How would this have helped me? All this Western gadgetry is no more use than this sacred ash unless you can give patient love and understanding. Naturally there is our own Ayurvedic tradition, diet and exercise, workings of heart, disorder of the bodily functions. We must know about these things. But as the saints say, the most important is love.' She packed up her bags with a cheery nod of the head. 'God bless you. Bye-bye.'

As the last light faded over the tank, we strolled round the outer courtyard and came to the sacred tree at the back of the temple. Many of the great Tamil shrines have such trees at the axial place – the mango at Kanchi, the *jambu* on Srirangam, the *kadamba* at Madurai. Here at Vaithisvarancoil is a huge and ancient *neem* tree which spreads over a courtyard with a lovely little roofed shrine built into its roots – a linga for the Lord of Healing flanked by Ganesh and Chandikesvara, the gatekeeper. Many were doing their own pujas here, and lighting lamps. Round the back of the tree a little crowd of people were camped, to sleep the night under its branches. In the shadows a young husband gently tried to coax his wife to be calm. She laughed and then cried out. Mala nodded sympathetically. 'Family problems,' she said, as she circled the tree;

but the women was clearly distracted in her mind or spirit, one of many people who come here hoping that the god – or just the peaceful atmosphere – will alleviate such affliction.

It was time to get the bus to Mayavaram. We slowly wandered back along the arcade of shops, which were now crowded with people looking at the fruit and flower stalls. Then out into the night with a last look back down the axis of the temple to the distant glimmering light in its heart. Ahead, the last pink hint of sunset behind silhouetted palms and the sound of birds chattering.

Mayavaram is a thriving busy town on the old Cavery river, a rail and road junction with a big bazaar teeming with shops: gold-smiths and silversmiths, electrical goods. 'This town is famous for lawyers and doctors,' said Mala. 'And Brahmin moneylenders,' she added, with a disapproving curl of her lip. The place was simply throbbing with life, much more so than Chidambaram. At the bus station we found Punnidah. Her husband, Shanmugan, seemed a gentle man, and they were both obviously delighted with their baby, Kailash. They were now living in an industrial estate outside Coimbatore, the big textile town in the north of the state, which proudly advertises itself as 'the Manchester of India'. We swapped family news; I showed them photographs of our daughters, which brought round an enthusiastic crowd of fellow travellers. Though the oldest of the four sisters, Punnidah was always the quietest and most introverted. She spoke little if any English and always seemed to be washing, cleaning or sewing in the background. She never wore the elegant saris the others did. But she seemed happy now, more assured, and her face would suddenly light up with joy, animated in a way one never saw before.

Mala was very pleased. She thinks Shanmugan is a good man (he was patient, kind and thoughtful), and she took great delight in her first and only grandson. We took some photos and then they boarded the bus. When they were gone we talked for a while in a tiny café in the bus stand.

'I hope my daughters will all find love and affection as well as security in their marriage. Love like you two love each other. You are lucky.'

'Well, why don't you let them have choice in whom they marry, let them marry the person they love?'

'Love comes with knowing and undergoing together. We believe arranged marriage is still the best way of making secure partnership for life: same people, same community, right age, right horoscope. They do have choice; they meet the boy, they have to like him, to see the seed of love is possible.

'Look at the divorce rate in your country,' she continued. 'Here marriage and family is still held in very great respect. In our community there is great respect between man and woman in marriage. God helps us find our mate.'

'Did he for you?'

'I respect my husband. He's a good man. He has been a good father to our children. I have affection for our lives together. We made the best of our marriage and we brought up good children.'

We made our way over the bus stand through the late-night crowds of travellers to find a bus back to Sirkali, and on to Chidambaram. Through the open windows the night air was cool; the bus lights occasionally illuminated the edges of palm forests and the roadside shrines as we careered down the pitch dark road back over the Kollidam bridge. Tomorrow was Thursday, so after one more day it would be the beginning of the pilgrimage: the night journey to Tiruchendur.

THE FAMILY HOUSE

The evening before the pilgrimage, Mala took me for a meal at her father's house, the house where she was born and grew up. It lies in a street south-west of the temple, in an old Vellala neighbourhood called Ellaiman Koil. The house had been built by her father's grandfather about 125 years earlier. At that time it had stood on the outskirts of town, and there were fields beyond the back garden; now it is hemmed in by ribbon development and concrete sprawl. It is a fine, three-bay house with a long pitched roof covered with curved terracotta tiles, in overlapping rows four deep which come right down to head height in the street.

The house has been an anchor for Mala; her children stayed there for long periods when they were growing up, when it was hearth and shelter for all the extended family. Over the years since she married she lived in many rented places which were not her own, but this was the family root. The Tamils call it their *ur*, a word which means your native place. It is an umbilical idea; ask a Tamil in a supermarket in London where his *ur* is and he may say India. If you meet in Delhi then he will say Tamil Nadu; but if you ask the same question of a Tamil in the streets of Madras or Madurai, he may tell you his current residence and home, but he will invariably qualify that by referring to his real *ur*, the place whose soil nourished his ancestors, the place where he was born or where his father's line comes from. Your *ur* carries a weight of associations. It tells you who you are. Its soil, so Tamils believe, is literally a part of you. This house is Mala's *ur*.

We went up the steps, through the vestibule and into the columned living-room: her father greeted us. He was a big man, an old man of eighty-eight; shaven head, stomach muscles sagging and an old man's breasts, but still a commanding presence. He wore the traditional dress, a loincloth, with a bare chest and ash stripes on his forehead. Like his daughter he was a devout Saivite who had followed the ancient ritual process from birth to old age. Here Mala appeared in a different light, no longer struggling alone to make ends meet in a rented room, but rooted in a strong and long-lasting family and caste tradition; and tradition can be airy and spacious as well as stifling.

Small landowners, all their lives they had made annual gifts to Nataraja and held special pujas for important anniversaries at other great regional shrines. They had founded a small *choultry* in East

Car Street to lodge pilgrims and still gave a part of their surplus as free food. They had never amassed material things, always giving a tithe to religion or charity. In the past they had also donated part of their paddy to feeding poor Brahmin scholars, for although the Brahmins were privileged in the karmic order of things, in the everyday economic reality of the countryside, they were mostly impoverished and needed support from those who shared their ideals. Such families had been mainstays of the old order, which was now changing so fast.

Mala disappeared into the kitchen while her father spoke to me. He had been born in 1907 and raised under the British (he was already forty when they left). Like his wife's father he had been headman of the town council at Chidambaram, so he spoke enough English to get by. His caste had done well under the British, but not so well in the Dravidian movement since Independence, which had been against religion, caste and the Brahminical order. There had been a massive redistribution of land, wealth and job opportunities in Tamil Nadu under DMK governments from the late sixties onwards, after Congress was booted out. Even more so since the eighties, when swingeing positive discrimination in favour of the lower castes had changed the whole social make-up of the state. It had been about time, most felt. But small Vellala landowners, still farming a few acres, committed to the ancient traditions, were stripped of any influence, and were now very much representatives of an older world.

Mala's father was such a man. In the old days they had farmed 120 acres of paddy and betel nuts with a few tamarind trees near Killai, on the road to the sea. 'That was in the days when there was no money,' her father explained. 'Only paddy. The workers who built the house worked only for paddy, and so did the field labourers.' Now Mala's brother, the active head of family, who lived here with his wife and daughter, farmed only the twenty-five acres which remained.

The father spoke slowly, deliberately, partly because of his age, but also because he was clearly someone who had been good at weighing up situations and people; he was a man who knew the value of things. 'Our community are the traditional farmers of Tamil country. Our name Vellala comes from *vellanmai* in Tamil speech. *Vellan* means 'water'; *anmai* means 'managing': we were people who managed the water here in Chola Nadu, which means the Cavery delta. And in rice country, the main job is water managing.'

Mala popped her head round the door: 'Our other name is Karkotta Vellalas: people who wait for the rain, save the rain; gathering it in tanks and saving it for irrigation.'

He nodded. 'Everything here depends on irrigating, bringing water,' he continued; 'this was the job of our community, for every community has its job. But we are the ancient people of the soil; full bred, not migrating.'

Mala's sister came out of the kitchen with tea and rice puffs. Above their father's head, running round the walls of the living-room, was a narrow shelf with pictures of the family: at their moments of rites of passage, the special pujas, celebrations, birth-days, marriages, lamented children. There was father's eightieth birthday celebration at Tirukkadiyur, the great shrine of Yama, the God of Death and 'Keeper of Dharma'. There was their mother's father too, wearing the black coat and hat of a clerk. And there was Mala's wedding photo from 1959. Mani was twenty-four, she was eighteen. Solemn faced. Unsmiling. They looked more well-to-do then. Now she had the marks of life on her.

'There are many stories about our origin,' he went on. 'They say that thousands of years ago, when the people knew nothing of cultivation and irrigation, drought fell on the world. People prayed to the goddess Earth to help; out of her own body she made a man carrying a plough who knew the secrets of agriculture, of how to till the soil. His offspring are the Vellala. Children of the goddess,' he said, with a little smile as if to anticipate my scepticism.

★

Mala's sister-in-law brought banana leaves, which she placed on the floor. Then in the light of oil-lamps we ate rice and *sambhar*: the men first, as is the custom, the women only later. Around us the wooden pillars and painted architraves, the photos, the pictures of the family gods, conveyed a sense of rootedness in traditional time. Mala's father's generation were almost gone now, and Tamil Nadu would not see his like again. They were, one imagined, not so far from the people recorded in the Cholan inscriptions of a thousand years ago on the temple walls, the free peasantry who supported the high culture of the Cholan kingdom in alliance with kings and Brahmins. It was an order which had sustained the south for two thousand years. But it depended on an unfree or semi-free peasantry working below it, and that could not survive India's revolution into democracy.

'We are Vaisya caste,' the father continued. 'In the time of the British, the Britishers tried to write down every caste, to fix things which cannot be fixed. In the time of my grandfather they made a census and wrote us down as Sudras' (the lowest caste above the untouchables: the labouring and servile caste). 'But this was mistake; we say we are Vaisyas. The ancient law book, the book of Manu, says Vaisyas are permitted to keep cattle, cultivate the land, give wealth, to sacrifice, read scriptures, and to buy and sell; this is our right and our tradition. It greatly upset my grandfather. We say we are the old community of the land from even before the Brahmins were here. We were never servants of the higher-quality people and cannot be Sudra.'

The British came to agree, and to value the Vellala's work ethic and moral sensibility in much the same way that they valued the well-to-do, church-going, industrial working class in their own part of the empire. (Funnily enough, I know a Vellala doctor from Chidambaram who was a GP in Blackburn for twenty-five years and found himself very much at home in the traditional Lancashire working-class ethos.) A later census described the Vellala as 'peace-loving, frugal and industrious; in the cultivation of rice, betel, tobacco they have perhaps no equal in the world . . . and will not condescended to work of a degrading nature'. The British also noticed that in religion they were more strict than the Brahmins: 'abstaining from intoxicating liquor or meat'. This is still true and is rigorously maintained by Mala's children, even when surrounded by the temptations of Madras.

These were the values passed down by their grandfather. 'We spent more time in his house than in our own when I grew up,' said Bharati. 'He told us, be honest, don't cheat people, work hard, stand on your own two feet, and you will do fine, earn enough to make a good enough living. Didn't you, Grandad?' Grandad nodded, amused.

'As for marriage, Grandad said if you have a good heart then you will find someone with a good heart.'

Mala said his advice to her was more blunt: 'Pray to Nataraja but make sure your money's safe in the bank.' At this he laughed and shook his head ruefully.

Later Bharati took me round the house and showed me some of its secrets. At the little staircase where you enter from the street, she explained, every morning before sunrise, grandmother brushes the ground and splashes the clean dust with fresh cow dung and water. Then she marks out the *kolam* of rice flour before the threshold.

'This is not only for auspiciousness,' said Bharati, 'but as a first sacrifice of the day, to show mercy and kindness even to the most inferior creatures.'

'What do you mean inferior creatures?'

'Insects.'

'Insects?'

'Yes: this is why it must be rice flour, so that they may eat it.'

Inside the latticed entrance porch is a kind of upper lobby, the *thinnai*, which has a raised platform for sitting or sleeping.

'Here grandfather would receive visitors and watch the world go by, or house pilgrims who needed shelter or rest: that is, strangers who would be given hospitality but not be invited to share the family hearth,' Bharati went on. 'Here in the *thinnai* at five every evening the family lights the traditional lamp for Lakshmi which will burn through the night.'

Then you go through the door into the living-room, where her grandfather and I had talked and eaten. This has a large square light well in the middle, which is surrounded by a row of old wooden columns. This space gives light and fresh air but here also the family pray to the sun and eat their rice milk and *jaggery* at Pongal, the annual harvest festival. The living space is divided by a curtain, there are two small rooms off it and a roof space above for the family treasures, bronzes, vessels and marriage gifts, including beautiful and ornate gold wedding necklaces.

The main part of the living-room has a bench along the wall. In the shadows are a TV and fridge. Here the family entertain guests and set the table – 'lay the banana leaf', as they say in Tamil.

The kitchen was at the back of the house. There was a little altar on a shelf with pictures of Murugan, Lakshmi, Venkateshwara, and three small statues of Vinayaka covered with flowers. Though the family deity is Nataraja, like all Tamils they have a special affection for the elephant-headed Ganesh, and on the family land they built and maintain a little temple to him. Here in the kitchen they do their morning puja and at dusk when they light the lamp in the front porch, they close the back gate and burn one here too.

Behind the house was a brick yard with a well and a latrine: by the kitchen wall were stone grinding bowls, one for *iddly* and one for chillies. To the left a little herb and flower garden with flowers for puja (red hibiscus and *nadiya vatai*, a delicate white flower) and an orange-flowering bush which is twined in women's hair as a decoration. In the middle is a clump of basil in a little stone pot; this medicinal plant is traditionally kept in every house (as it still is in rural Greece too). 'We call it the flower of Vishnu,' said Bharati. 'We boil up the root for fevers; the juice of the leaves is very good for children if they have a cold and also as medicine; we mix it with lime juice for skin infections.'

To the right through a gate were the remains of an old garden, with an ancient brick-lined well; further on under an arch was a brick and earth yard with a covered colonnade and a threshing platform. Here were the family's two cows and a calf, which provide them with ghee and milk.

Last of all, in between the yard and the house, there was a narrow storage room about six feet wide and twenty-five feet long. We pushed open the door and went inside. By the door were big sealed jars of this year's tamarind, red chilli, green dhal and paddy seed. There was a huge wooden tallboy for rice, taller than me, sealed at the top, accessible at the bottom through little trapdoors. Beyond it we climbed over a jumble of disused implements: an old planter's chair with swivel arms, its wicker bottom gone; discarded home-made wooden toys and a heap of children's cots. It had the feeling of a kind of memory room for the family; Bharati was visibly moved. Mala joined us, laughing at my obsessive recording of all the details but touched all the same by the sight of these relics of her children's childhood and her own.

'Houses have a life,' said Mala later. 'They are conceived like a person. When you make a house you have to have an astrologer to give a horoscope, to find the right time, the right alignment, the right soil. You must pray to Mars so that the house is properly grounded and then to Vinayaka; these influence the length of its life, and the life of the people who live in it. Correct performance of rituals helps all this. There is a puja for the laying of the foundation post. When my father's grandfather built this house, below the threshold he laid nine precious stones, for the nine planets: emerald, ruby, diamond and so on, to give the house wealth and long life. Then they did pujas when the work was finished, all prescribed and supervised by a priest.

'If you are buying a house which someone else built, you get a horoscope if you can, and also if you are building a new one. When you see a building site with a scarecrow this is not to scare off birds but to keep away bad spirits while it is being built. There was a house built close to Nataraja Talkies where attention was not paid to these things; it was left empty and the family went away. They could never sell it, and it was never rented out; a pawnbroker took the ground floor for his daytime business.

'You see a house has a personality like a person. Like a marriage, people and house must have compatible horoscopes so that they get on well. When you build a house you ask a Brahmin to name the auspicious time to start. Houses can be "heartly", houses can be lonely; auspicious and inauspicious. Certain houses have no companionship. This is an auspicious house, and will stay so, whatever ups and downs happen in the family. We have guarded its personality carefully, so it will stand like a rock.'

'There is a saying that with some houses, even if Yama the God of Death came to stay, no harm would befall its people. The life of a family can take on this strength. Well, this house is like that; I hope it may live two hundred years or more,' said Bharati.

Grandmother joined us from the kitchen: 'No, this was never a lonely house,' she said with an infectious laugh, which showed a still-splendid set of teeth. She slapped the thickness of the wall as if it were the rump of her favourite cow. 'Look how thick the walls are; they don't build houses like this any more. That's why we have not changed it. It's an auspicious house, so why change anything?'

Afterwards, at Mala's insistence, we walked in the darkness to Ananteeswaram, an ancient shrine at the end of a long sandy lane behind Bazaar Street. There were children sitting in the nave doing their homework and a gnarled old Brahmin shuffled over to unlock the inner gate. Mala explained she wished to do a puja for the health of my little daughters. Afterwards she was pensive.

We sat in the forecourt and Bharati told me a story about Mala and Ananteeswaram.

'When my mother was a little girl, two years old, she was very ill; it was thought she was about to die. She was then the only child. Close to my grandfather's house in Chidambaram there is a temple, quite a large temple. It is called Ananteeswaram: Ananta is the serpent. My grandfather in his distress prayed there to the god for my mother's life. He made a vow that if she lived he would make a special puja there every month. Also, that a portion of the income of his lands would be dedicated to Nataraja. He kept this promise. The offering is still made every month. My mother was very close to her father. She was his favourite. But he changed after she married. "How can I live without you?" he said. Now of course my uncle and his wife live with him in the family house. My grandfather has not been helpful financially even though he has seen the situation we are in. Half of his house is separate, and this is rented out to a merchant. When my mother and father were forced to come back to live here when my father went blind, my grandfather offered them to live in his house, but only at rent. Which they could not afford. But in any case they would have refused.'

I said I didn't understand why they couldn't live in the grandfather's house. And why had Mala refused?'

'Even to rent would be wrong. It is alright for a son to do this, to live in the father's house. But not for a girl. Once the girl has married, and her father has paid dowry to her husband's family, she has left. That is that. It is the husband's responsibility. It is my uncle who will inherit the house. The responsibility now is the husband's family.'

'So why can't they help?'

'My father's family have lands in their village and in Sirkali on the way to Vaithisvarancoil. They have a big house with a tiled roof and a very lovely garden, with some old mango trees. But my father's brother and his wife have cheated him out of his own share. This is the story.

'The house was an old-fashioned house with a tiled roof, like our grandfather's. It had a beautiful garden with many flowers and trees, and twenty mango trees, which in season gave abundant fruit of delightful sweetness. After my father married, he left his father's house and moved with my mother to Pondi, where his work took him. His brother, however, continued to live in the house, and when he married, he stayed in it. The understanding was that they would share it. But when my father lost his sight, his brother got him to sign papers which left him in sole possession. My father was always trusting and did not have a head for business. He did not think his own brother would try to cheat him.

'When my father went blind and lost his job, he came back to Chidambaram, and asked his brother whether we could also come to live in his family house in Sirkali. His wife, my father's sister-in-law, said she did not want us there. Even the profit made each year on the sale of the fruit of the mango trees they did not share. All that is left is a separate plot of land on the outskirts of Sirkali on the road to Mayavaram; this is still held jointly and my father will get half when it is finally sold. We feel that my father's brother must have planned to cheat him of his rightful inheritance from long before. Certainly his wife planned it. At one point they even asked my father to pay the overdue tax on the plot of land when they did not have the money and the land was threatened with confiscation. He is so generous that he did.

'When they refused to let us come to live in the house, my mother went to see them and she had a stand-up fight with her sister-in-law; in the end she was screaming at her. Now we don't speak to that side of the family at all. All we want now is that they sell the plot of land, father gets the money which he is owed, and that my parents can move from where they are now to somewhere better. We really want mother and father to come to Madras. But I do not think mother will ever leave Nataraja.'

5

The Video Bus

Just before nine on Friday evening we went down to the corner of East Car Street. Close by there is an old pillared *mandapa* in a sandy lane lined with tiled houses. This is Mala's neighbourhood shrine to Ganesh, whom the Tamils call Vinayaka, the jolly elephant-headed god who blesses the start of all enterprises. There are said to be exactly 108 Ganeshes around the temple at Chidambaram – Mala probably knows where they all are too – but this is the one she and her neighbours choose for their prayers before they go on any journey. The bus was parked by the shrine, its bonnet decked with a chain of marigolds, a sign 'Airbus 630' stuck inside the window. The driver was fussing over a few last-minute checks. On the dashboard was a little plastic Murugan hung with fresh jasmine, smoke curling up from a fistful of incense sticks. Next to it was a silvered bust of Balaji framed by birds and flowers, and Siva's silver trident studded with fake red jewels. By the cigarette lighter hung Our Lady of Velankanni, and on the wheel a little sandalwood Ganesh. And if that were not enough, there was a notice prominently painted on the side of the bus: 'Insured by Overseas Insurance Company Cuddalore'. We were in safe hands.

The bus was already jam-packed. The organizer, Mr Ramasamy, was clucking around like a mother hen, with his passenger list in one hand and a large bag of rupees in the other. He and two friends had hired the bus and driver, and organized the whole thing. Mala, as usual, had their measure: with sixty persons at 200 rupees per person she thought they would make 4000–5000 profit out of the whole venture: '4500 bus hire, petrol 5000, driver 150 a day. You see, they will make 5000 rupees.' She wagged her head. And as it turned out, for the wear and tear on his constitution, I thought Mr Ramasamy was welcome to every paise.

Mr Ramasamy was quite a card. He had a twinkly eye, buck teeth, a big nose, and a shock of greying hair, which always stood on end. He was an infant-school teacher and part-time life assurance salesman. 'Both these talents are very necessary for conducting a good pilgrimage,' he assured me. 'If you are requiring temporary cover I can oblige,' he grinned. 'Very reasonable rates.' Even when waking us up at four the morning he couldn't resist a joke, and at low points on the journey he would sometimes liven things up by reading out choice quotes from his supply of joke books, the sort of thing you bought on bus-station stalls along with crossword and game books, and movie magazines. He had *Good Jokes*, *Best Jokes*, *Famous Last Jokes*, but his favourite was *Aruvai Joks*, which, loosely translated, means 'Lousy Jokes' or 'Jokes to Make You Squirm with Embarrassment'. These he would deliver accompanied by loud guffaws, which he would then translate as best he could for the foreigner on the bus. I can't say I ever became a connoisseur of Tamil humour, but it is gentle, so far as I could tell. Crudity, violence and pornography are eschewed: word play, social jokes and movie jokes are preferred. Sex jokes are fine so long as they are discreet. Most were communicable in any language, mother-in-law jokes, as might be expected, being especially popular among the Tamils. (First man: 'My mother-in-law is a goddess.' Second man: 'You're lucky, mine's still alive!' Mr Ramasamy's own mother-in-law, by the way, was on board, sitting with his wife two rows back; she took it all with an indulgent smile.)

'We have saved you the place of honour,' said Mr Ramasamy with a grandiloquent gesture towards the front bench seat, right behind the driver. It would have been churlish to say so, but it was not the best place on the bus. There was no leg room (I am 6 feet 2 inches tall) and most of the seat was already occupied by an extremely fat man who seemed set upon maintaining a vow of silence all the way to Tiruchendur. The first stage of the journey, Mr Ramasamy announced, was to be nine hours non-stop through the night down to Rameshwaram. There was a great buzz of excitement in the air, the women carefully packing their tiffin boxes and spare saris into the luggage racks, the children all wide awake and thrilled with the prospect of the adventure which lay ahead. At last we moved off slowly down East Car Street, with most people still on their feet. By the temple gate more people got on, so it was now standing room only. Mutinous shouts rose from the back. Mr Ramasamy suddenly looked worried, and clapped his hands to get everyone to stand still for a proper count. Messages were shouted out of the window, and a little further on we stopped once more to take on board a dozen folding chairs to put in the aisles. The aisles were now filled up and everyone had a seat. Everyone that is, except a tall and gangling priest, who remained perched on the engine box. Raja was a Dikshithar from the temple; he had come with his friend Ganesh, another priest. Though off duty, both of them were resplendent in their Friday best: white loincloth, Brahmin's thread, bodies meticulously striped with holy ash, and hair done up in the traditional topknot. Suddenly, with one hand on the overhead rack, Raja vaulted with surprising athleticism over the aisle seats and launched himself on top of me. Ours was a seat for three people, not two, he pointed out. Could the fat man and I kindly make room? Clearly, five days of this was not going to be the most comfortable ride of my life. Still, we were off on pilgrimage, and for everyone else on the bus bodily comfort was the last thing on the mind. At least, that's what I kept telling myself.

Behind me, sitting with the ladies, their saris glowing in the red night light, Mala grinned at me and wagged her head. 'You'll get used to it in no time,' said Mr Ramasamy as I tried to massage my dead leg. 'This is a very good bus, the latest model, super de luxe,' he said showing off the threadbare furnishings and metal seats; 'very comfortable, no expenses spared.' He rolled his eyes and guffawed. 'By the time we reach Tanjore you won't feel a thing.'

We set off soon after nine o'clock, careering through the town with our horn blaring. We swept past the bus station and the Nataraja Talkies, swerving on the wrong side of the road round the Gandhi statue, and scattering unwary clientele at the almond milk stall. There were sixty-six of us in a fifty-six-seater bus. On top of that the driver had two assistants. One of them, a doe-eyed youth, seemed to be there simply to keep him awake. The other was the mechanic, and his main job was to keep the video working. He was to spend the next two hours fighting a losing battle with the picture, which kept disintegrating into a blizzard of white static and unbearable noise. Meanwhile tantalizing glimpses of a cool southern night flitted past in our headlights as we headed into the countryside.

The video bus is a new and popular form of pilgrimage in southern India. You have the spiritual benefit of visiting the sacred places and in between you see your favourite old movies. Unfortunately, in my place of honour, the screen and its speakers were about twelve inches above my head. It was a kind of torture. They stopped twice to try to fix the picture even before we left town, then again on the way to Sirkali and once more after Kumbakonam, obstinately trying to get a steady image. They then gave up until we had a brief night tea stop somewhere after Tanjore, when they finally got it working.

From 1 a.m. the old MGR movies rolled out. MGR had been the chief minister of Tamil Nadu from 1977 until his death in December 1988, and his face was still everywhere in the state. On political posters, pilgrim stalls and roadside shrines his furry white pillbox hat and dark glasses are as recognizable here as Churchill's trilby and cigar were once in England. This was a man whom a senior British diplomat once described to me as 'the most improbable politician I ever met'. But that hadn't stopped MGR gaining almost god-like status in the south. Among the poor he was credited with virtually miraculous powers. The story of his return from long hospital treatment in the US was famous. MGR had been gone for a year, during which the Tamil land had endured a severe drought. There had even been special pujas for rain held in the big temples, but to no avail. But within hours of his stepping off the plane at Meenambakkam, the skies just opened and every tank in the state was filled to overflowing. MGR evidently employed a good soothsayer (or a good meteorologist – one of the two). There were at least thirty suicides upon the news of his fatal illness, in the manner of religious suicide in the old days. More than two million attended his funeral on Madras marina, the site of which is now a place of pilgrimage.

Born of a poor Tamil family, MGR had been a movie star through the fifties and sixties, corny old song and dance movies, dramas of mistaken identity, lost twin brothers, wicked step-mothers, poor boys who had made good; movies full of dramatic clashes, pantomime emotion and fat-bottomed dances, all spiced with leering, coy cuddles with young starlets (one of whom was now MGR's successor as chief minister). During those early years he had been a member of the DMK, the Tamil regional party which stood for Tamil autonomy, atheism and anti-Brahminism, and his films had pushed a sentimental, watered-down version of the DMK ideology, using the party's symbols and colours on the screen. Justice for the poor, freedom in love for women, defeat for the corrupt, the triumph of the lower castes over the Brahmins – it was all there. Of course this was far from the reality of life for the poor labouring classes from whom MGR drew his fans, and subsequently his political support. But that was the point. His films acted out the fantasies of the ordinary people.

Cinema was – and still is – the great form of mass entertainment in the south, and films were the chief vehicle for the political message. Films can turn actors into chief ministers and stars into gods. Even if at the time MGR had no political ambitions (or, come to think of it, divine ones too) he had certainly tailored his image very carefully during his early movie career: unscrupulously, some would say. By the time he was forced to leave the DMK and form his own party, in 1972, his make-believe world had permeated Tamil popular culture. His eleven-year rule from 1977 to 1987, said a recent Indian study of the great man's career, 'was one of the darkest periods in the modern history of the state'. Under his aegis, his critics allege, profiteers, liquor barons, real-estate speculators and party magnates made fortunes, while living standards sank among the rural poor, the mainstay of his support. But, like a familiar and much-loved deity, MGR never lost the affection of the Tamil masses and consequently never had to answer the claims of conventional political morality. In the end he remained, an ageing and sick giant, inscrutable behind his dark glasses, surrounded by his soothsayers and courtiers, still disbursing his patronage while the cases piled up by the thousand in the offices of the Madras Corporation, which he had abolished. It was an almost incredible tale, which still rendered many of my friends in Madras speechless with pain and perplexity. When pressed, though, all of them admitted that if MGR had anything, it was charm: from the lowest to the highest, he captivated anyone who met him. 'He made them happy, even though the truth was the very opposite of what it appeared.'

Sitting next to me, and still somehow immaculate, Raja had two theories as to why MGR was so loved by the people: 'First, social themes. He cared for the poor, they called him their father, their brother, their son. They think he loved them. Second, is the way he acted. Watch this fight now.' I looked up to see what appeared to me to be a rather overweight and ungainly man in advanced middle age send two strapping banditti flying in somersaults across the set. 'Watch his movement,' Raja continued. 'You see? Very good, very strong, no one could beat him. Now here watch the way he dances too; Tamil people love the way MGR dances. Women especially. Many women admired MGR. Including the present chief minister.' Unbelievable, it all seemed to me. But there it was. Raja watched in approving silence for a while and then gestured once more at the screen: 'A very clever man. Mr MGR was getting four rupees for every bottle of beer sold in Tamil Nadu.' Even in a state where alcohol is frowned on by all religious people, and where partial prohibition was in force until recently, this added up to some kickback.

In the early hours, after two MGR films, they put on the new star Ragini Kanth. Modern stuff full of macho posturing and fighting. 'This man was a bus conductor before he became a star in films,' said Raja, who was turning out to be no slouch as a film buff, to add to his skills in Vedic *sloka*s. 'Actually it was the no. 17 bus in Bangalore. When he became famous he gave a great party for all the conductors and drivers on his old route.' Ragini Kanth's film was much more up to date in its pace and cutting, though still brimming with exaggerated fight sequences and dance numbers. 'He is a good man. Like a child,' said Raja. 'We like his sense of humour. He is one of us.' And indeed, Ragini Kanth's was an engaging screen presence. One could not help but laugh with him as he let his audience in on his jokes. Ganesh chipped in from his chair in the aisle: 'Watch this now. He has very good tricks.' Having wiped the floor with the villain, Ragini Kanth flipped his cigarette up into his mouth, quiffed his hair with his hand and gave a top-sided, quizzical smile to the camera. 'He is one of us, our brother,' Ganesh went on. 'He has fan clubs all over Tamil Nadu; social clubs which support him and do good works. I also belong.' So the Tamil movie star fan clubs even found their stalwarts amongst the world's oldest and most exclusive clan of ritual specialists. To Ganesh (should it even occur to him to wonder), there would be nothing strange in that at all.

The bus charged on through the night. On my right-hand side the fat man kept falling asleep and pushing me against Raja and both of us off the edge of the seat. I gave up trying to sleep and looked around me. We were a mixed bunch: more women than men, some children, Brahmin priests sitting with lower castes, a tax inspector, a schoolteacher, shopkeepers and housewives, a hotel worker. Across the aisle, there was a little girl called Minakshi. She was four years old, with a big smile and huge round dark eyes (like her namesake, the goddess of Madurai). She had come on the pilgrimage with her aunt and her grandmother, who were both very kind to this stranger. Though we had few words between us, they always offered to share their food with me, and better still, to share their feelings. Minakshi's mother had died in childbirth, and she had been brought up by her mother's sister, a rather shy, attractive woman who did not yet have children of her own. Minakshi always amazed me by her patience and good humour during the long hours on the bus. She had no seat of her own, and would sit and sleep on her aunt's knee, or on the wheel box with the driver's mate, on Raja's lap, or even my own, in front of the TV screen. Like most Indian children she had the knack of sleeping uncomplaining anywhere – unlike me, I was ashamed to acknowledge.

And so as the night progressed we all settled down with each other. Behind me, lit by the glow of the video screen, the women in their saris were slumped against each other, the Dikshithars with their elegant hairdos nodding with every bump of the bus. There was no room to fall over; we were so tightly packed that our sleeping heads rested on our neighbours' shoulders. In the morning Raja's stripes of ash had left a faint rime on my cheek. No one seemed to need any space, comfort or privacy: only I did, so un-Indian in my desire to find a comfortable position, and a tiny bit of private space. In the end I gave in and ceased to resist as the sleeping fat man slowly lurched over once more and pressed me in fleshy intimacy.

★

At six we stopped on a long straight stretch of country road. To the left the sky was streaked with pale mauve behind distant streamers of white cloud. Bleary and stiff, we all piled out, the women off into the bush at the back of the bus, the men to the front. I gulped the fresh breeze. We were near the sea.

As the dawn rose, the driver switched off the video and put on a sound tape – popular religious songs now, contemporary versions of ancient hymns which were as familiar to the people on the bus as MGR's movie songs. These were the hymns of the Tamil saints, the wandering singers who travelled the length and breadth of the south between the sixth and the tenth centuries, composing their poems about the Tamil holy places, drunk on the colours and fecundity of the Tamil landscape and the immanent presence of the divine. Their songs are played with a racy beat and jangling guitars now, but still to the immortal tunes which have been handed down for so many centuries: 'O simple heart, if you seek a good end, go to holy Rameshwaram: find salvation at the temple built with love by the beautiful Ram . . . simple heart go to holy Rameshwaram'. There are usually no end rhymes in Tamil poetry; it is the elegance of the rhythms and the refinement of the phrasing which Tamils love. Not every word is understandable today, but most are, and most Tamil people will know some of the saints' hymns off by heart: indeed it is still common to meet people who know the entire collection of the saints' hymns, the *Tevaram*. It is, let us say, as if English poetry of the age of Beowulf were still popular fare, and the *Hymn* of Caedmon as familiar to us now as 'Jerusalem'.

Soon we were running along the coast with the sea on the right-hand side. We passed fishing villages as the light came up: reed houses on wicker platforms, the sea around them like white glass with a gentle swell. Across the straits towards Sri Lanka the night boats were bringing in their catch, their stern lamps still glowing. We came to the bridges across to Rameshwaram island: the railway bridge built by the British in 1914 as a strategic link in their Far

Eastern empire; the road bridge opened as recently as 1988 by Rajiv Gandhi and named after his mother Indira. Until then pilgrims had come over by ferry as they had done for thousands of years. On the other side is a landscape of sandy scrub, dunes, acacia palms and umbrella trees, dotted with more thatched fishing villages and the picturesque ruins of old temples and *choultries*, their colonnades half buried in wind-blown sand. We stopped at the municipal bus park where the sellers of pilgrim knick-knacks were already setting out their stalls and the *chai* wallahs boiling up their first kettle of the day. We had arrived at one of the four holy cities of India, the southern point of the continent's sacred geography, 'Holy Rameshwaram, the temple built on the island by Rama when he bridged the surging ocean'.

RAMESHWARAM

On the map the island is shaped like a flying bird, nearly twenty miles down its length, its tail stretching out towards Sri Lanka to which it is almost joined by a string of islands known as Adam's Bridge – a two-hour crossing by steamer in the old days. The border had been closed now for some time because of the struggles with the Tamil Tigers, in which India had taken the side of the Sri Lankan government against the separatist guerrillas from the Tamil-speaking north of the island – an alliance for which Rajiv Gandhi had paid with his life. Now the straits were crossed by a new kind of smuggler, bringing arms from camps in the mainland, which at that time were covertly tolerated by the DMK government. For a period after Rajiv's death the disorder even threatened to spread to the Tamil mainland. But all this was far from our thoughts that luminous morning.

The temple stands on rising ground above a freshwater lake on the northern side of the island, a couple of hundred yards from the seashore. It is one of the great holy sites of India. According to the legend (and in India the truthfulness of legendary history has always been valued more highly than mere historical fact), Rama built the first temple here in expiation of his killing of the demon king Ravana in his invasion of Sri Lanka. The tale comes from the Indian epic, the *Ramayana*, which was probably composed in the first or second century BC but which, like the Homeric poems, refers back to much earlier historical events. As soon became apparent to me on the bus journey, the *Ramayana* is a tale which pervades the cultural life of India, just as Homer permeated classical culture for so long in the Mediterranean world. But the *Ramayana* is more than that, for its stories are common currency from the highest to the lowest in the land. It is probably no exaggeration to say that everyone in India is aware of the tale in some way or other, whether Hindu, Christian, or Muslim; it had a staggering success on TV, where it achieved the biggest ratings ever by any TV programme in the world. Whether in the hands of TV, movies, folk theatre or the traditional village storyteller, it still provides a model for human actions, right and wrong, good and evil. 'It is applicable for all times and all conditions of life,' said Mr Subrahmaniam, one of the pilgrims, as we walked across to the town bus stop. 'Everyone of whatever outlook, caste or education knows the *Ramayana* and loves wholeheartedly the hero and heroine, Rama and Sita; he is the quintessence of the noble and manly spirit, she the very image of the pure and loyal partner for life.'

Rameshwaram is a central place in this famous tale, for here Rama, the beloved incarnation of Vishnu, worshipped Siva after his destruction of the demon Ravana and his winning back of Sita. Here the great strands of Hinduism come together, and so the temple is revered throughout the subcontinent. All Hindus will try to come here once in their lifetime.

The town bus dropped us at the South Gate towards seven. Near by, Muslim custodians in white skullcaps were unlocking a little shrine – 'The Tomb of Cain and Abel', I was surprised to learn. The sun was already hot. 'First we bathe in the sea,' said Mala, striding off purposefully to the pilgrim stalls opposite, clutching her tiffin box and spare sari. Before any puja, or act of worship, there are preparations to be done: 'You never approach God empty-handed.' After checking the prices, she bought coconut, bananas, camphor, *vilva* leaves and a little boat of sewn leaves to make a puja lamp. Then everyone raced off to the beach in high spirits. The men stripped to their shorts or underpants to splash into the surf, the women went in full sari. After nine hours jammed in the bus being feasted on by mosquitoes, the swim was sheer bliss.

While I dried off, Mala plunged in, letting the waves cover her. Then she stood dripping on the beach, struggling to light her camphor as the breeze kept blowing out her matches. Finally she succeeded and said a little prayer as the little lamp boat went bobbing off across the waves towards Sri Lanka. I sat by her belongings while she went to change with the other women. Just around the bay to the right was a big fishing village with hundreds of boats, a jumble of masts and rigging, with heaps of nets and fish debris on the quay; an occasional pungent whiff came on the breeze. Out in the pearly haze we could see the shadow of the island on the horizon. Then it was time to go to the temple for *darshan*.

'Absolutely not permitted,' said the man on the gate, gesturing to me and then pointing to a painted placard: 'Only Hindus allowed beyond this point.' Mala was exasperated and told him off, but he would not budge. If I wanted to pursue the matter I should take it up with the committee. I was directed to the temple office where I waited like a petitioner. 'Not possible,' said a minion, wagging his head. Just then the head of the temple committee arrived in his office in a neatly ironed safari jacket and bearing a stainless-steel lunch-box.

'You are Hindu?' he asked.

'No.' I explained I was on pilgrimage with Tamil friends.

'But why?'

I tried the most unlikely explanation: 'It was my horoscope, you see: I was instructed to come by the astrologer at the Nataraja temple.'

He scratched his head. This was unusual. 'Come in, come in. Sit down.' He asked the boy to bring tea. Did I have reverence for Lord Siva?

'Certainly.'

'You see, usually we do not allow non-Hindus in at all. This is not a strict religious requirement in the scriptures. Indeed many Indian Muslims and Christians come here to worship freely. But problem is, we have many foreigners here; bus parties of French people and Italians in Bermuda shorts with cameras round their necks. If we let them all in they would impinge on the atmosphere for the real devotees who have come here from the farthest reaches of India.'

'I fully understand. But I would be most obliged, if you would be so kind . . .'

He relented. He launched into a potted version of the story of Rama's expedition to Sri Lanka. Then came fatherly talk on matters spiritual.

'The essential thing when you go in is to be pure-spirited. This is one of the holiest places in India. Inside is a most intense and emotional experience. Take this advice with you. Find a quiet corner. Get a few minutes to meditate in peace and calm. Then you will see some benefit of coming here.' He called for a dish of brightest vermilion and with his thumb daubed it emphatically on my forehead.

'There. Now you are pukka. I will write you a note for the people on the gate.'

Inside was absolute mayhem. Huge loudspeakers relayed religious music at nerve-jangling volume. Crowds surged backwards and forwards to a racket of bells, singing and shouting. Round every corner was a sudden rush and thunder of drums. And there was water everywhere. A constant stream of dripping devotees hastened in straight from the sea, many of them bearing pots of Ganges water, the traditional gift here, to be poured over the linga. Inside the shrine there are twenty-two sacred stations, many of them wells representing the rivers of India, and here the pilgrims, especially the young men, raucously pour buckets of water over each other. Around the main shrine was a rugby scrum. Wet from head to toe I headed for the outer corridors to try to locate the commissioner's quiet corner.

The temple forms a huge rectangle; its most famous feature is a double circuit of corridors round the inner shrines, dramatic colonnades more than 4000 feet long of thirty-foot-high monolithic black granite pillars. The oldest parts of the interior now standing are twelfth-century, made of dark, hard limestone cut in Sri Lanka. But the shrine is evidently much older than its surviving structures. It was already famous in the *Mahabharata*, whose traditions, like those of the *Ramayana*, go back to the first millennium BC. Ever since then the island has been one of the great pilgrimage sites, and the official guidebook carries pages of visitors' comments from Valmiki to Mark Twain, and from Marco Polo to Mahatma Gandhi. Encrusted with carvings, inscriptions and statues, the inner halls are a kind of religious memory store for India; their shelves, niches, shrines, alcoves, and wells form a kind of liturgical theme park for all India's shrines, a repository of pan-Indian traditions. In the treasury, engraved copper plates describe medieval kings weighing themselves in gold here at the 'beautiful *tirtha* of Sri Rama, where the monkey tribes built a bridge across the sea'. Among the bronzes is a lively portrayal of the faithful monkey god Hanuman, garlanded with beads around his head, who gingerly carries a large cylindrical linga like a gunner with a six-inch shell. Mr Ramasamy explained: 'The main idol is supposed to be the linga brought back by Hanuman himself from Mount Kailash more than three thousand years ago. You see, after Rama overcame Ravana he wanted to worship but there was no linga available. So Hanuman went all the way up to the Himalayas to bring one back. But Hanuman was unavoidably delayed, and Rama made another one out of sand. When Hanuman came back, he was greatly upset to find his efforts had been in vain. So Lord Rama installed Hanuman's linga also and gave it precedence. 'This is the very linga,' said Mr R pointing to a tiny black stone set in a round base and embossed with silver Saivite bands; he spoke with absolute conviction of the presence of the numinous. 'This we always worship first, in memory of Hanuman.'

Defeated in my attempt to find a quiet corner as the commissioner had recommended, I beat a retreat to a *dosa* stall for breakfast, shopped for a souvenir (a little framed picture of Rama and Hanuman), and then headed back to the bus for the next leg, the journey to Tiruchendur. Mr Ramasamy clambered over the folding chairs to count us all, and at about ten we pulled out of the coach park, music blaring, damp saris streaming out of the windows. Mala grinned; little Minakshi was wide-eyed with the fun of it all, while her aunt smiled as she combed the wet knots out of her long black hair, looking – to borrow a phrase – the embodiment of healthy and auspicious female power. And indeed we were all starting to let our hair down.

Pilgrimage has always been a vital part of Indian culture. In the *Mahabharata* there is a list of nearly three hundred holy places which forms a clockwise pilgrimage round India from the Himalayas to Comorin. Some of the key sites, like Lake Pushkar, go back to the Stone Age. Indian people have been travelling to worship at sacred places on rivers, mountains and seashores since before history. Very likely, the wanderings of holy men and women contributed as much as anything to the sense of the cultural oneness of India, which long preceded her political unity. Today pilgrimage is a massive industry, which has been totally transformed by cheap transport and mass communications. At the last Kumbh Mela in Allahabad, fifteen million people were present on the main night of a month-long festival. I can remember being at the home of a Tamil-speaking guide there when poor pilgrims from the deep south arrived from the station; without a word of Hindi, shivering in thin tropical clothes, they had had no idea India was so big, or the north so cold, but they had been drawn there to join in the greatest of all Indian pilgrimages.

The transformation has happened in little more than a century. When investment in railways was first mooted by the board of the East India Company in the late 1840s, there were those who doubted the viability of railways in India, because it was felt that the rules of caste purity and pollution would deter most people from using trains for fear of rubbing shoulders with the wrong caste. In fact, of course, those rules are infinitely changeable and adaptable (the system would hardly have lasted 3000 years if they were not). Knowing which side their bread was buttered on, Brahmin priests everywhere quickly agreed that travel by train did not mean losing the merits of pilgrimage. (No doubt in time they will also agree, if they have not already, to interactive puja disks and conference-call *darshans*!)

By the early 1900s, thousands flocked to places previously visited by hundreds in the days before railways. Now, in its turn, the bus has taken over, and with the increased popularity of gods like Murugan there has been a tenfold growth in pilgrimage in the south since Independence; indeed bus travel has turned a once obscure and inaccessible place, Subarimalai, into the biggest annual pilgrimage in the world, outstripping even Mecca.

'Of course times have changed,' said Mr Subrahmaniam, reflecting on this as we headed away from Rameshwaram: 'We do the *darshan* bus tour for speed and convenience. It is not arduous. Only we are fasting for the duration. This is all. In the old days these journeys were made on foot with only the barest necessities. This procured more merit than taking vehicular transport. But for us, time is not as before. Our fathers had more time. We have to be back to work Tuesday morning punctual.'

TIRUCHENDUR

The journey to Tiruchendur took us another eight hours in fierce heat along rough country roads through a baking wilderness of scrub jungle, crumbling red soil and thirsty palms. By noon the bottled water tasted as if it had just been boiled. In the afternoon the bus broke down in the middle of nowhere and the driver had to take the engine to bits while the women trooped off to do their toilet in the bush. Mala nervously paced up and down on the road as time ticked away: though she does not possess a watch she always knows what time it is, and she knew we were now likely to miss the key puja, the one Sivakami had told her to go to in her dream. Eventually we got going once more, and at last, towards five, we saw the *gopura* of the temple towering above the seashore.

Tiruchendur means 'beautiful holy town' in Tamil, and it is; a seaside town in a very picturesque position, cooled by the sea breezes from Ceylon, a holiday place for fresh air and fun. That Saturday it was bursting at the seams. In the sandy main street of the town we ran into a tide of people like a crowd emptying from a football stadium. To get to the temple from the town you have to walk up a long covered colonnade which stretches for nearly half a mile through the houses and up to the sacred precinct on the seashore: a processional way lined with stalls selling food, tea, flowers, incense, *kun kum*, astrological readings, children's toys, cheap clothes and pilgrims' souvenirs. We struggled up this walkway pushing against the flow of the thousands who were already leaving, and it was past six before we reached our goal. We had just missed the climactic puja of the festival. We pressed on, and suddenly the walkway opened out to reveal vast halls and thousands of people. To a thunderous crescendo of drums and trumpets a troop of elephants caparisoned in gold came sweeping past, followed by glittering palanquins festooned with bunting. We crested the last rise to the seashore and, choosing our moment, ran across the procession, ducking under the crash barriers and through the police lines. Ahead was the sea; as the light faded a truly fantastic scene was unfolding.

Stretching away to the southern horizon there were thousands camped on the beach, many taking a dip in the sea as the sun set – a million and a half people according to the police inspector standing by the Lost Persons' Tent. Beyond them was the deep blue sea, fringed by a line of crashing breakers. On the sand, the pilgrims had lit fires, whose smoke eddied round the beach and swirled up into the sky; the wind was now whipping up long streamers of sari cloths hung out to dry: gold, purple, emerald green, marigold, blood red, snapping in the breeze like the flags of some vast medieval encampment. To the east the sky was already darkened, with colossal thunderclouds piled on top of each other over the Palk Strait and the Arabian Sea. Along the horizon was a strip of pale golden light where the sun had gone. In front of us, the main gate of the temple reared up a hundred and fifty feet above our heads, covered in sculpture from top to bottom. Unlike most temples in the south, Tiruchendur's stonework is unpainted; scoured and bleached by wind and sun, it glowed an unearthly white against the ink-blue sky. On top, in neon lights, was the leaf-shaped lance of Murugan and the sacred syllable OM. ('It is visible from my bungalow in Tuticorin – seventeen miles away,' said a pilgrim who suddenly appeared at my elbow as if to read my thoughts.)

Below the tower the columned halls of the temple were hung with coloured electric light-bulbs. We went in, to be enveloped by the roar of the crowds. In the front hall on a raised platform a trio of plump Brahmin priests were doling out holy ash to crowds of worshippers and collecting their rupees as fast as they could, sweating profusely. Beyond them we could see deep into the temple where huge queues pressed behind metal barriers snaked off into the darkness, waiting for their brief audience with the god. Because of our bus breaking down we had missed the last puja, and the queues were so great that there hardly seemed time now to wait in line for *darshan*, that is, just to see Murugan for a few seconds. We had to be back on the bus down in the town at eight for the five-hour journey to our overnight stop at Cape Comorin. I was turning out to be not quite so committed a pilgrim as I had hoped. I was all for calling it a day. Tea and tiffin on the beach suddenly seemed greatly preferable to plunging into the barely suppressed riot which seemed to be going on inside. There might even be time for a swim. Lord Murugan forgive me, I thought; there'll be another time. Mala paced to and fro, disappointed at my lack of resolution though too polite to say so. Then I heard another voice at my shoulder: 'Kind sir, what is your native land?'

'England.'

'In all this great congregation of people, I have observed that you are the only foreigner here. Kindly tell me why you have come.'

He was a sweet-faced older man with grey hair, wearing a white short-sleeved shirt, a white dhoti and barefoot. Next to him was a young priest wearing a white loincloth, grey ash daubed on his forehead and his upper arms. The old man ran a packaging company in Tuticorin. In the present difficult economic climate the company had fallen on hard times. He had come today to ask the Lord for help. We talked for a while. I explained that we were late and had missed the puja. We said our goodbyes. Ten minutes later he returned with a second priest.

'You would like to have *darshan* of the Lord?'

Mala's face lit up. 'We would.'

'Kindly come with me, but first sir I must ask you to take off your shirt. Male worshippers must go before the Lord uncovered.'

A magic wand had been waved. It turned out the priest worked with the old man in Tuticorin. They had spoken to someone on the temple committee. We were taken to the back of the columned entrance hall to a side door through a high granite wall. The door was besieged by crowds, which were kept at bay by the police with an intimidating display of lathi waving. But after an anxious moment's push and shove, we were pulled through. We found ourselves in a cavernous corridor with immense carved pillars towering in the gloom, pillars capped by monstrous heads – griffins and basilisks glaring, snarling and biting their own tails. They led us down the hall, under more metal barriers, and through another door to join the pilgrims at the head of the queue outside the holy of holies. At the entrance the Chief of Police waved us on with a wag of his head, a friendly beam and a wiggle of his luxuriant handlebar moustache. 'Welcome!' he said. 'Come and see the Lord.'

We stepped on to a raised walkway of wooden duckboards and joined the crowd. First we came to the bronze processional image of Murugan, almost buried in flowers. Then the main stone image of the temple – god as ascetic, renouncer of the transitory and illusory. In his six abodes he has different aspects – Perennial Child, Eternal Youth, Warrior, Husband, Renouncer, Lord of the Tamil Hills – but in all he is benign and life-giving, Apollonian, 'grace-breathing', as Robert Browning puts it so memorably in his version of Aeschylus. His wars represent the triumph of good over evil; he destroys wickedness, decay and death. And his smile – the smile of Murugan – is the light of life and eternal youth. For two thousand years that smile has been a theme of Tamil poetry: 'radiating light, removing darkness from the world'. Finally we were right in front of him. They never fail, do they, these archetypal images? In the modern West we pay analysts to help us tease out some fragmented meaning from such dreams and urges, fulfilled and unfulfilled. Here it is all still out in the open. Child, goddess, androgyne, killer of the unborn child, whatever you fear or desire you can access directly in cult. The Greeks intuited their imaginal universe in the same way, in their gory myths of father castration and child cannibalism as much as in their mystic tales of renewal in the legends of Demeter and Aphrodite. Here in the presence of an equally rich and ancient body of myth, you can still understand what such stories mean.

'This is the God of Tamils,' said the man in front of me as he strained to see the inscrutable face. Then suddenly, as if he had locked on to a beam coming from the eyes of the image, his face was rapt and still amid all the hubbub. He raised his praying hands above his head and spoke some words from an ancient hymn on Murugan: 'Burning anger is wiped away. Scorched with the spark from your radiant smile, O leader of men with the leaf-shaped spear, lover of Valli the wild huntress.' He wiped a tear from his eye and turned to me. 'He is King of the Smile.'

All around us the energy and emotion was almost explosive, but all of it good-natured. The noise of the crowd filled the ears. On either side of the statue the priests were doling out holy ash into outstretched hands as fast as they could; devotees feverishly mouthed prayers. Pointing out the other statues, Mala tried to explain the main details of the myth – Murugan's wives, his conquest of the demonic forces, which took place on this spot – at the same time urging me to pray, while also hanging on in front of the image to snatch every last second of direct contact with Murugan's face – and especially his eyes – before the pressure of the crowd swept her on. In this narrow, dark, hot place the press of the crowd might have been frightening, except that the sense of excitement was quite overwhelming: the dim light, the puja flames, the damp heat, the thick, sweet smell of incense and ghee, the drenching scent of jasmine and marigolds, the sweat of our own half-naked bodies – it all combined in an intoxicating, almost sexual effect.

When we left the inner sanctum, the old man and his priest friend led us to another part of the temple, in one of the outer corridors, where there is an ancient Vishnu shrine in an underground chamber cut into the rock of the seashore. The image of the god sleeping on the coils of the undying serpent had been much re-carved and retouched but was evidently much older than the mainly seventeenth-century temple buildings (Pallava, according to our

friend; that is, eighth century). The existence of a shrine here
is known from the oldest surviving Tamil poetry, from two
thousand years ago, in which the deity appears as 'The Red One',
'The Spear Bearer', or 'The Bringer of Desire', as well as in the
form of Murugan ('the young, tender one, the youth'). But the
Tiruchendur region has yielded still earlier evidence of such a cult
in the south: in the 1890s a settlement was excavated on the
Tambraparni river which dated from before 1000 BC. Its people
were found to have worshipped a male deity whose emblems were
the spear and the cock. Intriguingly, the devotees also seem to
have worn mouth locks, just as worshippers of Murugan still do,
especially at the hill shrine of Palani. So it may well be that the
cult of Murugan and his peacock, lord of the hills and mountains,
goes back here deep into prehistory.

The six-day festival at Tiruchendur which climaxes on this day
is unique in India in its fastidious adherence to the most ancient
Vedic practice. The key event in the ritual takes place in a small
room deep inside the temple where the priest burns a hundred and
eight different herbs and magical substances – all to avert malaise
in the heart and malaise in the cosmos at large, a symbolic renewal
of the earth as it were, at the time of year when the monsoon is
about to replenish the land. This ritual is accompanied by some of
the oldest mantras in Sanskrit, which some scholars now believe to
be even older than human speech, mantras whose nearest analogue
we now discover is not human speech at all, but birdsong. (Here
we may have a clue to the origins of language itself. For if ritual
predates language – as it surely must do, since ritual behaviour is
known in the animal kingdom – and if mantras are indeed also
older than language, then was the first language developed by
Homo sapiens for ritual purposes? Curiously enough, this has long
been the assertion of the Brahminical tradition in India.)

As a last kindness the old man now led us to the room where
the chief priest was receiving guests. We were ushered in to have
his blessing. A tiny man with a gentle smile, he was unshaven and

looked worn out, not surprisingly, as he had just completed an arduous six-day ritual cycle in which the slightest mistake in syllable or gesture could cast a shadow over the whole of the proceedings. He had a few words with Mala, who could scarcely contain her excitement at the turn of events, and then he gave us special *prasad*, *vilva* leaves and holy ash, along with little wrapped packages from the great fire sacrifice. Last of all we were handed fresh *vetilay* leaves to chew. I hesitated, but Mala insisted, so I put them in my mouth. Their taste was very sharp and bitter and served as it were to wake us after such an otherworldly experience, reviving us as if from a dream.

It was almost time to go. We parted from our guide with effusive thanks. The old man sweetly asked simply that we pray for him and his business. Afterwards we crouched for a while in a quiet corner of the labyrinth around the shrine, our ears still echoing with the noise of the crowds and the distant sound of trumpet and drums. We looked at each other, ash and sweat running down into our eyes. Mala burst out laughing. From somewhere in the depth of the temple, a sudden gust of incense and ghee came on the wind, hot and voluptuous. Her face shone with excitement. 'We have been very lucky. The future is looking very bright. Many problems will go away.' For her, it all fitted together – the astrologer's prediction, my letter, her dream, my coming, the bus breaking down, the old man – everything had led to this auspicious end. Later, when we were back on the bus, she told the story to her lady friends. As it turned out, most people had managed to get a glimpse of Murugan and everyone was in high spirits. For the next few hours the discomfort of the bus was of no consequence. Even the MGR movie seemed, well, quite good.

It was after midnight before we reached Cape Comorin. With tired feet we trooped down smoky, dank streets lit by dim little pools of light, the cool sea breeze brushing our cheeks. Mr Ramasamy had not booked anywhere in advance, but in India, even at this hour, finding accommodation for a mere sixty-nine people is usually an easy matter. In the Amurath Pilgrims' Guest House we laid our pieces of cloth on the stone floor of a communal dormitory, and took turns to splash ourselves with buckets drawn from the hostel tank. Before lights out, Mr Ramasamy picked his way over our prone bodies with orders for tomorrow. A last joke. (Mother-in-law: 'That was a really funny book you gave me. I nearly died laughing.' Daughter-in-law: 'I'm so glad to hear it: why don't you try reading it again?') We had three hours until reveille. Tomorrow Cape Comorin and the goddess who resides on the southernmost tip of India. Then nine hours' drive to the sacred waterfalls at Courtallam. Mala grinned at me across the room and gently nodded her head in amusement. We all slept happy.

CAPE COMORIN

Before dawn, in that uncertain time between sleep and waking, I became aware of cool raindrops splashing my face, blown on a fresh breeze through an empty window. I reached out my hand. By my side the floor was wet. Outside there were flashes of lightning and rolling thunder. The monsoon had come. At 4.30, Mr Ramasamy came round clapping his hands like a redcoat at a religious holiday camp: 'Right, right, right! Time to rise up!' I pulled my dhoti over my face and pretended not to hear. Mr R was insistent.

'Shake a leg, Mr Michael: two hours to perform ablutions.' As there were only two loos and two taps, it struck me that this might have been cutting it a little fine. I turned over, discovering new mosquito bites to scratch, and then looked up to see a queue of ladies standing over me, toothbrushes and soap in hand. Mr Ramasamy had clearly already identified me as the potential weak link in tour discipline. 'Sunrise is at 6.30, Mr Michael. There is no time to lose.'

★

The idea was that we should get down to the shore to see the sun rise over the Indian Ocean at the same time as the moon set over the Arabian Sea. We would bathe, worship in the temple, and enjoy what Appar calls 'the fresh air of Comari'. All that before another long day on the bus. I drank a little tepid water from the bottle, ate an apple and then set off with Mala through the desultory little town. We walked down to the sea along a damp road lined with an untidy sprawl of hostels, cafés and concrete shops selling trinkets and souvenirs: tourist *mandapas* fringing a sacred shore. At the end, a rocky promontory opened out in front of us, indented with little coves and beaches, where the traditional eleven holy bathing spots are to be found. Behind us, tall palm trees shook their old heads in the wind, dark green against an indigo cloud bank.

Out in the sea, just beyond the southernmost point of the land, are two rocks half-submerged by the waves; these are the Pitru and Matru *tirthas*: they are reachable at low water along a path of iron poles linked by chains which were negotiated by the women slowly and gingerly, soaked to the skin as the swell slapped them in the face and tugged at their feet. These rocks mark the symbolic – and actual – limit of India, the holy land which stretches from this point two thousand miles northwards to the snowy peaks of Kashmir and the primeval wastes of Kailash and Manasarovar.

Every religious Hindu will come here once in a lifetime to take a holy bath and to make offerings to the memory of his mother, father and ancestors. Left to itself this would truly have been a divine spot, but like all famous sacred places it has gathered a wealth of unsightly accretions over time. On the beach the Indian government has constructed a large concrete 'Gandhi *mandapa*' to commemorate the place where the ashes of the 'Father of the Nation', the Mahatma, rested before they were consigned to the waves here. On an offshore island there is a memorial to the Hindu nationalist Swami Vivekananda, which rather resembles Bombay's Victoria railway terminus. It commemorates what is viewed here as a signal moment in the history of modern India.

On Christmas Day 1892 Vivekananda swam to the island to spend the night meditating on Mother India and the validity of her Great Tradition in the face of the challenge of modernity. Here he resolved 'to dedicate himself to the service of the Motherland and to spread the message of the Vedas'. So inspired, the next year he spoke at the Parliament of World Religions in Chicago, affirming the unity of all religion, as Gandhi would do after him, and, unlikely as it may seem now, announced that it was for America now 'to proclaim to all quarters of the globe that the Lord is in every faith'. At root, though, was the Swami's conviction that India's ancient traditions could be a vehicle for spiritual and cultural renovation in the future; an idea which it would seem is now being definitively rejected by the middle classes of Bombay and Delhi.

Above the beach were the old walls of the shrine: a massively built squat rectangle of weathered granite daubed with faded white and crimson stripes, the old colours of the deity: red for Siva, white for the goddess – the primary colours of life. You will still see natural stones painted like this out in the countryside, some the size of a house, and though it is difficult to prove, this custom must be prehistoric. We sat by the sea under heavy cloud, waiting for dawn, but never glimpsed the sun. At seven we went up to the gate for the first puja. By then a long queue stretched round the walls, poor people from the villages, many in loincloth, singlet and bare feet, some with shaved head plastered with bright yellow sandal paste, all coming to make a vow to the goddess; people who had probably come on a ten-rupee country bus trip from Tinnevelly or Trivandrum rather than a video bus from further afield.

The temple is one of the most famous of the sacred places of the Hindus, but is simple, bare and functional. Behind a big wooden gate is a sparse outer courtyard empty of ornament and swept by the sea breezes. Beyond is an inner enclosure with a covered colonnade around the central shrine. No subtlety of religious pageant here, no elaborate play for our entertainment. They wake the goddess up with conch shell and trumpet. She stands alone behind a curtain in the sanctum, holding a rosary, an ancient black stone idol with a white face like a Japanese Noh dancer. This is rare. Southern goddesses are usually dark, black, blue or green like Minakshi; but the Devi here is the Virgin, her face 'lovely as the moon' as it says in the *Mahabharata*. Her whiteness signifies the retention of female power, so her energy, her *sakti*, can overcome all evil: 'Marvellous in her serenity and beneficence', according to the pilgrims' guide I bought at Higginbotham's station bookstall at Trichy Junction.

Comari is one of the few places south of the Deccan which appear in the list of India's sacred sites in the *Mahabharata*, a list which may go back to the middle of the first millennium BC, and which in any case preserves a very archaic sense of her sacred geography. The ancient temple to the Devi was mentioned over two thousand years ago by the Greek geographers, starting with Eratosthenes. In a first-century Greek merchant's manual there is this fascinating note: 'Those who wish to consecrate the closing part of their lives to religion come here and bathe and vow themselves to celibacy. This is also done by women, for they say that the goddess dwelt here and bathed.'

So, as Indian shrines go, it is one of the earliest on record, and its early references invite questions: How old is the idea of India as a holy land? And who originated it? 'Aryans' or 'Dravidians'? Did Bronze Age sea-going merchants gain a sense of the shape and size of the subcontinent, from the Himalayas to the Cape? When we look at yogic gods in Indus seals, or Mesolithic dancing gods with tridents, it is hard not to think that the roots of Indian religion are earlier by far than her civilization.

After the puja we strolled down to the shore and bought some sea shells from vendors on the beach, little conches which are used by sadhus as talismans. Then we breakfasted in a café. I ate alone. A soggy *dosa* (there's tourism for you). Mala revealed that as part of her pilgrimage vow, she and her friends on the bus were fasting for the duration. She would only take some warm milk. Then we went shopping. My old sandals had finally broken and I looked for some flipflops, but Mala would not allow me to pay thirty rupees: 'too costly' she said with a frown.

Later we took the boat to Vivekananda's island across a 200–yard stretch of choppy sea. The sun was now starting to break through the banks of cloud. Up the coast was a big fishing port with a huge Christian church, its spire a gleaming white against a backdrop of damp green hills. Comari district has been a stronghold of Catholicism since Xavier's mission in the 1550s – though the Catholic fishermen still revere the Devi and participate enthusiastically in her festivals.

We sat for a while on the beach with one of Mala's friends, Mrs Vaideyen, a thin bird-like lady in her seventies with a lovely face and a big open toothy smile: she was still very beautiful. She wore a thin crimson sari, a Kashmir shawl and an old orange balaclava. She lived in Madras now near her grown-up children, having moved there after her husband died a couple of years earlier. She had come back down to Chidambaram to travel with old friends and neighbours on the Murugan pilgrimage.

As we talked I realized that I had met her late husband, a tall, distinguished, grey-haired man, who had been a schoolteacher. We had met one night some years before at Chidambaram's winter festival when he had stopped in South Car Street to teach us the opening verse of Manikavasagar's 'Maidens' song'. He had died the next year, she said, aged seventy-eight.

'He had been helping organize a special puja at Sirkali. He was rushing back and forwards every day when he had a heart attack, but when it began he still had time to put the ash on his forehead and to pray. He had the name Siva on his lips when he died.'

She opened her hands and shrugged her shoulders, raising her eyes heavenward; this had been a blessing.

'He was a primary teacher, but his great love was the *Tevaram*: he knew all the poems off by heart. He used to say that these songs were the heart of Tamil culture. In retirement he used to offer classes after school by the south *gopura* to any of the town's children whose families were interested in continuing the tradition.

'He learned them from the class of people here who sing in Tamilian, the *oduvar*s, the traditional poets of the Tamil lands. They are secular people, non-Brahmins, and you may still find them at places such as Sirkali, near Chidambaram. There the temple offered free instruction to popularize the *Tevaram*; my husband used to take the bus after school on Fridays and sit at their feet. Over the years he learned them all; many thousands of verses.'

I told her how her husband taught Rebecca and me a verse of Manikavasagar. She smiled. 'He was his favourite poet. He used to say: "No one sheds tears over the Sanskrit Vedas, but you have a heart of stone if you are not moved by Manikavasagar, wherever you come from." This was why he wanted to teach the children when he retired. He saw this as a religious duty. So the poems would be passed on to the young.

'We were a like-minded couple.' She smiled at the memory. 'When our children married and settled down, when we had discharged our duties as householders and parents, we set out on a great adventure. It had always been my husband's ambition to visit all the sites in the sacred journeys of the *Tevaram*: there are 274 of them. This we set out to do and over many years we did it. All except Kailash in Tibet and the two shrines in Sri Lanka. And in each place we stood together before the shrine of the god and sang the hymn which the saints had composed about that place.'

She smiled as if it had been plain sailing. Then she coughed and pulled her old orange balaclava over her head. She was feverish and after early rain the morning was still not hot. How many now, I wondered, would follow in her footsteps?

★

As we headed back to the bus, the wind swept the last of the clouds over the hills to the north. It was now a lovely day with a warm sun and a daffodil sky. Shining green paddies, rich glistening groves of coco palms, banana and bamboo; the rain had made everything come alive. Soon we headed off towards Nagercoil. To the right we passed the isolated mountain which marks the very end of the long chain of the Western Ghats, the spine of India. The dramatic pyramidal hill rises sheer out of the flat coastal plain, broken off from the main range which stretches off into the distance beyond. (It must be the one depicted by the English artists the Daniell brothers in the 1780s in one of their most memorable compositions.) This mysterious green mountain is called Maruda Malai – 'Medicine Mountain' – the place where healing plants grow. There is a legend about it, as there appears to be for almost every place in the south. This is the tale told me by Mr Subrahmaniam, a very sweet gentleman, who was travelling two seats behind me on the bus with his wife and teenage son. He was a tax inspector for one of the divisions of Chidambaram district.

'During the tale of the *Ramayana*, when Rama had crossed into Lanka by the magical bridge built with the aid of Hanuman and the monkey king, Rama's youngest brother Lakshman was hit by an arrow dipped in deadly snake poison, which was fired by a son of the demon king Ravana. Lakshman lay unconscious and near to death. Rama was plunged into great anxiety, and asked Hanuman the monkey god, his faithful companion, to hasten to Mount Kailash in the Himalaya to bring back the medicinal herb called *sanjeevini*, which alone is the antidote to all the world's poisons. Hanuman did so, but when he got there, he saw the mountain was covered with herbs and flowers, and he was at a loss to know which was the right one. So he uprooted the whole hill, which was called medicine hill, and brought it down to Rama. But as he flew across to Sri Lanka, a piece of the mountain fell here, near Cape Comorin, and this is the hill today called Maruda Malai.'

He smiled.

'Of course these are ancient stories in which the common people take delight. We need not take them literally; the point is that they are beautiful tales, and give entertainment. But they are part of the religion of the ordinary folk, and you will find a love of these stories of the *Ramayana* and the *Mahabharata* in every corner of India. Lately, of course, they have been very popular on TV, even among our Muslim and Christian neighbours.'

He looked out of the window.

'But it is a peculiarity of this place that in the rainy season, many kinds of medicinal herbs, which are used in the preparation of Ayurvedic remedies, grow wild on its slopes. They are a veritable pharmacopoeia of the traditional healing. The local people even cook the leaves of certain trees here, and the bitter grass which grows on the hill. It is said that after the battle with Ravana, and the conquest of Lanka, Hanuman installed a Siva linga on the mountain, as a thanksgiving for sorting out his medical emergency. And to this day, this linga is there on top, and visited and worshipped by pilgrims, particularly by those holy men and women who come down to Cape Comorin on foot in fulfilment of vows. It is one of the rituals they accomplish after bathing at the Cape, to bring their journey to a satisfying end.'

SUCHINDRAM

Suchindram. A big temple with an ornate tower standing by a pretty tank which reflected the old, red-tiled houses and the now cloudless blue sky. A notice outside in three languages stresses that the temple is open to all castes. Technically untouchables were allowed in all temples down here after Independence, but in practice this is still by no means everywhere the case. To enter, men must strip off and wear only a dhoti round the waist. I did so, and stood there by the bus trying to look inconspicuous, a foot higher than all my companions, my skin ghastly pale next to the luminous ebony of Raja and Ganesh. Mala and her friends laughed, as did the crowd at the pilgrim stalls. I was grateful to escape from the unsparing sunlight of the street into the shadows of the interior.

The temple is chiefly remarkable for its extraordinary sequence of epigraphical records, and for its very rich – some would say over-rich – stone carving. The chap from the local government was in his element, eyes glowing with justifiable pride.

'It is a treasure house of art and sculpture,' he enthused. 'Where else in the world would you see such things?'

He insisted I try out the four famous musical pillars. Each is cut out of a single block of granite into clusters of cylindrical rods which emit musical notes when struck by a wooden stave.

'There. This is the harp sound. And this the drum. You see, a symphony in praise of the Lord.'

I confessed that I could hear no difference. Perhaps I simply lacked the ear of faith? He wagged his head reprovingly. 'The point is, the Western ear is not trained as ours to detecting half-tones and quarter-tones,' he suggested, and clearing his throat, demonstrated with a scale from a Carnatic raga. My ear remained dull and blockish.

One of the halls of the temple is carved entirely with incidents from the *Ramayana*; another has Hanuman, Siva as mendicant and Krishna with his flute, a vast anthology in stone of all-Indian mythology. For good measure there were Pali inscriptions of Ashoka with Tamil translations. These texts from the third century BC, the time of the great Mauryan empire, are our first documentary records of the traditional dynasties of the south, the Cholas, Pandyas and Pallavas, some of whose descendants, it is extraordinary to recall, were still ruling in these parts when the British East India Company landed its armies in the eighteenth century. Around the back was a little sunlit corner: a gnarled old pipal tree caught in a pool of sunlight, a cluster of ancient stone lingas and snake stones entwined in its roots; it was strewn with blossoms and smeared with fresh sandalwood and vermilion, incense smoke curling across a beam of light.

We were about to leave when the local ice-cream man cycled furiously up to the bus on a three-wheeler with a wooden ice-box crammed with home-made lollies (the box lovingly hand-painted with flowers and lettered: 'Jothi ices, home-made of best ingredients'). Then we set off for Courtallam.

We left Tinnevelly behind, passing through little country towns and a landscape full of old buildings, temples and tanks out in the paddy-fields, their brickwork overgrown and crumbling; granite slabs lay displaced as nature took them back. The new is far less evident than the decay of the old. How strong here is this sense of dissolution and change as some key to life, as things decay back into their constituent elements, the elements celebrated in the temples. And even the greatest temples are impermanent, as impermanent in the eyes of Siva as the *kolams* of rice flour on the doorstep, blown away or rubbed into the dust at the threshold even before the sun reaches its height.

Travelling in this countryside gave a sense of why the Hindu religion is the way it is. Fecundity and barrenness; plenty and scarcity; violence and balm, a climate which alternates between benign calm and enervating extremes of heat; the irresistible violence of cyclone, monsoon or flood, when the ancient banyans along the roads are thrown on to their heads like clods of soil. Even the buildings, the ornate, pillared halls, the *gopura*s sprouting like petrified vegetation, seem to grow out of the palm forests like weird hybrids, part plant, part stone.

Not surprising then, given all this, that the myths of Tamil culture are given to the most intense extremes of expression, from the Cholan bronzes to today's Tamil movies with their make-believe violence and their barely suppressed sexuality. Even more than the rest of India, perhaps, Tamil culture is preoccupied with the attractions of excess, and the correspondingly extreme idea of restraint and control – and an awareness of the dynamic tension and conflict which inevitably comes out of their coexistence.

COURTALLAM

The day had grown very hot indeed by the time we reached Ambasamudram. No restaurant here could seat so many people, so they improvised, laying sixty banana leaves down in an upstairs corridor, where we all sat cross-legged like a line of beggars outside a temple *choultry*. Then the boy came down ladling food out of his buckets: vegetable *sambhar*, rice, curd, black-eyed beans, okra, a kind of celery in egg and lemon sauce, orange chutney, tamarind pickle: all beautifully prepared, and for seven rupees each.

Through the afternoon we pressed on down a winding country road, the wooded flanks of the Western Ghats getting nearer and nearer on our left-hand side. Gardens of nutmeg, clove, cinnamon and coffee; the velvet sheen of tea plantations in the lowering sun. Then we turned off into a bowl of hills cut by deep valleys. At 3.30 we reached Courtallam and stopped in the bus park behind the old Siva temple. Around us unfolded a beautiful landscape, which was often painted and engraved by artists during the British period when people came up here to take the waters and escape the heat. An Arcadian place, it was often said; it would take a Claude Lorraine to do justice to its ancient spirit.

Mala's husband used to come here when he was a boy, before he lost his sight, and it is one of his imperishable memories from the days when he could still see; how in July as the heat lessens after the first rains have fallen along the wooded mountains bordering Kerala, the waters rise above Courtallam, the river swells and the falls become full. Then, he said, on July mornings 'the spray hangs in the air in tiny droplets like a kind of mist, catching the rays of sunlight, casting a myriad rainbows around the sides of the falls'. To him, it was a vision of glory.

A new hydroelectric plant has been built now higher upstream so the flow of water is not what it was. But when the monsoon falls on Kerala in June, the Chittar river still swells and reaches full flow in July. It still has a good head in October, crashing two hundred feet, cascading over a sheer precipice which is broken about halfway down by a deep trough in the face of the rock. In the old days it was a wild place: cliffs hung with trees, ferns and creepers, pock-marked with caves, rock-cut terraces and carvings, where many sadhus, men and women, had taken up residence. (There are still a few.) Below the falls the temples, *mandapa*s and hostels were set back on the left bank of the stream in a very picturesque setting, drawn in the eighteenth century by the English artists, the Daniells, who did so much to fix the picturesque view of India in European art. Inevitably, with the huge growth of pilgrimage, the place has been taken over by modern concrete buildings plastered with advertising hoardings, and the river has an ugly new bridge draped with electric power lines. The place is still wonderful, but its divinity has been hedged by the modern world.

Dodging hawkers, we crossed the bridge, and I sat with Mala's bags and clothes as she went for a dip. There are three main sections to the falls here: the women's falls are at the left; the right-hand fall is mainly used by children and older people; in the middle there is a very powerful current and a concrete safety rail. Here the young men swagger and josh each other, having a laugh and a bit of horseplay. Some balance on isolated rocks as if daring the current to knock them off into the river below. Soon Mala came back dripping wet and went to change. When she returned I stripped off to a loincloth and headed for the young men's section to whistles from the crowd – again I was the only foreigner here. They held out their hands and pulled mé in. The force of the central flow was just about bearable; after a dawn start and six hours in a hot bus, it was deliciously cool and good to taste: the water pressing on my head, pummelling my face and rushing into my mouth.

'What conduces much to the restoration of invalids at this singular abode,' wrote the author of the *British Medical Report* in 1832,

> is the little waterfall, under which most of the Europeans daily bathe. The falling of the water, after the first shock is over, gives an indescribable feeling of pleasure; by its constant beating, it quickens the circulation and produces a fine glow all over the body; and has, besides, the further good effects of dispelling languor, raising the spirits, exciting appetite, and promoting digestion in a superior degree to any other kind of bathing that we are acquainted with. It has, in consequence of these virtues, together with the delightful climate of the valley itself, been the happy means of rapidly restoring many to health and comfort who previous to their visit to Cortallam appeared to be hastening to their graves.

Feeling suitably rejuvenated I went back to Mala, who immediately shooed me back into the water: 'It's not enough – this is too short a stay. You must stand for a minimum of ten minutes to get full benefits.' So back I went. Then we all decamped from the main falls to the Five Falls, a tree-shrouded fairy grotto where five streams pour down crevices in the black rock. There we went through the same ritual again as the sun sank behind the hills and the skin tingled with cold. I was photographed with half-naked priests (Raja and Ganesh), the beaming tax inspector, the manager of a worsted mill from Coimbatore and the back four of a football team from Tinnevelly who somehow got in on the picture. Eyes twinkling, Mr Ramasamy barked out one more of his *aruvai joks* as I snapped him, while the now chilly water dripped off the end of his beaky nose. Mala then took the camera to take some pictures of her neighbours. The tax inspector shepherded us all into line; everyone by now seemed excited and there was a great feeling of togetherness. Soaked to the skin, little Minakshi's face was lit up, her huge eyes wide, as she held her aunt's hand for their photo. Her aunt allowed herself the faintest of smiles as she balanced on a glistening mossy rock in a clinging marigold sari, still managing to exude auspicious female power even when she looked as if she'd been pulled through a mangle.

The tax inspector came over in a voluminous pair of underpants and gave me a fatherly smile. 'So now you are getting into it. Now I am sure you will begin to feel the benefit of our Indian holy places.' I was. I can remember other memorable dips in Indian sacred waters: at the freezing confluence of the Ganga and the Jumna; in crashing breakers at Puri; in the Ganga in Benares in the late summer when the river is high and has the temperature and thickness of strong brown tea; but the falls at Courtallam surpassed them all; they were exactly as Rajdurai had promised. Perhaps the tax inspector was right: I was beginning to feel that I might after all garner a little spiritual merit from this journey.

Early in the evening we drove into Tenkasi. Set back from the road was a gigantic *gopura*, pale in the half light. Inside were wonderfully sculpted halls depicting scenes from the *Mahabarata*. The local tax inspector was now warming to the whole thing. 'These stories we imbibe with our mothers' milk,' he said, describing the 'Exile in the Forest'; then came a hall with Siva's dance portrayed, the fierce and smiling dance on adjacent pillars and the constantly recurring myth of Siva's dance competition with the black goddess Kali. 'See how they have been carved, such huge figures, with such delicacy. Here the artist's hand found speech.'

After puja we sat together in the arcade.

'These holy places we call *tirthas*. In Sanskrit this means crossing place of a river. In ancient times many sacred places were on holy rivers. But also *tirtha* means crossing place between human world and divine. God appeared on earth in these places. So they are especially suited to approach the deity now. They are crossing places between different worlds. In your country?'

'In my country, Mr Subrahmaniam, we have completely lost the sense of two worlds.'

With that he turned to me with a worried look, hesitant, as if anxious not to offend.

'Tell me one thing, Mr Michael. This has perplexed me during our journey. You are Christian. How do you reconcile this in your conscience with attending our rituals?'

Outside, big drops of rain were falling again. Sound of rain pattering on leaves.

'I cannot really call myself a Christian,' I began. 'I don't go to church or anything like that. I suppose you might say I'm just curious.'

'About the god?'

'About Tamil culture, about being Tamil. Anyway, I thought Hindus think the truth of all religions is ultimately the same?'

'Indeed, this is what Lord Krishna says to Arjuna in the *Gita*.'

'I think that too. And still, as Mrs Mala says, I feel a great heartliness in being here.'

'It is all that matters in the end. As the saints say, the key is not in the temples or the idols or the holy baths, but in your own heart.'

Outside, flashes of lightning suddenly illuminated the horizon of townscape, silhouetting the *gopura* black against the night. Tremendous thunder. We hurried across the enclosure as the drops of rain fell on our backs. We ran past a huge tree hung with prayers and requests. The rain started to pour. We left the town with the wipers on monsoon setting. How on earth could the driver see through it? There followed a death-defying journey to Srivilliputtur, driver and assistant craning forwards as water cascaded over the windscreen. On the narrow road, buses and lorries approached head on out of the night, swerving with inches to spare. I kept flinching. Raja just laughed. Above our heads, MGR danced on.

SRIVILLIPUTTUR

At nine o'clock we reached Srivilliputtur. A great Vaishnavite shrine with a gigantic *gopura* soaring nearly 250 feet in elegant curves, the entire structure swathed in bamboo scaffolding and rattan screens. Vast and truly impressive. This is a temple to Vishnu but is celebrated all over the south because of the legend of the mystic poetess, Andal, who lived here in the ninth century. Here we stopped for our evening meal.

It is a huge campus. We had missed the last puja so people went off to do a bit of sightseeing as the priests locked up the sanctum, and we all bought bags of *goa*, the milk sweet for which the town is famous. The big nave was packed with Vaishnavite pilgrim pictures and souvenirs, including cassettes and books of Andal's songs; but supposing myself to be temperamentally more of a Saivite, I gave them a miss.

Outside the nave was a wide sandy approach with gardens over to one side. My dhoti was in tatters after the frolicking at Courtallam, so I went out into the street to buy a new one at a textile stall run by an old Muslim gentleman in a white embroidered cap; Srivilliputtur's Muslim weavers are one of the town's mainstays. His cavernous shop had polished wooden shelves, and an open carpeted floor where rolls of cloth could be spread out. Behind his desk sticks of incense were burning by a row of holy pictures just as in any Hindu shop. Here, though, they showed Mecca and Medina; he had scenes of Indian Muslim saints performing supernatural feats of endurance, riding tigers and charming snakes just like Hindu holy men. He also had a poster which is popular throughout south India: it depicts Buraq the magical horse who transported the Prophet on his night journey and on his ascent to heaven – an elaborately bejewelled winged centaur with pink body and peacock-feather wings and, to cap it all, a beautiful woman's face with made-up eyes and lipstick.

The wonders of Indian Muslim art remain emphatically Indian. When we see the gorgeously half-human Buraq, or the Shia Imam Ali represented as an avatar of Vishnu at Lucknow or Hyderabad, or even the Prophet himself with the attributes of Krishna (as he appears in Tamil literary epic), we understand that in India Muslim art could never quite break with the Hindu vision.

Islam's battle with representational art makes a long and fascinating story. It starts as early as the remarkable Hellenistic-style figural art from early Islamic Jordan. Later, in the fertile artistic climate of medieval Persia, the iconoclasts could only ever have been partially successful. Here in India they were forced to give way before the overwhelming need to make images of everything.

In the busy main street Mala paced up and down searching for a good eating place. Though she was not taking food herself, she was concerned that I had a clean place with good cooking. Eventually we found brightly lit 'hotel' with *dosai* and she watched me eat. She looked tired: but then she was now in her third day of fasting. I asked her about the legend of Andal, the patron saint of the town. It turned out to be a tale which rather resembled that of the bride of Christ, Teresa of Ávila, though with distinctly erotic undertones.

'Andal was a foundling girl, discovered in a basket by the river: she was fostered by a priest at the temple.

'From very young age she was seized by the desire to marry Vishnu. Secretly each morning she was decking herself in the fresh garlands with which her foster-father was supposed to adorn the image of Vishnu. This was sacrilege, as it is forbidden for anyone even to smell fresh flowers which are to be dedicated to the deity.'

The girl would fantasize about union with Vishnu: what it would be like. ('What will his kiss be like: does it taste like fresh lotus blossom, or camphor? Or is it as sweet as honey?') When she put on the flowers, she would look in the mirror to see if she was lovely enough to be his bride. She saw nothing wrong in this: she was pure-hearted. Certain of her poems indeed are frankly erotic

('Enter me and leave the imprint of your saffron paste on my breasts . . . mixing, churning, maddening me inside'). Mala says these are less well known, and not often publicly performed.

The waiter came over to lay a fresh green plantain leaf on my table, which I sprinkled and brushed with water, leaving a shower of tiny droplets over the soft matt ribbed surface of the leaf. Then my special *dosa* arrived: a crisp pancake of ground rice and lentils, two feet across. I discovered I was ravenous. Mala continued the story.

'When her foster-father discovered her sacrilege, he was upset and prayed to Vishnu to ask him what to do. Vishnu then appeared to him in a dream saying that Andal gave an added fragrance to the flowers which was dear to him. So she was blessed, chosen by god. Aged sixteen she went to the island of Srirangam, the greatest Vishnu shrine in India, and vanished in the sanctum; she was never seen again. Taken by God.'

(Andal's cult had already spread across the Tamil lands by the twelfth century, when there were special recitals of her works. Later generations could not resist filling in the gaps in the tale by providing love letters to her from Vishnu.)

'In Margali month, which is December time, all over Tamil Nadu she is celebrated every morning on the radio; there are recitations of her Tiruppavai poem in temples and at home gatherings. You can buy it on cassette. Young girls especially sing verses of it to make a happy marriage; often they make vows to rise before dawn each day to bathe and recite the entire poem. Each morning a special puja is still done here, where garlands are put on Vishnu after first being put on Andal; this is in memory of the tale.'

As always, Mala had infinite patience with my questions. Where, I wondered, had all this knowledge come from. Had she always been religious like this? It was something I had never asked. She answered by going back into her past life:

'After we married in 1959, my husband worked as a clerk in Pondicherry, and the children were brought up there until the loss of his sight during the late seventies and early eighties led to him losing his job and returning to Chidambaram on a tiny disability pension to live. It was then, about twelve years ago, I started to find out more.'

'So when your husband went blind?'

'From that time I started to question an old religious lady in the town about the religious stories. She was a widow, over seventy years old. She knew the poems of the saints, the *Tevaram*, and had visited most of the sites in their sacred journeys. She was also a Saiva.'

(Among Tamils, I should add, you will often find a sense that Saivism is the indigenous religion of the south; Vaishnavism is more identified with the Sanskritic, Brahminical, pan-Indian culture, especially in the figures of Rama and Krishna. Saiva is held to be the 'old religion' and this has left its marks in the language. For example, when you sit down at table to eat vegetarian food, as we were doing, this is called in Tamil '*Saiva sapede*', 'Saiva food'.) Mala continued her tale as I demolished my *dosa* and ordered another.

'Till then I had been religious, but only as most people are in our community. But from that time I became filled with the desire to know.'

So she started to learn all the *sthalapuranas*, the myths of the individual temples, the special qualities of the different shrines. Following the sacred paths, she made trips all over the south, scrutinizing the almanac and mastering the seasonal calendar for festivals, eclipses, days of largesse, days of abstinence, the special properties of *vilva*, *neem* and pipal. She could recite all the great sites and days: the sacred marriage in Madurai in May; Tiruvan-namali in November, when a huge fire burns for three days and nights on the summit of the pyramidal mass of the Red Mountain, which rises sheer out of the central plain; Tirupugalur in April, when, in one of the most enthralling rites anywhere in India, Appar is celebrated at the very time and place of his death, in the sanctum in the dead of night, when the lights are extinguished and his last poem is recited: 'Lord now I am come to your lotus feet.'

These values she had passed on to her children. Yet at the same time she had fought to give her four daughters the best secular education they could manage. She had got Bharati into technical college in Nagapattinam, and when relatives wouldn't help take her there, Mala took her there herself. She wanted to equip them for the modern world, even though she herself was still committed to the old ways of caste and stars. For her the two were by no means incompatible. She still believed, for example, that this was the best way of finding a good husband, a compatible person for a marriage within the community; 'god will make sure you get on.' So she took on the male duties of householder, while falling back on the old powers to shore things up, keep things from breaking apart, protect the family and children in hard times. Yet in the end in her heart of hearts I suspect she knew that only hard work could mitigate the pains that flesh is heir to.

It was time to go. We trooped back on to the bus for the last journey of the day – three hours more to Tirupparakunram. Even Mala was nodding by now. A tiring business, the pilgrimage.

THE ROCK OF SIKANDER

Towards one we turned off the Madurai road into the long lane which leads up to the temple and the great rock. They had had no rain here, and when we got down from the bus there was soft dry sand between the toes. The street was gaily decorated for the temple festival, hung with flags and figured cloths; in the middle was a big marquee canopied with sewn elephants and peacocks. Beyond was the entrance *gopura* draped in fairy lights. Tirupparakunram is another of the abodes of Murugan and was in the middle of the same ten-day celebration that we had seen at Tiruchendur. A lovely atmosphere lingered around the late tea stalls as we asked around to find somewhere to stay. There was no room in the first *choultries* we asked. One was for Brahmins only. We of course were of many castes (though there were no untouchables on the bus). Finally Mr Ramasamy came out of a darkened building with a sleepy-looking *choultry* manager, and we were ushered into an old-style pilgrim lodge on the approach to the temple: they had a vacant communal room upstairs: a hundred rupees for the whole party.

We found ourselves in a columned entrance hall with latticed screens over the windows; on either side a narrow stone staircase led to the first floor where there was a long dormitory with a hard floor of painted lime plaster. A heavy old fan with a nose like a Spitfire propeller wobbled alarmingly in the roof. The first ones to get up the stairs had already earmarked the floor underneath it. We made space for ourselves, spreading our dhotis or sari cloths on the floor ready to lie down for the rest of the night, women, children, men all mixed up together. The wash place was outside, downstairs at the back; it was rather like the backyard of a temple, with water drawn in buckets from a stone tank under a starry sky. To one side was a row of cubicles for loos which in no time were hung with sari cloths. I stretched out to get some sleep while Mr Ramasamy delivered the next day's programme. I'd brought a mosquito net, but somehow I'd have felt a bit of a cissy trying to use it. In any case, where would one hang it? Now it came into its own as a pillow. Mr Ramasamy came over:

'Here's a good joke for you, Mr Michael. One lady says to her neighbour: "I like your new milkman; he is handsome as a movie star: What's his name?" Neighbour replies: "Paul Newman".' (He pronounced Paul as Paal).

A blank look from the floor.

'I don't get it, Mr Ramasamy,' I said.

'In Tamil *paal* is milk. See? *Paal* Newman – new milkman! Good?'

He shrugged his shoulders despairingly. 'Mr Michael, you are needing to learn much more Tamil if you are to enjoy the Tamil sense of humour.'

I slept like a log till 4.30 when Mr Ramasamy's wake-up call interrupted my dreams of many-armed gods and goddesses and smiling anthropomorphs. We had the usual two hours to go through our ablutions before the first puja in the temple. The washing area was crowded by the time I got down. Raja had another plan. The temple itself had a particularly spacious bathing tank which would be great for an early morning bath. Did I fancy that? Certainly, I said. They didn't offer to show me the way. So off I went on my own at five, still pitch dark, in a thin, small dhoti clutching my soap box, walking down the streets of Tirupparakun-ram. The air was blissfully fresh and cool. I got a cheery wave from the tea stalls where they were heating up the first brew of the day. But otherwise, no one paid the slightest bit of notice to this thin foreign body, pale as a ghost, wandering their streets in search of a holy bath.

I found it at last, a lake-sized reservoir with stepped sides and a columned *mandapa* on an island in the middle. As the sky faintly lightened to the east, I could see that it was cut mainly out of the living rock and filled by water courses which channelled rainwater off the great bare shoulders of the hill – cold, deep water into which I did not wish to stray too far in the darkness. The water closed over my head with exhilarating sharpness. Standing up I sucked in my breath and swore to myself in pleasure; after a short while I tried to climb out, and feeling for the slimy steps I tripped and fell over.

'Bugger.'

'You are from which country?' said a sudden voice from no-where. White short-sleeved shirt and whites of eyes; gradually I made out a young man clutching a spring folder. Naked and dripping I picked myself up, grabbed my dhoti, and tried to look perfectly normal while he stared, faintly bemused, and kept the conversation going with series of questions. It transpired he was on the way to the bus stand to go to the college in Madurai where he was studying English literature.

'Did you see Mr Peter Brook's *Mahabharata*?'

'Mmm.'

'What is your opinion?'

'I saw the stage show: very exciting. Loved it when they set the stage on fire. What did you think?'

His face puckered.

'This was cheap magic. Not satisfactory. Generally it was not liked in India. How can you put the world's longest poem into seven hours when recital takes seven days? Also Indian people do not behave like these actors. And Bhima was played by an African; this did not go down at all well with an Indian audience. Bhima has a wheaten complexion; he is not a black man. We consider the TV version of Mr Ramanand Sagar was wholly preferable.'

'Why?' I asked, squeezing out my wet dhoti and wrapping myself with the towel. I squeezed out some toothpaste and brushed vigorously.

'They spoke like gods to start with. In epic style. We did not understand it all. Even the actors did not understand it all. But it was in the language of the gods. Every Sunday morning people even did their pujas in front of the TV screen. Ninety episodes. It was biggest-ever audience on TV. Even the Muslims were fans.'

'Really?'

'Really.'

'Also they looked like gods. You see we know what gods look like,' he said, with absolute certainty.

'Krishna in particular is strong, majestic, powerful and noble. And he is blue. This Krishna was the wrong colour. This is the last straw. You might as well have had Prince Hamlet played by a girl.'

'Actually we have.'

'There,' he said, 'this only proves the point. You have lost touch with your tradition. The important thing is not innovation, but following of the tradition. In India this is what the people love best. Mr Brook's Krishna was strong and powerful. But he did not speak like the god. And he was the wrong colour.'

I made as if to go.

'Do you have a visiting card?'

I rummaged vainly for a moment in imaginary pockets.

'I'm sorry . . . I'm afraid I didn't bring one.'

The light was coming up fast now on the brown pyramid of rock behind us. I scribbled my address on his pad, and agreed to correspond further on the matter of Mr Brook's dramaturgy. I then hurried back to meet Mala and Minakshi and her aunt and grandmother at the tea stall by the temple gate.

The temple at Tirupparakunram is another ancient and famous place on the Tamil pilgrimage routes. It is dramatically situated at the bottom of a precipitous granite rock known as Skandamalai, which rises over 1000 feet straight out of the plain. The rock is dotted with ancient caves and rock sanctuaries and holy springs; it has been a place of worship since prehistory and sacred at one time or other to Saivites, Vaishnavites, Jains and Muslims. Orthodox pilgrims not only climb it but circumambulate the base where there is a path with wayside shrines. Right on top there is an old Muslim tomb which is still visited and revered by Muslim pilgrims from the region; they call the hill Sikandermalai, 'the rock of Sikander', the Indian name for Alexander the Great. The tomb, however, dates from the brief and dramatic heyday of the Madura sultanate when Tirupparakunram was the capital of the Muslim state down here; it was the scene of one of the most dramatic episodes in the history of the south. The tale takes us back to one of the most momentous events in the long history of India, the coming of Islam.

Muslim armies reached the Indus valley in 711, less than a century after the Prophet's death. Between the tenth and twelfth centuries the Muslims overthrew the Hindu kingdoms of northern India in a bloody and traumatic irruption into Indian life, severing the people for ever from their native religions. But in the south this period was the zenith of Cholan power and achievement, with its unsurpassed temple architecture, bronze and stone sculpture, and literature. The Cholan navy ensured the south remained inviolate; in 1017 they even sent an army to the Ganges. At that time the kingdom based on Tanjore on the Cavery river conquered Sri Lanka and despatched fleets to the Maldives, Java, Sumatra and Malaya, leaving Hindu culture, which has survived till today in islands such as Bali. Their mercantile embassies visited Sung China and Chinese junks came to the Coromandel coast to trade their silk and porcelain – which is still found by the beachcomber, pounded into the surf line at the mouth of the Cavery.

Until the end of the twelfth century the Tamils were still a strong and wealthy naval power, people with whom the Chinese could do business, unlike the later Western buccaneers and entrepreneurs. For unlike the Westerners they were people who had not dispensed with their rituals, and in Chinese eyes this was the chief mark of a civilized people.

But through the 1200s, even as the last great building projects were under way at Chidambaram, Cholan power began to decline and the Muslim rulers of north India began to eye their wealth covetously. By now, of course, Islam was dominant from the Mediterranean to the Ganges. In the early fourteenth century the first large-scale attempt was made to attack the south. Plunder was no doubt the first objective. Sultan Allauddin Khilji of Delhi must have heard of the great temples and the extraordinary treasures kept in them; at Tanjore alone Rajaraja the Great had given 400 pounds of gold to his temple in 1010, along with many other treasures which were still there three centuries later. And Tanjore was just one temple among thousands. With the south now riven by civil war, and the Cholan dynasty in terminal decline, the chance must have seemed too good to resist.

The campaign against the south by the sultan's general Malik Kafur began on 18 November 1310 and lasted for a full year, during which the southern Tamil lands were overrun, temples demolished, towns looted. In January 1311 they hit Trichy and attacked the great temple of Vishnu on the sacred island of Srirangam. The temple staff had no time to flee and a terrible massacre took place. The temple chronicle records the events of the time. A strange legend still told by the temple priests told how the cult statue of Vishnu was taken to Delhi, where it was rescued by a Muslim princess who fell in love with the face of the Lord and eventually restored it to the temple.

Many of the ancient temples in the Cavery valley must have been terrorized at this time, and some of the buried treasure troves uncovered in recent years must represent the desperate efforts of the priests to hide their old bronzes and temple treasures before the onslaught. It is tempting to think that this is the explanation for the great collection of temple bronzes from the eleventh century found in the 1950s buried around Tiruvengadu in the Cavery delta. The eighty bronzes found in a secret room in the 1960s in Chidambaram, which were mainly from the tenth to thirteenth centuries, may also have been concealed at this time. In many cases inscriptions record that a temple had collections of bronzes in the eleventh century which are represented today only by fourteenth-century or later copies. Rajaraja the Great, for instance, had sixty-six bronzes cast for his temple at Tanjore in 1010; of these only two survive today, one a damaged and repaired masterpiece.

As the destruction of the accumulated artistic treasures of a civilization, Kafur's year-long campaign had few parallels in south Indian history. Are we to see it simply as motivated by greed? Or by religious fanaticism? The work of murderous bigots or of brutal warlords who, as in our own time, from Sudan to Bosnia, have used religion as a means of dispossessing minorities and lining their own coffers? At the time, it must be said, both sides saw the destruction as religiously motivated. The Koran, of course, provides both justification for, and explicit rejection of, such persecution. But for the more orthodox Muslims of the day, holding to the austere monotheism of their sacred book, worship of Hanuman the monkey god or the elephant-headed Ganesh was beyond the pale.

However much Hindu philosophers might claim the linga of Siva as an aniconic 'mark' of god, in many temples it was all too explicitly phallic. No matter that Muslim and Hindu met in the more elevated doctrines of the Sufis and the *bhakti* singers; popular Hinduism to many Muslims was irredeemable (as it was to some British imperialists, even in our own century). Stories of the 'womb chamber' in Tanjore, where milk libations were poured over a twelve-foot-high polished black stone phallus with head and glans delineated, must have brought shivers of horror among the ulema in the durbar halls of Delhi. No doubt then it was as easy for Kafur to travel with chapter and verse in his baggage as it was for the Conquistadors. The scientist Al Biruni put it succinctly: 'India is full of riches, entirely delightful, and, as its people are mainly infidels and idolaters, it is right by order of God for us to conquer them.'

In March 1311 Kafur reached the frontier of the Pandyan lands which were then rent by civil war, and marched on Madurai, raiding towns and villages and desecrating temples on his way. Alerted by events on the Cavery river, the priests in Madurai had time to hide their main treasures. The 'womb chamber' with the main linga of Siva was filled with earth and bricked up, and a new false linga built outside in the vestibule; scores of bronze processional images were buried; the statue of the goddess was hidden in the *vimana*, above the shrine; the gold treasures were carried off.

When Kafur reached Madurai on 10 April 1311, like Napoleon at Moscow, he found an empty city, for Sundara Pandya had fled with his family retainers and treasures. The chronicler Amir Khusru says, 'They found the city empty, for the king had fled, leaving two or three elephants in the temple of Cokkanatha. The elephants were captured and the temple burned.' Though the Pandyas were subsequently able to mount a counterattack and forced Kafur to retreat, it had been a disastrous time for the towns of the south, especially for their great and ancient shrines, full of the hoarded-up treasure of centuries. According to a relatively sober source, Kafur retreated with a vast baggage train loaded with loot, including 612 elephants, 20,000 horses and ninety-six measures of gold, the equivalent to 100 million gold coins. 'At every corner,' continued Khusru, 'conquest opened a door to them, and in all that devastated land, wherever treasure remained hidden in the earth it was sifted, searched through and carted away so that nothing remained to the infidels of their gold but an echo, and of their gems, a flaming fire.'

Kafur's raid was the prelude to an attempt at full-scale conquest and the brief and still obscure period of the Muslim sultanate of Madurai. It is a story which has attracted little attention in modern times; short, brutal and enigmatic, the tale is only now being untangled from the surviving remains of that time. In the following decade the south was subject to more raids; then Muslim governors appear in the Madurai region. In the 1340s these nabobs had proclaimed a sultanate of Madurai, in the story of which the hill of Tirupparakunram played a key part.

When the greatest of all travellers, Ibn Battuta, came here in 1342, he describes the Muslim capital of the south as a large city with well-built streets four miles away from old Madurai by the Vaigai river. His description of the capital matches Tirupparakunram, a Muslim planned town built at the bottom of the great rock. This must be the 'city of Ma'bar' recorded by Muslim historians: the capital of the sultanate, during the half century of its life, where eight sultans reigned until the last, Sikander Shah. Indeed, according to local Muslims the tomb on the hill at which they worship is none other than the tomb of this last sultan, killed here in the dramatic battle when the sultanate fell to the forces of the revived Hindu empire of Vijayanagar in 1377.

The end of this ill-starred venture is recorded by the Delhi historians. According to Shams Siraj, the last sultan had gone native, and worse:

He began to perform acts of indecency in public . . . when he held court in the audience hall he wore women's ornaments on his wrists and ankles, and his neck and fingers were decked with feminine decorations. His indecent acts with pederasts were performed openly . . . [and] the people of Ma'bar were utterly and completely weary and out of patience with him and his behaviour. Then the Hindu army from Vijayanagar entered Ma'bar with a large force and magnificent elephants. They captured [Sikander] alive and killed him and took over the city of Ma'bar. They destroyed the whole of Ma'bar, which was a Muslim city, but also the Muslim women were taken by the Hindus. And [their leader] established himself as ruler of Ma'bar.

No doubt we can take the story with a pinch of salt. But Sikander was not the first – nor the last – to go native in the perfumed climate of Madurai. Most celebrated was the Jesuit Roberto de Nobili, who in 1605 donned the saffron and translated Tamil scriptures (the first Westerner to do so), attempting a meeting of Hinduism and the Bible through Christian Neoplatonism and Upanishadic mysticism. For forty years this unlikely figure walked the streets of Madurai with a shaven head and Saivite marks and was a strict vegetarian. He became known as the 'teacher of reality', Tattuva Bodhakar (as he still is among the older generation in the city which erected a statue to him not so long ago). It was perhaps the most extraordinary missionary experiment ever undertaken; he only drew the line at offerings to the linga in times of drought. Inevitably in the end the Vatican lost patience with the bold flights of his syncretisms.

There were others. In the early nineteenth century a British collector, Rous Peter, earned the nickname Peter Pandya from the locals for his lavish native lifestyle, his ability to ride elephants and shoot tiger, and his devotion to Minakshi (to whom he gave gifts which are still in the possession of the temple, allegedly for saving his life when a storm wrecked his house). The British were a little more robust about going native, at least in the East India Company days. Peter was remembered as a good chap and elicited admiring comments from the sober author of the local gazetteer a generation later.

It would be pleasing to think Sikander had gone down the same path. But the tradition told today by Muslim pilgrims at Tirupparakunram is somewhat different. To them Sikander was no sybarite or unbeleliever but a pious and saintly king who was martyred together with his faithful vizier and a handful of loyal soldiers surrounded by the Hindu army. His followers' tombs are pointed out halfway up the hill; his own, on top, is supposed to be on the spot where he fell.

But Tirupparakunram's pre-eminent shrine is of Murugan; it is one of his six abodes and is mentioned in some of the earliest Tamil poetry from the first centuries of our era. This was the goal of our visit: we met up back at the hostel at six and took tea in the lane before making our way to the shrine entrance. The fairy lights on the *gopura* were still on in the half-light, with the dramatic backdrop of the great rock; at the entrance, the temple servants were washing the steps.

'This is one of the six abodes of Lord Murugan,' announced Mr Ramasamy. 'The legend commemorates the marriage of Murugan to his main wife, Deivani, daughter of Indra. Because of this story, at the auspicious time in early February, thousands of couples come here to solemnize their marriage or to be blessed. Incidentally, as Murugan has a second wife, the wild gypsy huntress Valli, there is also a little shrine dedicated to her on top of the hill, so that she is not left out.' In the summer, he added, vast crowds attend Lord Murugan's birthday. 'Then you will see all sorts of strange happenings: people fire-walking on hot coals, piercing of the body with metal spears and locks through the mouth, people pulling carts hooked to the back.' He pulled a face. 'They are all getting a little carried away.'

The main temple is at the bottom, where a town has grown up since the Muslim occupation in the fourteenth century. It is spectacular. Because the sacred core was an eighth-century rock sanctuary a hundred feet above the street, the medieval builders constructed a series of massive terraces to incorporate the ancient features, and you climb through a series of grandiose halls to reach the sanctum.

We entered through a columned hall about forty yards square, supported by a forest of carved pillars. To the left are pilgrims' stalls, offices and other temple buildings leading to a smaller tank; to the right are further storehouses, including the elephant shed, where the elephant was getting a vigorous scrub from two servants who stood on him, wielding long, hard-bristled floor brushes. The elephant looked up with a beady eye, wriggling with pleasure, as a first rush of early pilgrims came in. While the elephant and I scrutinized each other, Mala hurried over to the office to check with someone from the temple committee that, as a non-Hindu, I would be allowed to go right up to the sanctum. There was no problem: Murugan temples are usually open to all, including untouchables. Most Saivite shrines in the south are also generally welcoming to the respectful visitor, except in big places like Kanchi and Madurai which are on the tourist track. In my experience it is the more orthodox and 'Sanskritic' Vaishnavaite temples which invariably refuse entrance to outsiders.

We walked on through the hall. This main *mandapa* was used as a field hospital by the British when they took the place over in the 1760s, when once more the temple suffered seriously under foreign occupation. It was, said a British observer of the time, 'the most beautiful rest-house I have ever seen . . . all hewn of stone with a roof supported upon a number of splendid pillars covered with carved figures . . . lofty, wide and long'.

At the far end you go under the main *gopura* and up curving stairs on to the second level and then up two more flights of steps on to the third, where there are a number of shrines. You then climb more stairs on to a fourth level, which leads to the sanctum itself. This is actually built around a series of rock-cut caves dating from the late seventh or the eighth century: at the back of the sanctum are carved panels, black with the constant burning of oil-lamps.

We were among the first people in the central shrine after the temple opened at 6.30. At the sanctum they were getting ready for the first pujas and a very helpful priest explained the rituals: 'here we only do the libation on the lance of Murugan' (i.e. the ritual libation); he washed the lance and, after a prayer, placed it on Murugan's lap. Mr Ramasamy and several of the group including his wife and daughter were with us, and the priest waved us round the rail and into the area of the old sanctum itself, so that we could inspect the carvings close up, including a splendid Siva doing the cosmic dance, watched by Parvati and Nandi. In the main cave facing the entrance were Murugan and Ganesh at the two ends, and the goddess in pride of place in the middle. Below the shrine was a warren of subsidiary caves and long dark passages full of eighth-century carvings which included Murugan on his peacock: all in all one of the most remarkable collections of Pallava sculpture to survive.

He pointed out the line dividing the original rock-cut part from the later additions. For my benefit the priest explained the tale of Murugan's marriages; everyone chipped in. Mr Ramasamy was a devotee of Murugan; this, after all, was a Murugan pilgrimage including his three major abodes. Mr Ramasamy became animated as he told the story: again the reference to Murugan as the God of the Tamils. Mr Ramasamy speaks of him and the family as if they were rather elevated neighbours, or better still movie stars, the kind of people whose lives and houses are shown off in the Indian equivalent of *Hello!* magazine, people whose peccadilloes were rather engaging and a constant fund of gossip. Murugan himself was clearly a bit of a lad: 'This was his first wife, major wife. The second wife Valli was a gypsy; he could go running off to her in the hills.' He snorted. 'This is the prerogative of the god.' He grinned and rolled his eyes.

'But why is Murugan a child, Mr Ramasamy?'

'God can be father or mother. Or a child. When god is a child, the devotee is like a parent and his worship nourishes the child. In return the child gives the devotee joys which a parent has from children.'

The priest chipped in: 'This way too the devotee is helped to see himself as a child: to develop childlike skills, playfulness. A child at play is centre of attention, centre of life, worthy of devotion. You see, Tamil people adore children.'

After *darshan* in the sanctum the priest tidied up. 'We were occupied by the British. There was a hospital here two hundred years ago. A certain Major Hewitt told his superiors he did not use force against this place, but he did, and a priest committed self-immolation in protest. This was not the action of a British officer and gentleman. Where are you from? London: I have a cousin in Acton.' Then while Mala and Mrs Vaideyen went for breakfast I headed up the hill path by the temple.

From the top by Sikander Shah's tomb the plain is spread out before you. It is a lovely spot: some trees in rocky gullies shading a spring, and gnarled and bent umbrella trees bracing themselves against the winds which sweep across the top. On the summit is the tomb chamber and a little mosque with standard fifteenth-century Hindu-type monolithic columns with flowery patterns and brackets. The mosque was added later; it has a domed pavilion on top and a little wooden-roofed colonnade of carved stone columns, again of standard south-Indian type. Probably the tomb was expanded a few decades after Sikander's death when the Hindu rulers no longer saw Muslims as a threat, and the memory of the terrible attacks of the 1300s had gone. Now a shrine, it is one of the most revered Muslim sites in the region, but you will often see Hindus who have made the climb going in to pay their respects.

The hill of Tirupparakunram is just one of a series of dramatic granite outcrops which fringe the plain of Madurai like enormous boulders left over by some ancient age of fire or ice: Elephant Hill, Snake Hills and so on. In the early morning haze their weird shapes fringe the horizon of the plain like petrified monsters. They are graphically described in one of the first British accounts of the region in 1868. At that time most had never been climbed or visited by outsiders. James Nelson of the Madras Civil Service describes Snake Hills:

> They are wild and uncultivated, covered with rocks of all sizes, from stupendous blocks of naked granite down to boulders and stones, and of the roughest and strangest shapes. Only the scantiest vegetation clothes their slopes: thorns and stunted trees alone form their jungles. No wealth of any kind is extracted from their summits and scarcely a pagoda has been built upon them; so that neither the natives who live in their neighbourhood, nor the officers who collect revenues from those natives, are often tempted to climb their gaunt and burnt-up sides.

In the early morning after a little night rain the sky was clear and the air fresh and, apart from a gentle haze over the city, you could see all the way from Tirupparakunram across to the Alagar Hills. The whole of the Vaigai plain stretches out like a natural theatre, widening out into the blue haze in the direction of the sea, fifty miles or so to the east. This was the heartland of Pandya civilization, the southernmost of the three great historical zones of Tamil Nadu, the sacred landscape which animates the temple myths of the Pandyan land. Looking from the top of Tirupparakunram, modern suburbs stretch out across the plain on both sides of the Vaigai river, and in the centre, visible despite the early morning haze, are the four main *gopuras* of the Great Temple of Minakshi, which lies at the heart of one of the oldest and most famous cities in the whole of south Asia: Madurai.

THE GREAT GODDESS OF MADURAI

We headed in along the long straight road from Tirupparakunram and soon hit the teeming streets of Madurai. Home to a million people, the second city of Tamil Nadu after Madras, it is a thriving commercial city, famous for its textile mills and transport work-shops, and has a very busy shopping centre. The streets were blocked with lorries, cycle rickshaws and bullock carts. Auto-rickshaws buzzed like angry hornets. Marco Polo spent two months here in 1273, not long before the Muslim sack, and called it 'the most noble and splendid province in the world'. Polo got hot under the collar about the scantily clad women, for it was the custom for women to go bare-breasted, as it was even recently on the nearby Malabar coast. Today the city is as famous as in the Venetian's day for its commerce and in particular for its quick-witted street sellers and rickshaw-men, who are proverbially out to con the unsuspecting strangers and country folk, who pour in in their thousands every day to do pilgrimage to the goddess of the 'fish eyes'.

The bus slowed down to walking pace behind a ruck of bullock carts. 'Mr Michael, be very careful with your money here,' said Mr Ramasamy with a concerned look. 'People here are out to bamboozle you. Not as bad as Delhi, but this is the reputation of Madurai; watch your purse. Don't be persuaded to buy things; they will have the very shirt off your back.'

Madurai is booming these days. New buildings are going up everywhere. The entire place is being rebuilt in concrete, with a profusion of new hotels near the station, but the modern city is shaped by the ancient. The streets form a series of concentric circles around the temple, a layout which has always determined the city's topography and which probably goes back at least to the first centuries AD. The inner streets are named after the Tamil months and were part of the ritual layout of the city from its earliest days; this is planning as laid down in the religious texts for the sacred city, the cosmic city. It is an ancient idea you can see in ruins at Teotihuacan in Mexico or as a museum in the Forbidden City, but here it is still living.

Madurai in fact is one of India's oldest cities, mentioned in Indian and Greek texts from the fourth century BC onwards. From the first century BC, when Greek navigators discovered the secrets of the monsoon, their merchants could sail regular return journeys every year to trade in spices; soon they started to settle in Madurai. In Tamil sources the Greeks here are described as mercenaries living in some sort of colony. Epic poems refer to the *Yavanas* – the Greeks – walking the streets gawping like tourists. There are even tantalizing references to Greek sculptors working here. Hoards of Roman coins have been picked up in the city and across Tamil Nadu, proof of commercial links with the Roman empire, and these are detailed in one of the most fascinating documents to survive from the ancient world, the Alexandrian merchants' manual known as the 'Periplus of the Erythraean Sea'.

Following leads from the 'Periplus', Mortimer Wheeler excavated in a creek near Pondicherry on the eve of the Second World War, and uncovered the Roman warehouses of Arikamedu crammed with Aretine wine for the Tamil middle classes (a first-century consumer boom?). In Augustus' day a Pandyan embassy went from Madurai to Rome, and soon enough a temple to the emperor was erected on the Kerala coast at Cranganore. (Victoria was not the first Western ruler to have her statue set up in an Indian garden.) The biggest demand on the part of Western consumers was for spices. If we are to believe the geographer Strabo, in his day the Roman balance of payments ran deeply into the red to fill the pepper barns by the Tiber. And even today some of our words for spices – pepper and ginger, for example – are loan words from Tamil which came into Western speech via Greek.

The cultural pre-eminence of Madurai dates from this period.

Tradition holds that the city was the centre of the Sangam, or academy, of Tamil poets. In Tamil literature there are, in fact, legends of still earlier, antediluvian *sangams*, but the one in the Roman period is real enough. A famous Sangam poem, 'The Garland of Madurai', paints a brilliant image of the city in the days of the second-century Pandya king Nedunjeliyan when, it was said, the perfume of flowers, ghee and incense from the city could be smelt from miles away: 'a city gay with flags, waving over homes and shops selling food and drink; the streets are broad rivers of people, folk of every race, buying and selling in the bazaars, or singing to the music of wandering bands and musicians'. The poem describes the stalls round the temple, 'selling sweet cakes, garlands of flowers, scented powder and betel pan', and the crafts-men working in their shops, 'men making bangles of conch shell, goldsmiths, cloth dealers, tailors making up clothes, coppersmiths, flower-sellers, vendors of sandalwood, painters and weavers'. All this could be today's city, and indeed Madurai has known an amazing continuity from that day to this; the Pandyan dynasty had its ups and downs, but a distant scion of the dynasty ruling in Strabo's day was still ruling when the British Raj took over in 1805.

We parked by the north gate and walked round to the east entrance usually used by pilgrims. Here custom dictates you enter not under the *gopura* but through the goddess's *mandapa*, the hall where the eight attributes of the goddess are represented. Where Chidambaram is the god's house, this emphatically is the domain of the goddess. The road outside is crammed with shops and stalls hung with decorative canopies. Here at festival time the streets are closed to traffic and you cannot move for stalls selling clothes, shoes, tools, utensils, tiffin boxes, toys, cakes, scaly-skinned *jak* fruit. Right by the entrance are tea shops with old brass samovars where they boil up the first brew at four, just as the temple is opening. Behind the shops is one of four big covered stalls where the thousands of visitors leave their shoes before entering the shrine.

Before you go in, just opposite the entrance, there is a grand *mandapa* built as a *choultry* for pilgrims between 1626 and 1633 by Tirumala Nayak, the great builder of early modern Madurai; beyond the temple are the remains of his Nayak palace, constructed in a showy Saracen Gothic. He also built the huge festival tank outside the old city walls. But the *mandapa* is perhaps his most magnificent, and certainly his most tasteful piece of work: 333 feet long and over 100 feet wide, it has four rows of elaborately sculpted monolithic pillars supporting a flat roof of huge granite slabs; in the central aisle are portraits of the dynasty. A haunting series of glass-plate photographs – now in the India Office library in London – taken in the 1850s by Captain Edward Lyons, shows this wonderful building at the time of the Indian Mutiny, unencumbered, its floor an undulating expanse of polished flagstones. But for a century now the building has been leased to tailors and the place is packed with stalls, shops, workshops and booths heaped with bales of cloth, curtained with figured drapes. Walk through here any time of day and you will be besieged by importunate seamsters offering to run up a suit for you by the end of the day – or sooner. It can be a struggle to stay clothed.

'Hello, sir. Kindly tell me what is your native place? You are from which country? England? Very nice. I have many English friends. Do you know Hull? I am a tailor, sir.' (Hands card.) 'Seven generations of my family are tailors here by the East Gate. Come into my shop. Sit; sit and have some tea. No obligation to buy. Just look.'

He stared at my shirt.

'This is a very old shirt.'

'Actually it's a very new shirt. I got it as a Diwali present. But it has only taken the dhobi in Chidambaram one wash to beat the life out of it and break all the buttons. I think the dhobis and the tailors must be in cahoots.'

He laughed. 'Dhobis are tailors' best friend, sir. But you are most definitely needing a new shirt. If you will take off your shirt here and now, I will measure and copy it by five clock. Exact. I will make two: one white, one blue. Best Kanchi silk. No? You don't want shirt? Look, your trousers have ripped. These I can remake.' (Takes tape measure from round neck and threatens inside leg measurement.) 'What time does your tour bus leave? I will bring them to your hotel. Take them off straight away! Take them off please!'

'I'm sorry. I'm going to the temple now to do puja. I can hardly visit the goddess with no trousers.'

'All right then, what about a sari for your wife?'

'This is not my wife.'

'No problem, sir. Still you can take a present for your wife too. Maybe you want to change dollars? Very good rate. Better than Indian State Bank. Pounds? Deutschmarks?'

As he ran after me his voice dropped to a hissed whisper: 'You want some nice Kerala grass?'

Above you smile voluptuous, life-sized, stone goddesses adorned in real saris, rouged in vermilion, cooled in sandal. Below, the aisles chatter and rattle all day and half the night with the sound of treadle sewing-machines.

Leaving the *mandapa* and coming back to the east entrance, the one traditionally used by pilgrims, we plunged down the steps into the goddess's entrance hall. It has an arched roof supported at the sides by double rows of columns on stone platforms above the pavement. The front rows have carvings of the eight attributes of the goddess; these are life-sized granite caryatids with powerful shoulders, muscular breasts, elaborate suspenders and freshly vermilioned foreheads. Above is a clerestory of painted stucco figures; the ceiling is gaily painted with flower designs enclosing five *yantras*, ornamental mandalas peculiar to the goddess. At the inner end are stone statues of Ganesh and Murugan, the children of the goddess whose house we are about to enter. Tied up framing the entrance were fat stems of banana plants, sagging under tumescent bunches of green fruit: everywhere images of fecundity.

The entrance literally seethed with life. Set back behind the columns were brightly lit stalls selling all the usual offerings for puja. Through it you come into what is almost a town within a town, for the outer halls of the temple are given over entirely to commerce. Even if you have seen it all before on the Tamil pilgrim trail, as I had, still the pilgrim stalls of Madurai come as a staggering spectacle: you pass through caverns of bangles in coloured glass, plastic and cheap gilt and walk down arcades of gaudy religious pictures, showing gods and goddesses of every faith, and some unheard of. Airbrushed eyes follow you round under cascades of travel bags, peacock feathers, clockwork birds and fluffy toys. There are trays of conch shells, emeralds, beads, sandal bars. There are heaps of the most dazzlingly intense scarlet, saffron and purple powders (on one table alone I counted a dozen dizzying shades of crimson). In the central colonnades are twenty or thirty flower stalls piled with beds of cut flowers, and hung with garlands as tall as a man, kaleidoscopes of cut blooms individually strung and bound to make adornments fit for the necks of politicians or gods. Around them the floor was littered with leaves, discarded blooms, broken coconuts; the air was drenched with the perfume of jasmine and incense. Finally, at the central crossing, you stop under four vast bracketed piers, and stand rubbing your eyes trying to take it all in, while the crowd jostles past you into the interior. Then you feel a soft moist breath tousling your hair and look up to see two temple elephants standing benignly over you, bright yellow *yantra*s of wet sandal on their foreheads. Shifting gently from foot to foot they receive the pilgrims and their proffered rupees amid a cacophony of noise, chatter, laughter and music, while sudden flurries of drumming and squeals of trumpets echo in the depths of the interior. And we had yet to set foot inside.

Mala came over to pull me away from the pictures and brusquely handed back to the stallholder the one I was about to buy, a silver-framed trio of lissom young goddesses sitting lotus fashion in red saris in a crimson-draped boudoir. (By now I confess, I was becoming irresistibly hooked on the most tawdry superficialities of Hinduism.)

'It's really nice, don't you think?' I said hopefully. It cut no ice with Mala. 'He is charging too much. Twenty-five rupees is too costly. Now we are going in. Put it down and come.'

I protested feebly and then did as I was told. A few days on the road and we were beginning to behave like a married couple.

In Madurai, contrary to the usual custom, the goddess is always worshipped before the god. As far as the pilgrims are concerned, this is her temple, not his. And so, offering baskets in hand, Mala and Mrs Vaideyen led the way past the Ganesh shrine which stands in a lovely little garden opposite the elephant house. The paving-stones were damp after their early morning wash; a *kolam* on the floor, fresh marigolds on a cluster of lingas and snake stones under the *vanni* tree. In the garden a group of pilgrims were reading religious texts aloud with their guru. In the early morning light under a clear blue sky the temple looked simply lovely.

From everywhere you can see the *gopura*s. These form the distinctive skyline of the city. Madurai city laws forbid building higher, as also does old Tamil popular belief. 'Building higher than the temple *gopura*' is a proverbial description of hubris. That day the west and south towers were covered with scaffolding, wooden poles and wicker cladding – undergoing a major renovation, the first in thirty years, to restore and repaint the sculptures on the towers. There are no fewer than 1500 sculptures on the south tower, and the west and east towers have over a thousand each. Now faded to a pleasant pastel shade, they are to be restored to a garish Hindu Disneyland, as we could glimpse from the glaring tangerines, greens and kingfisher blues under the rattan screens.

Here the Tamil *gopura* reaches its apotheosis, sweeping up in elegant parabolic curves covered with sculpture from top to bottom. There is none of the restraint of Chidambaram, with its sedate measured rows of dignified deities; here they are swarming with demons, gods, goddesses, monsters, animal-headed creatures, figures of myth, fantasies, dreams, nightmares, wriggling, prancing, dancing – giving the impression of a myriad life forms. Energy itself shooting up into the sky. Here you think that if Zen is about the distilled essence of life, Hinduism is about its amazing and infinite variety. Or, as Edward Lear put it when he came here in 1874, 'its myriadism of impossible picturesqueness'.

It is not everyone's cup of tea, it must be said. Though an artist like Lear could describe the Dravidian temples as 'stupendous and beyond belief', this architecture was disparaged by the architectural historian Ferguson, who raged at its barbarity, finding it all a prodigious wasted effort, and to make matters worse, 'all for a debased fetishism'. He thought nothing here aspired to 'the lofty aims of the best works of the Western world', and reserved his most scathing comments for the design of the *gopuras*: 'As an artistic design nothing could be worse,' he thundered. 'The bathos of the *gopuras* decreasing in size and elaboration as they approach the sanctuary is a mistake which nothing can redeem; it is altogether detestable.' As for the idea that 'the altar or statue of the god should be placed in a dark cubical cell wholly without ornament' – well, that left him finally speechless. 'If only the principle could be reversed,' he burbled, 'such buildings would be among the finest in India.' Which only goes to show how even the best scholars can utterly fail to escape the preconceptions of their own time and culture, and, what is worse, fail completely to divine the purpose of the architects who made these great buildings.

The temple forms a rectangle about 850 × 750 feet on its longest sides, so it is by no means the largest of southern shrines, but inside this is the final baroque flowering of the Dravidian style we saw in an earlier phase at Chidambaram, and whose origins lie in the seventh-century shore temple at Mahabalipuram and the early shrines at Kanchi. Inside you enter a labyrinth of corridors around the shrines, monolithic sculpted granite columns thirty feet high, with huge stepped overhanging brackets to carry the roof, many of the columns highly sculpted into the form of monsters and capped with the snapping heads of mythical beasts. Leading off the corridors are many sub-shrines, including the thousand-pillared hall built in 1572, which is no longer used for worship now. About 250 feet square, it has 985 granite pillars brilliantly carved with mythological figures. A wide central nave leads to a shrine of the dancing Siva, with vistas down the full length of the hall. At the far end a large bronze Nataraja is now inappropriately backlit with Hammer House of Horror red gels.

In front of the main shrines the corridors open out into pillared vestibules in the 'baroque' style of the Nayaks. Most impressive is the Kambattadi *mandapa*, a vast shadowy arcade in front of the entrance to the Siva shrine. Lit by dazzling shafts of light from the roof, this space has the baroque magnificence of the contemporary Bernini. But where the Italian master constructs floods of light with gold, paint and sunbursts of gilded wood, here the astounding elaboration of the carving (and in such a hard stone) is coupled with a sensual energy which positively bursts out over the iron rails. Such was the last flowering of the Pandyan tradition. Though in fact only erected in the early seventeenth century, it actually looks as one might imagine the House of Atreus had it never fallen; smelling of hoary antiquity and glistening with vermilion and the oil of sacrifice.

Originally, the *mandapa* was lit only by artificial light – the light wells, like the neon strips, are modern – and you passed this lamp-lit zone before plunging down the axis to the silvery chamber of Siva, whose starry lamps flicker deep in the interior. In few architectures has the world of the spirits been made so concrete. In front of you, rearing up behind iron rails, are the twenty-four forms of Siva carved in the round on the sides of eight huge pillars around a tall gilded flagstaff which rises through the roof. Among these is the marriage of Siva and Minakshi–Parvati, which is still celebrated every year. Between them, facing Siva's sanctum, is his faithful bull Nandi, a stone monolith which is usually covered in heaps of *darba* grass and a snowfall of salt offerings.

This colossal arrangement is faced by another group of four monolithic granite statues each over ten feet high, and each a masterpiece of the stonecarver's art. There is Siva in his fiery 'terrifying' and 'non-terrifying' forms, the *urdhva tandava* (the impassioned dance), and also Bhadrakali, the ever-present black incarnation of the goddess. These statues are the object of much veneration for today's pilgrims, and in front of them there is always an attendant seated at a little table with a large tin bowl containing lumps of ghee floating in water (to stop it melting in the heat). These the pilgrims buy for a few paise and throw at the statues for good luck; it is an ancient custom but no one could enlighten me about its origins. By mid-morning the figures are spattered head to foot with yellow ghee, which is scraped off every hour or two by temple servants on ladders.

The *mandapa* creates a tremendous brooding impression: the dim light, the giant statues, the lamps and puja fires, the glint of brass and silver, the shafts of sunlight coming down from the light wells, not to mention the noise and the smell – an impression quite overwhelming to earlier generations of visitors, who rather like Forster's Miss Quested entering the Marabar Caves, found it all 'frightening' and 'incomprehensible to the Western mind'. Hinduism here was 'a religion without possibility of salvation'. Francis Yeats Brown, a well-known thirties Indophile, could not bring himself to enter ('I was afraid'). 'Here one may see the very essence of Dravidian idolatry,' wrote one old British hand in the twenties, admitting nevertheless that 'the whole effect upon the mind of this majestic hall is powerful and strange in the extreme'.

It is easy to sit for hours here and watch the world go by, the ebb and flow of visitors, the ritual cycle of the temple's day. Or to wander the corridors and subsidiary shrines; outside the door of the Siva shrine, for example, is a little group of altars to the planets; oil-lamps burn from dawn till night dripping fire on to the stones, and pilgrims are constantly moving past them. At a huge, pot-bellied Ganesh devotees leave sticky sweets and pray for good luck. There are shrines to the legendary Sangam poets; there is even the preserved trunk of the *kadamba* tree where the temple was founded in mythic times (rather as in classical Greek times the stump of Athena's olive was preserved along with her archaic statue in the Erechtheion at Athens). And all through these spaces lamps burn and pilgrims congregate, mill around, pray and perform their own intimate rituals with a bewildering variety of gesture and movement. Tapping the forehead with the knuckles, smacking cheeks in a kind of chastisement, holding the hands above the head, pirouetting, bowing, prostrating: the halls echoing all day with the susurration of a thousand private prayers.

But we had no time to wander. Mr Ramasamy's timetable admitted no slack: our Darshan Video Bus tour had to get to Palani by early evening, so for us it was straight to the goddess. Mala led the way, through the inner gates, framed by a huge metal arch holding a thousand oil-lamps, which are lit at festival time, so that the pilgrim passes through a gateway of fire. We walked past the lotus tank, along a spacious and airy sunlit arcade to the Kili Kudu-mandapa which lies outside the goddess's shrine, a space with an elaborately painted roof supported by rows of pillars carved with roaring lion-like creatures with their tails in their mouths. Outside the door is a Nandi and a big painted *kolam* on the floor like an intricate geometrical pattern, and a circular lotus mandala in a square frame inlaid in the floor; here many devotees prostrate themselves before going in. To one side is a row of shrines with parrot cages. (Goddesses in the south are often shown with parrots, but the parrot is Minakshi's particular emblem: they are held to signify peace and happiness. Until fairly recently the temple kept real parrots, which were taught to speak the deity's name: this was discontinued, according to Mr Ramasamy, because of 'maintenance problems'.) Above the door there is a big illuminated sign identifying this as the goddess's domain, and only Hindus may go beyond the threshold. Mala explained my presence to the guardian on the door and after some discussion with my fellow travellers I was allowed through.

*

When you go through the door the echoing sounds of the exterior world are left behind, daylight lost. You have moved literally and figuratively to an inner world, the antithesis of all that lies outside the door: peace. Where Rameshwaram was riotous noise and confusion, the atmosphere here was quite different, and for this obviously the pilgrims were responsible. There was a warm hush of expectation, a suspension of reality and the projection instead of a land of dreams. You go under an early-thirteenth-century gateway into a large chamber lined by a double row of columns, with brackets holding up the stone slabs of the roof. This is the outer of two enclosures which surround the goddess's sanctum; it is a spacious columned walkway circling the inner shrine, allowing circulation of air in the stifling interior. In front is the gilt and brass flagstaff of the goddess, where her long linen flag is raised at festival time; on either side of the stairs up into the inner area are shrines to Ganesh and Murugan, the two sons of Siva by the goddess, emphasizing that Minakshi is another form of Parvati. On the inner wall to the left you see a group of plaster images of the temple's great benefactor the Nayak king Tirumala Nayak and his two queens, in painted stucco, sensuous and pot-bellied; he was a patron of gunpowder and sandal, sponsor of dancing girls and gladiators, protagonist of the beautiful but violent world which was seventeenth-century Tamil Nadu on the eve of the European invasion.

We circled the corridor and then, coming back to the front, entered the inner enclosure, up the front stairs, through a door flanked by two copper gatekeepers. You step into a darkened inner chamber built in the fifteenth century, in which the goddess chamber stands. This is the most atmospheric part of the temple, despite the neon strip lights. In front of the goddess's shrine the roof is held up by forty granite columns which are covered with chased copper. The room is lit only by artificial light, and the effect is very striking, fire glittering on surfaces of metal – especially when the temple is open at night for special pujas, on eclipses, and full moons. Counting inwards from the old walls you have now passed through four concentric rings of processional streets, and four rectangular enclosures within the temple: in other words, a kind of huge man-made mandala, a vestige of the ancient city planners.

Now we were in the heart of the labyrinth. In front of us was a stone chamber fifty feet long by twenty-five wide, 'the womb chamber' in whose rear part the immovable image of the goddess is fixed. The sanctum, which only the priests may enter, is raised by three steps above the floor of the inner court. The pilgrims wait below the steps on either side of the rail, the nearest fifty feet or so from the image. The goddess stands in a narrow corridor of darkness, lit by hanging oil-lamps, and by a ring of lamps behind a horn aureole on the back wall like a circle of stars, creating the strange effect of limitless space in the darkness behind the image. Only when the priests do puja and hold fire before her is her face dimly lit in the flickering flames.

In the womb chamber the pilgrims come face to face with the image which is their goal. It is a human image, much more personalized and specific than the aniconic linga. Here the transaction is with another person, albeit divine. This is what we in the West call idol worship. Better though to quarry its original meaning in the Greek: *eidolon* means 'something seen', whether concrete or phantasmal, and hence a material image which evokes a shared imaginal world in the minds of those who see.

The image of the goddess is a little smaller than lifesize, her skin of green stone (emerald according to more than one pilgrim I spoke to, but probably green porphyry mined in the hills north of the city). She stands in contrapposto, right leg slightly bent at the knee so that the left hip is accentuated, emphasizing her procreative powers. She is crowned, and though the statue as carved is clothed – as are the bronzes – she is always dressed in a real robe too. Her costume changes each day; she wears a white sari at night to symbolize the retention of her sexual powers, and red during the day, signifying blood, the colour of female potency, so that she is charged with the aura of sex and fecundity. In one festival in particular, Navaratri, different symbolic meanings are expressed by costume shifts and liturgies on each of the nine days. She holds a parrot and a bouquet, 'radiating love and compassion' as the local guidebook for pilgrims puts it.

At the rail Mr Ramasamy, Mrs Vaideyen and Mala lean forward, craning to see; Mala strikes her cheeks, right with left hand, left with right. As the Brahmin comes along the rail with the tray bearing camphor flames and ash, she drops a few paise on to the tray in return for ash and daubs her forehead with it. (The scented whitish ash which comes from the camphor flame is the colour of the god; the vermilion dot seen on Indian women's foreheads the world over is the colour of the goddess.) Then she resumes her fixed concentration on the image and completes her prayer. There was a kind of urgency to the action, especially a pressing need to see the face – *virtus* comes from the face and specifically from the eyes. *Darshan*, the act of worship, means 'seeing'.

There was a hush as they stared into the black chamber: the flickering flames of the puja lamps caused the air to quiver in the hot airless room; a smell of sweat and incense; stillness. As the atmosphere seemed to vibrate in front of my eyes, I had the uncanny sense that the statue was moving; it was as if the pilgrims' love had infused the image with life.

('Senses stilled and indrawn,' says the famous Tamil poem by Tirumullar, which is known to all the pilgrims. 'Surrender to the Beloved is as when a man and a woman lie together in embrace and loving caress. When that becomes this then you will find peace and bliss.' Having nothing from my own culture with which to compare, at that moment I found myself thinking of the strange story of *The Winter's Tale*, in which, in a mysterious lamplit shrine, the statue of a mother is brought back to life by the faith of her lost daughter and her grieving husband. How very Indian, Shakespeare's strange puja in that late romance.)

The Madurai temple legend according to Mala is this: Minakshi, the daughter of the Pandyan king, is born deformed, with three nipples. She is told that when she sees her future husband the blemish will be removed. She becomes queen of the Pandyas, but she is an Amazonian, wielding spear, bow and chariot, conquering her male enemies; ruling and acting as a man. Then, on Kailash, as promised, she has a vision of Siva and is restored. In fact she is none other than an incarnation of Parvati, the embodiment of auspiciousness within marriage. She returns to Madurai to dwell in the temple and hears the appeals of the childless and blesses their future offspring. Married into the Brahminical pantheon, but a Dravidian warrior queen, she retains a strange status, which is summed up in her role in the temple. She has primacy in the cult, she is worshipped first, before the male god and stands apart from him. Having been self-created in the sacrificial fire, she passes from being the Amazonian three-breasted queen who led armies and ruled as a man, to being the epitome of domesticated femininity, married and a mother. But she is none the less the independent mistress of the shrine. Her role in the year's festivals reminds the pilgrims of her more dangerous side; and she always stands alone to receive her pilgrims, not as an appendage of the male god. Mr Ramasamy had something to say about this.

'We have a saying in Tamil Nadu,' said Mr Ramasamy; 'In a marriage you either have a Madurai house or a Chidambaram house.'

'What does that mean?'

'If it is a Madurai house, the lady is wearing the trousers.'

'Which one do you have, Mr Ramasamy?'

'Well, we live in Chidambaram, but reverence Minakshi. Ideal balance.'

Mrs Ramasamy raised her eyebrows with a twinkle.

When we left, big mirrors in the roof above the door enabled the pilgrims to see the goddess still above the crush, to glimpse her image behind them as they walked away. At the door Mala turned again, standing on tiptoe, to look one last time, saying goodbye. Like a child, or a lover.

On the way out near the door there is one last image at which the women pray: a simple crude stone relief carved on a column. It shows the goddess as the Earth Mother; it is an image prayed to especially by women hoping for children. Big-legged and round-bellied, she stands naked, legs akimbo, while her female essence is drunk from her *yoni* by a tiny male devotee; the whole pillar is smeared in *kun kum*, and glistens blood red in the semi-darkness. The Tamils believe the life juice is possessed in much greater quantity, and more potently, by women than men. Like the ancient Greeks, they think that women's sexual power is much greater than men's, and hence it is vital in seeking a partner in marriage that the horoscope shows the right balance of attributes. Preferably the man should be some years older than the woman, for in all things – age, personality, caste, physical attributes, sexual appetite and proclivity – a mismatch is destructive to the male. Visceral and unambiguous, this image is the very symbol of tantric religion, a literal representation of the force which through its long history India has assigned to Sakti.

I was fascinated by our encounter with the goddess. It felt like meeting someone once known but long forgotten. Aphrodite, Artemis, Athena, Demeter, Persephone, Nut, Isis, Ishtar. We know their names and attributes but we meet them only in the residue of their aura, in books, paintings, symbols, and in archæological monuments. We try to trace her epiphanies in broken Greek majuscule at Eleusis, or on the starry zodiac of Dendera where her genitals and breasts have been gouged by Christian fanatics. We stand uncomprehendingly before the black-faced, gilded Diana in Naples, her neck hung with bulls' testicles; we confront Ishtar's haunting visage in Baghdad, she who knew 'the rules of the underworld'. But to meet her living incarnation was, to say the least, exciting. Nowhere on earth as in India is the goddess worshipped in such splendour. There is an archaic, irrepressible current in Indian life which has never been done away with by the westernization or modernization of our own times.

We walked back outside into the blinding glare of the sun. By the tank, I talked to Mala while her neighbours packed holy ash into their bags. Everyone was satisfied: it was as if they had taken food or drink. I pondered this as we ate that lunchtime in the crowded Sree Ganesh mess: a dank subterranean place, friendly and overcrowded, which served the office population near the West Gate.

I asked the women about Minakshi's eyes: Why does she have 'fish eyes'? Beautiful women's eyes are like a carp, they said, 'long and shapely as a fish'. Also fishes' eyes are round and unblinking, to look at they are liquid and glitter. (This is an ancient semantic cluster in Tamil, for the word *min* is the root of both fish and star; originally perhaps meaning to shine, it probably comes from the most archaic stratum of the language, for this combination of fish and star occurs on the pottery of the Indus civilization.) Someone also mentioned an old folk belief that fishes have the power to hatch their eggs by a mere look. Today in Tamil Nadu, they said, there are many popular stories about the fatal power of the glance: between men and women a glance is said to be almost as significant as the loss of chastity. Eyes, like sex organs, contain love: 'Love at first sight,' we say. Souls are said to mix through the eyes – to my mind a true insight into the overriding power of physical attraction in choosing a partner and falling in love.

Mala said that this is what should happen in an arranged marriage when you meet the prospective husband or wife. The horoscope may be right, but if you don't have the feeling through the eyes, then you should seek elsewhere. Sarasu, for example, had been looking for two years now; some of her suitors had been perfectly compatible, but she had felt nothing looking into their eyes. One of her friends added the popular etymology of the word for husband in Tamil, *kanavar*, as *kan*, 'eye' and *avar*, 'he', that is, 'the one to whom the eyes go' or 'are given'. The first sight of the

THE SEASON OF RAINS

potential wife or husband has the kind of resonance of *darshan*: a recognition, a powerful encounter involving the exchange of spiritual and sexual power (as real *darshan* is with the goddess). 'You see,' said Mrs Vaideyen, 'when Sita and Rama meet and fall in love, Kampan says their eyes met and a shaft of love entered her which later expanded and spread into her whole being. He invaded her heart, she said.'

With its grandly conceived annual ritual cycle and its great festivals, with its simple daily round of pujas, music and sacramental meals, Madurai reminds you that very simple rituals, by their beauty and antiquity, have the power to satisfy everyone, not merely the gullible and the illiterate. It is a mnemonic of a culture: a focal point, a crossing place, as the tax inspector had said. Behind the so-called idol lies the mental image: an imaginal world and a whole culture. It is not only, or even chiefly, about belief, but about being Tamil. In Western culture, Isocrates thought the mysteries of Demeter at Eleusis the most important legacy of the Greeks, for such things connect both with the whole body of myth and with social belief as well. At Madurai I felt myself in presence of (as Quintilian said of the Greek gods) 'things which never were but are always.'

THE HILL OF PALANI

'Now you can see the hill, Mr Michael,' said Mr Ramasamy, shouting from the front of the bus. I jerked awake; the afternoon heat on the bus had been stupefying. It was now five. We had by-passed the rock of Dindigul, through Virupakshi, and entered a great bowl of wooded hills cut by deep valleys ahead. Rising up on the left were the cloud-topped foothills of the Western Ghats, the great massif of the Kodaikanal hills. Mr Ramasamy was excited. The last goal of our pilgrimage was in sight. 'There, there, see now. You see the hill? It is one of the most charming places in all of Tamil Nadu.'

We were at the edge of a great lake, the Vyapuri, looking across it towards the mouths of two big valleys separated by dramatic cliffs, their pale ochre crags boldly etched by the sinking sun. Framing the eastern side of this beautiful prospect rises the steep rocky hill of Palani, a perfect dome 450 feet high, not unlike the Acropolis of Athens. On top is the famous shrine of Murugan, squat and flat, with red and white striped outer walls and a small *gopura* on the west. Below it you could see the sacred way which winds round the base of the hill, lined with shrines and *choultries*, and the wide stone staircase which climbs up the hillside to the summit.

As dusk comes on lamps are lit all the way up these paths, giving the impression of a hill draped in a garland of fairy lights. The natural setting was indeed, as Mr Ramasamy had said, quite charming. More than that, though, the surrounding bowl of hills lent an added majesty to the mysterious shrine on the summit; it was not a place to be passed through, or casually stumbled upon, but must be deliberately sought out in its mountain lair. Celebrated two thousand years ago in Sangam poetry, it is another tap root of Tamil culture. In the evening light of a quiet October day, across the rich cultivated plain, the green rice fields, the groves of palms and the vast silent range, it was a memorable sight, and the spirits of everyone on the bus visibly lifted with anticipation.

Like Lourdes, Palani is an out-and-out pilgrimage town. The mile-long road from the station to the foot of the hill winds through the town, round temples and shops and food stalls. There are hostels, *choultries* and lodges for the thousands who come in each day for a short stay: these are owned by different temple bodies, caste associations from all over the south. I strolled into the Sri Venkateshwara lodge to use their bathroom; it was a vast barracks painted bright green, the front hung with banana leaves and palm fronds for the festival; the foyer was heavy with the smell of Mysore incense and disinfectant. The place was crowded and buzzing with excitement, officious managers, booking clerks, and catering officers rushing to and fro. The whole town seemed to be geared to servicing the shrine. As you neared the foot of the hill, the religious buildings crowded the road: washing places, cloakrooms, left-luggage halls, hostels. We parked near the bus stand:

'Right. Right,' said Mr Ramasamy. 'Three hours; leaving at eight o'clock. Take tiffin before we leave.'

There are two main things for pilgrims to do here: first you walk round the hill on a path called the Giri-Veedhi, a mile-long sandy road dotted with shrines, stone images of the peacock and memorials set up to commemorate wealthy devotees; it is a pleasant walk in the evening under the spreading branches of *kadamba* trees, Indian oaks. Many bathe too in the sacred river, the Shanmuga. Then you climb the hill. At the big festivals, especially in May, hundreds of thousands do this, many carrying a yoke across their shoulders and pots of milk for lustration. Some, usually young men, go further in self-mortification, piercing their cheeks with a kind of mouth lock, using a little metal spear with Murugan's leaf-shaped blade: apparently the same ritual as that uncovered by the archaeologists on the coast near Tiruchendur.

I left my shoes in the temple office cloakroom and started up the 659 steps. On the slopes there are little gardens fed by streams from a perennial spring and shrouded by creepers with mimosa, bougainvillea, white-flowering vines and peacocks. Large signs tell the visitor they are sponsored by the Indian State Bank, the Vijaya Bank, Dindigul, even the Catholic Syrian bank, Dindigul. In leafy glades you catch sight of lifesize tableaux of mythic stories: there are shops, too, for drinks and snacks. Along the path sit the poor and the sick, and the holy renouncers: a line of ash-smeared ascetics with white whiskers.

From the parapet opens out a view of the great Vyapuri tank, the causeway and the town with all its lights coming on. On top of the hill is an open forecourt where a big crowd had camped out in the balmy light, listening to religious music relayed through loudspeakers; fires were burning at an open-air altar. To the north, the great circle of mountain peaks shaded off one behind the other. Then the sun burst through the clouds, glinting orange on the lake and the flooded paddy over four hundred feet below, far from where we were, in the domain of Murugan, Lord of the Hills.

The queue for *darshan* was predictably long: I had taken the precaution of buying a special ticket at the bottom of hill for 10 rupees: to 'save waiting' I was told.

At the top I showed my ticket to a man with an official armband.

'Please wait.'

'How long?'

'One or two hours, please.'

'I thought this was a special ticket and I could go straight in.'

'Ah, you need to buy twenty-five-rupee ticket.'

'Fine. Here's the extra fifteen.'

'Sorry; refund not available; ten-rupee ticket is not valid to exchange. You must pay the total: twenty-five rupees.' Seeing my face his expression softened. 'It is very nice; you will be sitting very close to the lord.'

I sat right by the entrance to the inner sanctum, across which was drawn a black curtain embroidered with the characters OM. I could hardly see a thing in the smoky half-light. Then drums struck up, and the curtain was whipped smartly aside to reveal a doll-like figure in gold garments and scarlet underclothes, a gold cummerbund and a conical gold hat. His smile was decidedly jaunty, like that of Rajini Kanth in the movies. There was so much incense smoke that he appeared to be standing on a golden cloud. It was, I learned, just one of several costume changes Murugan has at different pujas (one, as a girl, is no longer done). We of the twenty-five-rupee tickets sat right in front while the hoi polloi behind the rails were ushered through cheering like a football crowd. When the curtain was drawn open, an old man next to me who had brought his ten-year-old grandson burst into tears. The atmosphere was one of unalloyed pleasure and joy, as if people were sitting in front of a fire which warmed them to their hearts. When puja was over, *prasad* was handed out for us to drink. As I sat for a few minutes watching this strangely lifelike little face in its smoky golden room, the fat man who had sat next to me taciturn for almost the whole bus journey turned to me with a look of deeply serious happiness: 'India – best gods.'

Outside, the sun had set and crowds were promenading around the wide terrace which covers the summit around the shrine; music playing through the loudspeakers added to the holiday atmosphere. The ranges of mountains were now receding into the twilight; over the paddies the light was fading into a misty softness and plumes of smoke were hanging over the fields below.

'You are from which country?'

He was in his thirties. Handsome face, square jaw, honest, open face, short, curly black hair, moustache, kind eyes: friendly but guarded.

'I am Christian. My name is Salvin. Same as your archbishop.'

'Salvin?' I said, and had to think for a moment before I cottoned on: 'Ah yes, Selwyn. Catholic, Syrian, C of E? Evangelical?' I asked, trying to be heedful of the diversity of any Indian religion. Even with Christianity these days in India one has to be a little careful: as the Catholics turn against Syrians in Kerala; and Pentacostalists and Evangelicals against everybody everywhere.

'Protestant.'

'Ah, me too,' I said, surprising myself.

He turned out to be a telecommunications engineer from Madurai working in Palani. 'So you have seen Lord Murugan,' he said pointing to the blobs of sandal paste on my shirt.

He told me the story of the idol in the Murugan shrine. According to legend it is made of the nine poisons: special herbal medicines amalgamated into a wax-like substance over a thousand years ago by a mysterious magician, a *Siddha* (the sect still exists by the way). His name was Bhoga; he disappeared into a cave under the hill, where he will reappear like Merlin at the end of the Kali Yuga, this declining aeon of ours whose end is now in Hindu terms imminent (i.e. in a mere few hundred thousand years).

'So you've seen Lord Murugan here, Selwyn?' I said, slightly surprised; he was Christian, after all.

'Many times. I work here in Palani you see. Lord Murugan is the most popular of the Tamil gods,' he continued, and then added: 'I have great faith in Lord Jesus.'

How welcoming Indian religion is, I thought. Here naturally, Jesus is another Indian god. For Selwyn perhaps he is more efficacious than Murugan, personally he is more drawn to him; but to have faith in him was to deny neither the existence nor the power of Murugan. You can see them arm in arm on pilgrim posters and murals in Madras. Despite periods of persecution under the likes of Malik Kafur and Aurangzeb, Indians lack our ideological baggage from inquisitions and crusades; the point of view of the man and woman in the street is ecumenical. Selwyn in fact happily goes between the Catholic shrine at Velankanni, Murugan of Palani and Muslim Nagore. Perhaps, I reflected, Indian Christians and Muslims are in a sense Hindus too, in that whatever faith Indian people follow, their mode of worship remains Indian. It is an old adage: Hinduism is India and India is Hinduism. Best gods indeed!

Though he had never been out of the south, Selwyn was well read and widely informed about the world. He was also a real believer in Gandhi, the first I had met to hold firmly to Gandhi's ideas on non-violence and the unity of all religions. These days young Hindus never speak of him, but for Selwyn Gandhi was still the key. Look at the events in South Africa, he said. Mandela's success proved that Gandhi's principle of non-violence was still valid. 'He is the greatest man alive: he forgave his enemies, you see.'

'How old are you?' he asked.

'Forty-four. And you?'

'Thirty-four. You look younger. And I older. Look at my face. I look older than you, I think. This is living in a poor country.' He smiled as if embarrassed. 'You are married?'

'Yes, I have two little daughters. You?'

'I have been married for two years. My wife Sundari works in local government. She is Christian too. We do not yet have children.' There was disappointment in his eyes. 'We have little time together you see: I am six days a week in Palani, then one day in Madurai. At present we are saving, both working. I have applied for a transfer to Madurai, but not yet successfully; it is hard to live apart like this.'

Somewhere in the courtyard I could hear Mr Ramasamy calling us all together. I left Selwyn sitting on the parapet looking out to the mountains with songs still drifting from the loudspeakers. At the top of the steps a great crowd sat around the flaming altar while the temple elephant tapped tonsured children on the head; a couple from Coimbatore waved goodbye. We had reached the end of our pilgrimage and I think felt very heartily, as Mala would say. We had a group photo taken by a bank manager from Bangalore. 'So you see, Mr Michael, this is the joy of pilgrimage: the companionship, the doing it together,' said Mr Ramasamy, beaming: 'Now I ask you this: would you have had so much fun if you had gone privately with a driver in an A/C Ambassador car?'

We took nine hours back to Chidambaram; it had all been a bit of a whirlwind, and it was over so quickly. I couldn't sleep. Mr Subrahmaniam, the tax inspector, and I sat together. Now and then he interrupted the conversation to point out of the window to something quite invisible in the darkness, for all I knew miles away, but clearly to him vividly present, exerting a spiritual force field which could easily be felt on the bus. Passing the island of

Sriringam, for instance, he told me the story of a secret garden there, many acres in extent, surrounded by high granite walls:

'There only the flowers sacred to Ranganatha are grown. These are then plucked and woven into garlands by special celibate priests. No one else may ever enter that garden,' he said. 'Even those who carry the garlands must tie a cloth around the nose so that they may not accidentally smell the fragrance before it is offered up to the god.'

His eyes lit up. Mr Subrahmaniam, as I knew by now, had both a subtle grasp of the higher flights of abstract thought and a childlike love of spectacle and mystery; needless to say this appealed to me greatly. In the early hours as we nodded in the glow of the red night light, he became more reflective.

'Pilgrimages like this take place at the time of great natural phenomena, full moons, eclipses, the ends and beginnings of the cycles of heaven. To be there on such occasions, you feel a part of it. Part of Nature. Part of human society, of civilization. This is what it means to belong to a tradition.

'Now here this tradition has a very special quality. It is a memorizing tradition. And memorizing gives certain very important things: a tremendous command of the language; a refinement of expression; a vision of poetic imagery which has survived many centuries. And in this tradition, what are the things which are valued as great? Sound, meaning, images, landscape, myths and stories, but also values, attitudes to life and respect for tradition itself.

'This is being lost now. This is true all over the world, of course; I know, as we read in our newspapers. Traditional societies are being replaced. Tamil Nadu, I am sure, is not peculiar in this, although I have never travelled beyond it. But Tamil Nadu had a very deep commitment to it, and it survived even to the end of the twentieth century. But now it is on the way out. I think the damage has been done now. Traditional scholars are no longer being trained in the old ways, only in Western method. Temples

THE SEASON OF RAINS

have lost individual traditions which went back nearly two thousand years. Also, a memorizing culture needs time and who these days has time; where in the next generation will there be young people who want to devote the time to learn all this? When it is lost you cannot get it back.'

'But don't the politicians say now they want to revive it?'

He smiled sadly. 'Ah. But they no longer know what it is.'

Dawn came with smoky lilac mist around Sirkali. The bus arrived back at Chidambaram around five. The streets were still dark as we came up East Car Street and stopped by the Ganesh statue outside Minakshi's aunt's house. Mala and her neighbours did a quick prayer at the little locked grille where the oil-lamp was burning low. It was still dark as our tired band trooped home to prepare for work: Mr Subrahmaniam to the local tax office, Ganesh and Raja to the temple, Mr Ramasamy to school. He was looking ragged and unshaven.

'So, back to school this morning then, Mr Ramasamy?'

'Yes. Out of the frying-pan, Mr Michael. Good training, you see. Handling busload of pilgrims or class full of children. Same, same.' He grinned.

'So what next?'

'We go to Tiruvannamalai next month: only one night, 110 rupees. But next year I am planning a big pilgrimage for Sivaratri festival: we will be going from Chidambaram to Kashi, Benares, in north India. And many other places: Haridwar, Rishikesh, Gaya, the Sangam at Allahabad. It will take two weeks: super-de-luxe bus, no hard seats like these, reclining chairs: cushioned seats.'

'So you are not planning to renounce the world just yet?'

'Ha! I am expanding. This will be the best yet: 2200 rupees, two meals daily included.'

'What about accommodation?

'No accommodation.' He laughed. 'This will be provided free by various *adinam*s: Tirupannandal, Dharamapuram. They provide food and lodging at Benares in *choultries* for the Tamil pilgrims. Everyone makes only the donation he can afford.'

'And movies too?'

'A galaxy of stars. By next year maybe even Hollywood movies dubbed in Tamil. Spielberg! So get your booking in soon, Mr Michael. Book now to avoid disappointment!'

6

Journey into the Delta

THE CYCLONE

So by a circuitous route, and quite unplanned, I went to Tiruchen-dur, just as Rajdurai Dikshithar had said I would. When I had come to Tamil Nadu I had had no intention of making the journey laid out for me in Rajdurai's horoscope. But now, after my adventures on Mr Ramasamy's video bus, I felt compelled to complete it: to visit Jupiter at the Sun temple at Suryanarcoil, and especially, as Rajdurai was so insistent, to see Saturn at Tirunallar. Mala was tied up on family business for a few days, so I decided to get the train south and go alone up the Cavery river. Later we would go together to Tirunallar. But at that moment my plans were interrupted.

It was seven at night and I was sitting in the tea stall in East Car Street when the cyclone came. Suddenly a huge black cloud came over from the south-east and rolled up the sky like a blind up a window; then came flashes of lightning so tremendous that the night sky over the town momentarily turned day blue. By the time I got back to the bus stand, there was a sea of mud, and in VGP Street the auto-rickshaws were up to their axles in water. Frogs roared outside my room all night, almost drowning out the late show at the Marriappar Cinema.

By the morning the water in the canal was rising fast: up the ghats by the bridge where the poor shanty-dwellers wash their clothes, covering the steps and rising inexorably towards the earth levee on which their grass houses stand. In Bazaar Street drenched Muslim ladies hurried by under veils; scavenger dogs and bed-raggled hogs scuffled by the hackney carriage stand, where a lone horse stood stock still, stupefied, ankle deep in muddy water, eyes lowered, water dripping off its abused back.

Outside Mala's room the passage was soon an inch deep in water and the street was flooded from her wall to her neighbour's porch. Water dripped through a gap in the roof tiles. Everything was wet: strings of damp clothes hung across the room. Even the animals were coming in for shelter. Every so often Mala got up to shoo frogs away, for 'wherever they are the snakes will follow'.

Through the afternoon the rain still poured, rain as I have never seen it. Outside Mala's room the water was now up to the door sill; frogs, lizards and rats huddled under the eaves. A goat was bleating in the alley. By six the downpour had abated enough for us to go to the temple. That night Jupiter was changing station, and it was an important astral date for Tamils; despite the atrocious weather there were big crowds in the temple. In the great north corridor they gathered by the black-faced Dakshinamurthi, pouring offerings of ghee into a big metal bowl, which flamed up in the gloom, gilding their faces. Near by a press of people filed round the planetary shrines, nine squat black statues all freshly decked in clean bright wraps and flowers; Saturn, as always, was heaped. As the main puja took place, torrential rain began falling again, like a curtain outside the colonnades, streaming in a neon-lit waterfall off the golden roof of the sanctum.

All the time the rain seemed to be growing in strength. Then the power failed. The entire town was now blacked out, for the whole night as it turned out. And in that magical time the temple was returned to its ancient presence: the immense halls lit only by oil-lamps. At Dakshinamurthi the faces of the crowd were lit only by the flickering bowl of fire, the granite columns touched a warm golden colour in the light of the flames. A vision of ancient days. Behind the shrine there is a hundred-yard-long back corridor which is normally closed; here are kept sixty-three stone statues of the saints, ancient icons rubbed oily dark with soot and ghee, inscrutable little black sprites. Tonight the corridor was open, pitch black apart from tiny lamps glowing at the feet of the big three saints. It was a delicious sensation to feel one's way past them in the vast echoing colonnade as squeaking bats fluttered and dipped around one's head; tip-toeing as it were through the secret memory rooms of Chidambaram. By eight the rain was a deluge, even dripping through cracks between the granite slabs of the roof. Outside the sanctum were jostling troops of black umbrellas. Rain, darkness, oil-lamps, trumpets: the modern world was erased.

In a lull I made a break for the gate but the downpour grew again in intensity. As I fumbled with the key of my bike in East Car Street, I heard a shout: 'Hello! Hello! Poor wretch that bides the pelting of this pitiless storm! Michael! Come in! Where are you going in all this wet?'

It was Radu, who had just arrived back from Holland, with a typically literary flourish. I took shelter in his house, where part of the roof by the light well had caved in, and the whole family were struggling to anchor a plastic sheet which flapped noisily in the teeth of the gale.

Radu wrapped himself tighter in his shawl and laughed ruefully: 'We are dissolving in rains, I think.'

'Sorry?'

'This is Shelley, Shelley.'

'Ah.'

His son brought us some hot coffee. We sat in the living-room with an oil-lamp. His face was fatter. Beard trimmed. A few months in Europe had changed his look. Still twinkly-eyed though. He's in his mid-forties now, I'd guess, the long, flamboyantly curled black hair starting to go grey. Radu had been one of the first of the Dikshithars to take me under his wing years before: I had been ill with a bout of amoebic dysentery, exhausted after losing two stone in a week. I was sitting at a brown Formica table in the coffee house on East Car Street, staring blankly at a mural of a sunlit Alpine view, when he breezed in to rescue me. He cheered me up with a blast of his enthusiasm and promptly hauled me off to his house 'to eat some good rice'. Then he presented me with a tub of foul-smelling Ayurvedic medicine. ('This will do the trick,' he said. 'Where do you rub it on?' I asked. 'You don't rub it on; you eat it.' It was foul. But I did get better.)

He is a remarkable man; he did his first degree in English literature by correspondence at Annamalai University. Then he took an MA in Indology. To say he's eclectic would be an understatement; he can and does quote Simon and Garfunkel, Keats and Robert Pirsig in the same sentence: 'the body is the bike; the soul is the rider.' ('Actually, Michael, this is from the *Gita*, with a minor change converting Arjuna's chariot to a Harley-Davidson; technology may advance but spiritual reality remains the same.')

Radu stands in an extraordinary position *vis-à-vis* the archaic community to which he belongs. In the old days in India the Brahminical taboo on going overseas was rigidly observed, but it has been dispensed with in modern times. From the Minakshi temple in Houston to the Murugan shrines in East London or Singapore, pukka Brahmins are serving and doing rituals overseas without having incurred pollution by leaving their native soil. It is not so in Chidambaram. Here the Dikshithars have stuck to the letter of Manu's law. Virtually alone among temple priesthoods, they haven't budged on the old rules. Radu was the first serving Dikshithar to go overseas. And he suffered the inevitable consequence. No longer pure, he was struck off the puja rota, with all that means in terms of lost livelihood.

So Radu branched out. He did a two-year MA in one year and published odd articles on the temple for Indian magazines. Because he speaks excellent English, he had long been a source of information for scholars who came to Chidambaram seeking to learn more about this notoriously secretive community. (Several of them indeed have made careers out of the temple.) Radu has also done translations from Tamil and Sanskrit; he once showed me a fragment of a mysterious unfinished novel. But for all his questing, in reality he was still part of the Dikshithars' world; as a Brahmin priest with a large extended family to support, the pressure he was under was becoming intolerable. Money and social status are everything in his society; now he was in trouble. The collapse of his house roof that night seemed to symbolize it.

We moved back from the inner room to the hall, which was dry, and sat there, an oil-lamp at our feet, looking out over the darkened street towards the albino's tea stall, where the awning sagged under the weight of water. Radu fulminated: 'The Dikshithars don't like change; they are stick-in-the-muds. But where is it leading them? Have you seen the latest Lonely Planet guide?'

This is the most popular guidebook, even among Indians; it carries travellers' reports, which are often scathing and always on the look out for the rip-off.

'Can you believe this? It says the Dikshithars are money-grabbing: it says visitors are only taken into sanctum for money. Well this is not how it was and not how it should be. They are in danger of losing a priceless gift, Michael: their integrity.'

I asked him about the report in *India Today* magazine, which said they have money troubles which may finally unravel the whole thing and endanger their independence. He would have none of it; according to him they have enough. His fourteen-year-old son returned and we rushed back inside to help fix the sheet once again. Radu was almost in tears.

He is no doubt a sensitive soul who takes all hurts deeply, whether real or imaginary. Unfortunately the roof and the Dikshithars were not the end of his problems; he said that there had been a campaign of Chinese whispers. He wouldn't elaborate, but the story was well known in the town. He had developed too close a relationship with a foreign scholar. In a small town like this it is impossible for anyone to have such a friendship without everyone knowing, and such friendship is not countenanced, especially between a Brahmin priest and a foreign lady.

The gossip was damaging to his relationship with his community. He didn't wish to talk about it and I didn't wish to press him. He had more immediate concerns.

'Look at this situation; we are plagued with power cuts here. Really I need my own generator for light, especially to help the children's education. I wrote for help to one scholar I know in the US, but I received no reply. This was the most unkindest cut of all.'

'I'm sorry,' I said.

'*Julius Caesar*,' he added, in case I needed reminding (which I did).

'They are jealous of the course I have taken. They are objecting to my growth, to my development. But I have no option but to carry on down this path. Build up my lectureship in Holland. Trouble is, so far I am making almost no profit out of it. Air ticket costs 56,000 rupees; it takes almost all my fee. Still, there are changes coming. Soon Lufthansa will try to break the monopoly; then you will see the prices tumble. And other things have improved greatly. Look, you can phone Chidambaram from Holland now. Direct. This is great. Digital! Faxes too. This Rao is a wizard! One day soon there will be e-mail in East Sannadhi, the vedas through the ether! No really; I am serious. There are more things than are dreamed of in their philosophy.'

The rain was still incessant. I told him about my bus journey, and of the projected trip to Tirunallar. He raised his eyebrows.

'They are the richest priests in India. Just look when you are there: Rolex watches and Mercedes cars. Believe me.' He finished his coffee. 'Let me show you my latest project.'

He crossed to the bookcase to retrieve a translation he had done of Chidambaram's *Mahatmya*, the official version of the temple's founding myth. It is the story of a leprous king who was cured by bathing here and then built the first temple. Not so long ago a German scholar tried to prove it all a twelfth-century concoction, which Radu doesn't accept.

'I have done it in verse: friends who have read it compared my version to the poems of A. K. Ramanujan.'

It did indeed read well.

After an hour I decided to brave the storm and got out the plastic mac I had bought in Bazaar Street (75 rupees). Radu held up the lamp.

'You don't look so good,' he said as I was leaving.

'It's been like this since Palani; my eyes are sore with conjunctivitis, I've got a bad throat, a mild dose of malaria, a dicky stomach and I'm getting a cold. Apart from that I'm fine. I think I prefer it when it's hot.'

He wagged his head. 'Well, well. Travellers must be content.' The twinkle came back to his eyes. 'Shakespeare: *As You Like it*.'

I waved goodbye, dived into the flood and started pedalling furiously. Before I reached the corner tea shop, my hat blew off, and was dexterously caught one-handed by an old lady struggling calf deep in water while she clutched with her other hand a covering made out of an assortment of plastic carrier bags. I gave up on the hat and held it in my teeth as I pushed on down East Car Street. The town was still blacked out, and my hired bike of course had no lights and threadbare brakes. The familiar landmarks of East Car Street were shifting fast in a black lake populated by shadowy semi-aquatic creatures: hogs, cows, bullock carts, parked rickshaws, a lone sweet vendor pushing his carriage and, in the middle of the road, a hapless holy man, bald and white-bearded, wrestling with a large metal trident and a disembowelled umbrella.

At the corner of East Car Street the road comes off the plateau where the temple stands and slopes down towards the canal and the bus stand. There I ran into trouble. At the junction a torrent was pouring across the road, ripping away the crumbling remains of the tarmac surface. All the way down to the bus stand the water was now a foot deep, and with every stroke of the pedals, my trousered leg went into a river of sludge, fuel oil, refuse and sewage, while the bike slewed over broken bits of road. Finally I careered into an open stretch of sewer by the roadside and came off. As I stood there sodden, the man in the pan and *beedi* store shouted a greeting from his perch, sitting snug and secure on the wooden drop-down front of his shop, three feet above the flood. An oil-lamp burned comfortingly by his side. He waved expansively at the swirling water underneath his little kingdom: 'This is all from the drains,' he said, with inexplicable enthusiasm.

Calf deep in water I pushed the bike past the Nataraja Talkies into VGP Street. There, to my amazement, the flower stalls were still open, their storm lanterns casting a marigold glow across the oily pond of the street; though what nautical passing trade they hoped for was hard to guess. At that moment, headlights sweeping the gloom, the Sirkali bus swerved past the Talkies into the bus stand and sent a rippling tide across the street which knocked me over again, to applause from the flower sellers. I decided to walk the rest of the way home.

At the canal bridge the river was now all the way up its banks; it had risen six feet in forty-eight hours. Perched on their muddy berm of rubbish the shanties by now were nearly flooded, surrounded on three sides by fetid swamp and fields of bobbing water hyacinth. In a couple of houses, lamps were still burning. By now their owners must have secured their belongings in the roof, and crowded up the slope to the road, to huddle under makeshift plastic sheets, lashed by the rain. The houses nearest the river, carefully built of palm stems and fronds, salvaged wood, wattle, daub, twine and other people's throw-outs, were now starting to move; their swept floors, the *kolams* by the door washed away. The man who recycles paper litter was desperately bagging his 'savings' in sodden bundles; the woman who collects coir sacks full of broken plastic carrier bags and the boy who gathers the metal tops of soft-drink bottles were scrambling away from the rising tide. For them, it was going to be a long night.

I aquaplaned out of the dark into the hotel forecourt, cape flapping like one of the four cyclists of the Kali Yuga, dripping from head to toe. The night staff and the kitchen boys watched with amusement.

'Your macintosh is not buttoned up, sir: this is why it is not keeping out the rain.'

'Thanks for the tip.'

'This is monsoon season, sir.'

'Ah, I see. That explains all the water in VGP Street,' I said, trying to be funny. 'What food is left?' I continued brightly. 'Meals are available?'

Inscrutable smile and wag of head which may mean yes, may mean no: 'Restaurant closed, sir.'

'But it's only five to ten.'

'Yes, but no one was here, sir.'

I moped disconsolately to my room and lit a candle to find various winged creatures of the night and half the mosquito population of town. They would be too miserable to bite, I hoped.

I got a beer upstairs in the bar of the former permit room. There in the half-light of the hotel generator was a hard core of drinkers: a travelling salesman, a couple of medical students and a balding professor from the university who was drinking Golden Eagle beer with rum and Thumbs Up chasers. (On the wall, a faded old notice: 'Tourist information. Temporary liquor permits for foreign tourists can be had from the government TN Tourist Office, Chidambaram, or the District Collector'.) The waiter mournfully mopped up with a heap of sackcloth at the doorway.

'Cyclone is now 350 km off Nagapattinam,' said Prof, turning over the pages of *The Hindu* with gloomy relish. 'River Vaigai dam is opened and Madurai city itself is flooded. There is derailment at Dindigul Junction due to line being washed away.' He ordered another rum. 'Trees have been uprooted in Madras and ships grounded. The elephants in Madras zoo have run amok.'

Life was tasting better by the minute. He turned to me. 'During the last big cyclone electricity here was cut off for ten days; for eight there were no trains or buses. My wife luckily had laid in a great supply of dried vegetables and fruits and pickled delicacies. Our rice store lasted the time so the hardship was not great.' He smiled; he seemed to be quite looking forward to a repeat. 'You are staying long here?'

'Difficult to tell,' I said, queasy at the prospect of being marooned in Railway Feeder Road.

Later I went down to the foyer to secure an emergency supply of mosquito coils. If I was not to eat, I thought, at least I would try not to be eaten. The light was on in the restaurant. Inside the boys were tucking into a hearty meal of steaming *iddly* and other delights.

'I thought you said the restaurant was closed?'

'Staff meals, sir.'

'I see. I don't suppose there's a chance of a cup of tea?'

'Sorry, sir, not possible now; restaurant closed at ten o clock.'

Back in my room the mosquitoes had dried themselves off and regained their appetite, so I retreated behind a prophylactic smokescreen, and as the mosquito coils curled up, I dosed the tap water, fearing it could not be long before the local water supply mingled with what I had been cycling through – a groundless fear as it turned out. I went to bed to the sound of rain pattering on the leaves of the banana trees in the garden and a torrent sloshing on to the soil out of a broken gutter. It was, I imagined, like having an incontinent bull elephant urinating all night outside one's window. Eventually I fell asleep and dreamed the hotel was floating down the canal to the sea. The boys were still smiling.

KUMBAKONAM

The worst of the cyclone passed down the coast during the night. The main damage was to the north of the state. We settled down to a period of continuous monsoon rain, when nothing ever seemed to get dry. But my time was running out. Leaving aside the growing dangers of trench foot in VGP Street, and eyes permanently red with conjunctivitis, I felt I couldn't wait any longer to finish the journey Rajdurai had given me. When I had come to Tamil Nadu the idea of going to Tiruchendur had been the last thing on my mind. But after the adventures on Mr Ramasamy's video bus, I felt not merely curious but driven to complete it, to go to Suryanarcoil and the sites on the Cavery river, and to visit old Saturn at Tirunallar. Maybe I would even get to see Kamala's fabled Tiruvidaimarudur. To see them entailed a journey into the Cavery delta, the heartland of Cholan civilization. Mala had to go off to Coimbatore, so we agreed to team up at the end of the week to go together to Tirunallar; I would go on my own to the Cavery. I decided to get the train south.

Two days after the cyclone, in a lull in the rain, I donned my mac and went along to Chidambaram station to find out the time of the down trains. The lines were flooded, goats queuing up the stairs to the railway travellers' retiring rooms. I walked on to the platform, and bought a tea from the stall as a new storm advanced down the line and engulfed the station, drumming on the platform roof and thrashing down on the Cholan Express, which had just come in heading north.

Suresh, the ticket inspector, was in a jolly mood. 'So would you like to go to Madras right now?' In my mind's eye I saw a dry hotel; a hot-water shower; scrambled egg instead of the interminable *iddly*.

'Well, I would like to go to Madras. But I have to stay here in Chidambaram for another ten days; I have to go to Tiruvidaimarudur.'

'Whatever for? It's a small place with an old temple in disrepair. There is no hotel. And now it is flooded by the Cavery river.'

The porters were still loading the goods van, while passengers ran on and off the train, covering their heads and clutching steaming cups of tea from the stall. Suresh put his flag under his arm and brushed the water from his jacket. 'You see, in Tamil Nadu there are six seasons. Now is the rainy season, *kar* in Tamil; then is winter; then in the New Year *munpanni*, early dew; February/March we call late dew; then April/May is *ilavenil*, time of young warmth; June/July is *mutirvenil*: this is the ripe heat. This is when it is very very hot and we sleep out on the rooftops or in the street. After the ripe heat come the rains again; the best time for tourists to come is in the winter: December and January. Next time you should come then.'

'But which time is best?'

'Ah,' he said as another sheet of rain sprayed us off the roof of the carriage, 'hottest. Hottest is best.'

It was time for the train to go. He shook the water from his whistle, blew, and waved to the guard: slowly the train rumbled off into the darkening morning and soon disappeared behind a veil of rain. When it had gone, the proprietor of the tea stall emptied his sock of tea reflectively into the bin while on his roof two monkeys hugged each other for warmth. The station master strolled back into his office to take his seat once more beneath his garlanded picture of the Goddess Lakshmi, and the goats in the booking hall bleated in sympathy.

That afternoon I took the slow passenger to Kumbakonam via Sirkali and Mayavaram Junction. The Coleroon was high now, a fast swirling brown flow half a mile wide. Everywhere the paddy-fields were flooded, only the winding baulks standing above the water. Lines of palms disappeared into a grey mist; the horizon closed down to a few hundred yards. The rain was continuous, whipping up in intensity every few minutes and then falling away to a steady drizzle. In a field near Sirkali we trundled slowly past a farmer in a loincloth who stood sharing his umbrella with a brown cow, the two of them staring at his ruined groundnut crop.

From Mayavaram the route turns westwards, inland along the old track of the Cavery: you glimpse the river through the window at the little halts. It is no wider than the Thames as it winds through the meadows of Windsor, and is overhung with a jungly tangle of palms and creepers. At every halt were dripping banyans and temple *gopuras*, with little station signs: 'Alight here for worship at Uppiliankovil.'

In the delta we entered a watery world: a flat land of dykes, canals, streams, rivers, rivulets. It is less than a hundred miles across but there are over thirty main rivers and numberless streams, drains, lodes, cuts and sluices. Across the paddy the snaking patterns of the field baulks formed a tracery of green across sheets of water which mirrored trees and clouds. Every acre of this landscape has been elaborately and intensively tended since ancient times. Easy here to imagine people like Mala's father and his ancestors, the 'keepers of the water', who tilled it under the kings of olden days: a world without history or landmarks until it was shaped by the irrigators with their dams and anicuts.

The British thought the landscape of the Cavery delta the most fertile of all their Indian territories: 'It affords annually three luxuriant rice harvests,' wrote Colonel Fullarton in his *View of English Interests in India* (1785), 'the forests abound with valuable trees, the country is overstocked with sheep and cattle and teeming with an industrious race expert in agriculture. Such are the natural benefits it enjoys that no spot upon the globe is superior in productions for the use of man.'

This landscape has been celebrated in Tamil poetry for 2000 years; there are hymns to the sacred Cavery in the Sangam poetry. But it is above all the landscape sung by the saints between AD

600 and 900. Their hymns form a kind of litany of the land, encapsulating the myths of a society and a civilization, myths about the primeval spirits of this alluvial world: folk deities of water, juice, rain, sperm and sap, gods of mango tree, *Vili* tree, *jambu* tree. Their shrines form the landmarks in a network of sacred journeys created by the ancient poets: an imaginal landscape which gave form to this fluid green wilderness.

This enchanted land is the core of the Tamil sacred geography: it is perhaps the most intensively mythologized tract of India. More than half of the 274 Saivite sacred sites are to be found in this compact triangle of the delta, from the sea to its apex at Tiruvadi; Nowhere do you have to travel more than a day's journey on foot to find a shrine sung in the *Tevaram* hymns. Pilgrims will find shelter and food for the night in an ancient network of *choultries* and *adinams*: hostels where, as it says in the religious guidebooks, 'free meals are provided throughout the year . . . free accommodation for all classes . . . meals gratis to Brahmins . . . supplies given to Bairagis for three days'. And there will always be religious people like Mala or Mr Subrahmaniam who will shelter and feed the pilgrims before sending them on their way.

The paths which link these shrines take you all the way from the Western Ghats to the sea, and from the north of the Coromandel down to Cape Comorin, a journey of over five hundred miles. They are paths still followed today, 'from the shining Pennar river swelled with the monsoon clouds . . .' to Tiruvidaimarudur 'on the south bank of the cascading Cavery which throws up on its banks its precious cargo of sandalwood, aloe and wild mountain rice'. It was these invisible but still trodden tracks through the modern world of Tamil Nadu which marked out the last stage of my journey.

The train reached Kumbakonam at seven in the evening and I found a room in a hostel overlooking the back of the Nageshwara temple: a tiny cell-like room with bare, blue-washed walls marked by unidentifiable stains. There were metal grills over the door, and a plastic jug and mug on a battered Formica table; clearly the hostel catered for a rougher sort of clientele. In the upstairs corridor were Indian-style loos and at the back a row of open shower cubicles where a balcony gave a sunset view over freshly painted *gopura*s. In the shower I talked to a jolly travelling salesman.

'This is the town of maths and *muth*s. This Sarangapani Street is the home of Ramanujan, the greatest mathematician of the twentieth century. He came to your Cambridge University at the behest of Professor Hardy of Trinity College, but he experienced sickness of heart due to leaving Tamil Nadu and died in London age only thirty-two. He was a man who knew infinity. Mathematics is a great Hindu science; the numerical system which is today used by the world, with absolute zero and decimal point, is a Hindu invention. All the wonders of modern science would be impossible without it.'

He laughed. 'We have 33 million gods: so you can see we have to be good at maths! Ramanujan was all his life a Hindu: a child of the sacred Cavery. He said this: an equation has no meaning unless it expresses a thought of God.'

Dawn came with clear air, damp streets and temple bells. The river, which was high, runs right through the busy town. There are many temples. At Nageshwara the sculpture is exquisite, the unpainted stone weathered to the softest finish. In the niches around the shrine is a series of languidly graceful female figures, probably queens and princesses of King Aditya's household, and masterpieces on a par with anything you will see in India. (They are dated 886, the time when Alfred the Great was struggling with the Danes.) Other subjects are mythical: a melting Ardanari, half-man, half-woman; Siva as the enchanting mendicant, attenuated limbs, breathtakingly delicate. These figures bring to mind the finest Gothic, the equivalent perhaps of the Portail Royal at Chartres.

Though bronze casting shows little diminution of quality over the entire Chola period, stone sculpture in Tamil Nadu had gone decidedly off by the time you reach Rajaraja at Tanjore. (Gigantism? Imperialism?) It bucks up again at Gangakondasolapuram in the 1030s, but this early flowering is the very best, by common consent the greatest stone sculpture ever produced in the south.

At lunchtime I went to change money at the State Bank of India. I am reluctant to use the word, but it was truly Dickensian. An open floor crammed with tables, teak bookcases, cabinets, fans whirling in the ceiling; it was populated by a hierarchy of cashiers, clerks, underclerks and apprentices. Across the floor the tea boy shimmied with a circular aluminium tray full of glasses which he grasped by a central holder like a puja tray, expertly negotiating the crowded floor and the incessant circulation of weighty cash books. In the centre of the clerks' area was a large polished walnut revolving cabinet whose compartments carried sixty to a hundred big ledgers: 'next year we will be computerizing', says the clerk to whose desk I am ushered.

In the meantime, half a dozen forms are to be filled in to change my travellers' cheque; the clerk has Saivite marks on his forehead and behind him there are enough deities on the wall to make up a football team; the airbrushed faces of the goddesses are disturbingly like real photographs subtly idealized. No wonder they are so sure what gods look like.

Then I went to the Mahamaham tank right in the middle of town, a huge stepped basin lined by a dozen pillared *mandapas*; incessant mantras are relayed through loudspeakers all around the tank. This was the scene earlier in the year of the Mahamaham festival which takes place only once every twelve years. Now there is a baked cloudy leaden sky, stovy somnolent heat building up for another storm; a few bathers in a scum of debris and litter, bits of leaves and vegetables. In the corner of the tank is a man washing his bum in the holy water. Incessant, tuneless, distorted drone of the loudspeakers.

In the festival last February two or three million turned up on the key day, jamming every access into this already congested corner of town. Coincidentally or not, the day appointed by the astrologers was the birthday of Chief Minister Jayalalitha, MGR's former co-star and protégée. For the occasion the tank was lined with enormous cut-outs of the 'living legend' sporting her distinctive poncho; there were stories that bathing at the most auspicious bathing time was delayed to allow her arrival by helicopter to have the maximum effect. When she landed a wall collapsed under pressure from the crowd and forty or fifty people were killed in the rush. There were murmurings about culpability, but the victims' families swiftly received state payouts, and the living legend's reputation did not suffer. Like her mentor MGR, her cult is growing now. Her image is proliferating all over the state, even the state bus corporation has now been renamed the Hon. Dr Jayalalitha Bus Co. She gives no interviews (always politic, if it can be managed), is ever more unapproachable and autocratic, or so it is whispered. Her most zealous MPs and party workers practise full prostration in her presence, a tribute even Mrs Thatcher did not receive. Divinity surely beckons.

A number of people were sitting on the steps of the tank, including a family from Tuticorin: husband, wife and teenage son. They were on pilgrimage to Tirupati via Kumbakonam where the wife's father lived. He wore Western clothes, she a sari; the son was fed up and not at all interested. Dad was a scientist at a coastal research establishment, a specialist in heavy water. They offered to share their food so we sat by one of the *mandapa*s on the steps and opened our tiffin boxes to eat rice and *sambhar*. Then up came another woman, a renouncer.

She carried a small cloth bag of her life's belongings. She was not very old; had an androgynous look under a dusty lion's mane of hair. She sat and waited, didn't force herself on us but did not ignore us; whenever I looked up she was looking into my eye. I felt conspicuously greedy dipping my hand into the tiffin box. Who was this young woman, wandering the streets of south India, blown by the hot wind around the scum-filmed tanks of the holy city of Kumbakonam, begging for alms? (Of course the point about renouncing is that it gives liberation not to be born again: 'Grant me the boon not to be born.')

The wife, who has said nothing, goes over and puts food on to her plate. The woman eats.

We got up to go. Abstracted, the woman muttered to herself, head on one side like a bird, as if she had been listening and had a question. She gets up and walks with us along the side of the tank; walks past and stops. She has nothing and no one by the look of it. Remember Appar: 'We have nothing. We fear nothing. We are free.'

In the evening I took a bike to Darasuram over the river; there were immense banks of blue cloud to the north-east. A few big drops of rain and then it lets loose, torrential rain lashing the road. Tremendous flashes of lightning light up the palm forests; roads soon swimming in water; cows huddled soaking under trees; crowds of frogs hopping across the swirling road, which appears alive, green, wet and pullulating.

TANJORE

On the next day I took a bus to Tanjore, the old capital of the Cholas in the tenth century.

Rain was still falling when I went inside the big temple, spattering the eroded orange stone of the gates. Inside, the campus is 1200 by 800 feet, surrounded by a pillared cloister along a magnificent forty-feet-high granite wall with an external double dado and pilasters, a beautiful and austere classicism to set beside the frenetic activity of so much Tamil architectural decoration. In the centre is a huge pyramidal *vimana* 216 feet high, which when it was built, in 1010, was the tallest building in India. In the spacious courtyard they were erecting bamboo marquees for Rajaraja's birthday puja. Sheltering from the rain was a group of boys trying to organize a sponsored cycle ride round the world for charity. As the rain fell once more, I went into the shrine where there is a twelve-foot-high black linga wrapped in a white cotton skirt. Inside the ambulatory passage are eleventh-century murals which were recovered in the thirties, revealed beneath rain-damaged paintings of the seventeenth century. Little Cholan painting survives, and the ones that have been exposed and conserved here are magical.

The technique is true fresco, painted on wet lime plaster. It affords an extraordinary glimpse into the lost world of the Cholan empire, when Cholan arms spread Hindu culture to the Maldives, Sri Lanka and Java – a strange mingling of militarism and the most exquisite delicacy. Blood and flowers, evoking strange parallels – feudal Japan? Aztecs? Soft blurred outlines as if seen through a smoky mist: lapis lazuli, *terre verte*, white lime, lamp black, yellow and red ochre. There are girls dancing, celestials, naked but for their waistband, bangles, anklets and elaborate hairdos.

Inside the ambulatory there is an extraordinarily lifelike portrait of Rajaraja himself, fleshy lipped and golden skinned, deep in conversation with his white bearded guru, the poet laureate Karuvar Devar. There is Siva the destroyer of cities, full of bulging-eyed rage, tracers of paint swirling around him like time-lapse headlights. Here are the royal family worshipping their family god: the shadowy image of dancing Siva in his ring of fire, shimmering jewels faint, as if on a photographic negative, and behind the cult image is the unmistakable bowed roof of the Chit Sabha at Chidambaram.

Upstairs in the upper ambulatory galley, unfinished at Rajaraja's death in 1014, is a great sequence of relief panels of the 108 poses of the dance, the Bharata Natyam, in the exact sequence of the ancient textbook, the *Natya Shastra*. These temples were huge establishments; of 850 temple employees, 400 were dancing girls brought here from all over Chola Nadu for the dedication in 1010.

They lived in the streets adjacent to the shrine, and they are all named in inscriptions on the exterior walls, giving the address of the house and the name of their native village. Now the most intimate and revealing remains of their time are hidden in dank interior passages smelling of stale ghee and bat droppings.

The town art gallery is in the old sixteenth-century Nayak palace approached through two quadrangles, three old brick gateways and a courtyard crowded with pots of rubber plants and mother-in-law's tongue. Here, too, is a huge sixteenth-century library of Sanskrit and Tamil palm-leaf manuscripts, its treasures include not only classical poetry but de Nobili's manuscripts, the first Western attempt to square the Indian vision with Christian and Platonic idealism. In the old durbar room are scores of bronzes. The best are the stunning pieces from Rajaraja's time, especially from the Tiruvengadu hoard dug up in the fifties, all swaying lines and lovely curves: louche, androgynous divinities with a hint of puppy fat above their jewelled waistbands. Ancient themes: the dancing god, the yogi, the dark mother, the benign wife – themes still endlessly reinvented today in cinema and TV. The best, perhaps, is a four-foot-high masterpiece cast in 1011 in the delta at Tiruvengadu. It shows Siva in his archaic role as Lord of the Animals. But here the wild boy of prehistory is a sinuous cowherd with a turban of snakes, legs nonchalantly crossed, left arm hanging provocatively by his hip; he is naked but for the skimpiest wrap round his thighs, which serves only to draw attention to his heavenly attributes.

'You are from which country?' It was the museum director.

'England.'

'Hm.' He rubbed his nose. 'Your own prime minister was most impressed by this image of the Lord,' he said teasingly.

'Oh yes. Which prime minister was that?' I said, sceptical.

'Mrs Margaret Thatcher,' he replied, as if I should have known all along.

'When was that?' I said in disbelief. (When could the Bronze Lord ever have crossed paths with the Iron Lady?)

'In 1982, February. He was taken to London for Festival of India exhibition. Mrs Thatcher was performing the opening ceremony. She was not I think enamoured or understanding of Indian art, but when she came to this, she stopped and stared for some time before remarking on his beauty.'

It almost cast Mrs T in a new light.

The bronzes are displayed on pedestals around the old durbar hall in the palace of the Tanjore Nayak kings. This was built after the break-up of the Hindu empire of Vijayanagar in 1565, when independent local kingdoms like this one were formed across the south. Tanjore in particular remained for over two centuries the centre of a brilliant culture, especially of music. But these small kingdoms were always prey to outside attack. In 1683, in the courtyard outside, the last of the Nayak kings fell in internecine warfare with his neighbours. Tanjore was under attack by the king of Madurai and the walls of the old fort eventually succumbed to a combination of grapeshot and tantric magic. Leaving no spell unturned, the attackers' guru had filled the Cavery with thousands of squashed pumpkins, magically charged so that whoever drank the water would desert to the conquering army. Duly finding himself without an army, the last king put on his best outfit and went to an anachronistic death in golden garments studded with gems, his eyebrows pinned up with golden wires, as they were so bushy with age that he could not see out. Singing hymns to Vishnu he walked to his death with swords strapped to both hands, having ensured the immolation of his harem by a gunpowder explosion in the palace yard. A weird harbinger of the end of Tanjore's ancient glory.

At the back of the durbar hall, on a platform of black granite, is a white marble statue by John Flaxman of Sarfoji, the last but one Maratta ruler of Tanjore (the kings who followed the Nayaks). He wears a triangular pointed cap and his hands are joined in prayer; he was to oversee the final dissolution of the old polity in the south. In the late eighteenth century Tamil Nadu, or the Carnatic, as it was then known, became a theatre of war between the French and the British. This was a revolutionary period in the south, the real dividing line in south India between the ancient world and the modern.

For thirty years European armies with their native allies and mercenaries trekked back and forth over the Chola lands, devastating the once fertile countryside. They turned the great enclosures of the holy sites into fortresses bristling with cannon and took pot-shots at the statues on the *gopuras* for target practice. Between 1749 and 1781 Tanjore and Chidambaram (along with many others) were attacked and occupied several times by the British or the French and their ally, Hyder Ali, the Muslim sultan of Mysore. In Tanjore the missionary Frederick Schwartz saw 'the dead lining the streets and the living like wandering skeletons'. At Chidambaram the young Devon seaman James Scurry saw the courtyard full of chained British captives and famine-stricken Tamil refugees. Back home the names of the temples became familiar to the British public as they read gripping yarns of our brave boys imprisoned by the cunning and cruel Hyder Ali. They thrilled to the exploits of such as Lt Wilson of the Yarmouth and his bold night escape by rope over Chidambaram's 'stupendous walls'.

But in truth these events were very far from heroic. Neither side had any scruples about desecrating temples or oppressing the native population. The poor and the pious had no defence. Well over a million Tamils died of famine and war. Massacres were commonplace on both sides. In one horrendous incident, four hundred wounded and exhausted Tamil women were stripped of their possessions and raped by rioting British soldiers; many committed suicide. In the Cavery delta the French general, Lally, shot Brahmins from his guns when they refused to reveal the where-abouts of their temple treasure. Eventually, British arms triumphed and the son of Hyder Ali, Tippoo Sultan, was trapped and killed

on the island of Seringapatam in the Cavery river, a story immortal-
ized in Wilkie Collins' novel *The Moonstone*. (Tippoo's relics,
incidentally, are still to be seen in England: his dream book in the
India Office Library; his green velvet quiver and poisoned arrows
in Windsor Castle, along with the splendid quilted helmet which
had been dipped in the holy well of Zum Zum.) It was not the
most honourable phase in the imperial history of either French or
British. The south Indians, though, bore surprisingly few grudges.

THE BRONZE CASTER

On the way back to Kumbakonam is Swamimalai; this is where
the *sthapathis* live, the hereditary bronze casters who make the
temple idols. Their workshop is near the Murugan temple behind
an unprepossessing modern shop front. The head of the firm sits at
his chair in the tiny reception behind a desk with a little Ganesh
and a big pad of order forms. On a display shelf to one side are
specimens of his work. White ash on the forehead: deep, narrowed
eyes always staring at a distant horizon even when in a little room.
He has made idols for temples in the United States and England as
well as all over south Asia: on his wall is a framed letter from a
Murugan temple in East London thanking him for the quality of
his work and 'the divine expression on the Lord's face; your efforts
were surely guided by a higher hand'.

'We follow the old patterns,' said the proprietor. 'We are not
allowed by the government to do exact replicas the same size as
some of the ancient masterpieces because there is so much theft of
bronzes from temples these days, with the substitution of modern
copies. But we follow the traditional patterns. Sometimes we are
asked to do statues of mythological themes that do not exist in
earlier bronzes and we improvise on the theme as we see fit.'

He picked up his brochure, which illustrated about a hundred
patterns: mostly famous ones, the kind you see in Tanjore museum,
and some variations on a theme to suit modern taste.

'Mostly we follow tried and tested time-honoured formula; this is what people like for their living-rooms. People like the old ways and of course for a temple this must be so.

'We still make by the lost wax process, called in Sanskrit *madhuchchishtavidhana*. Come, come.'

He led the way from the foyer to a grimy darkened storeroom heaped with half-worked material, stuff waiting to be worked, and partly stripped rough casts. Behind that room was a thatched workshop which opened on to gardens at the back. Here under a rattan and palm roof were heaps of slag, broken moulds, tools and the earth pits where they bury the moulds. Two workmen were digging a hole. It took no effort of the imagination to see in these people the descendants of the creators of the brilliant pieces in Tanjore.

'The model is made of bees' wax, according to the classical proportions, the nine measurements; it should be light yellow in colour and pleasing to the eye. Into it we cut some of the detailed modelling. They can be very big: we have done a six-foot-high Nataraja. We then attach long tubes to the back, each with a flared mouth like a *kasa* flower. Then we apply the clay mould; again the proportions must be right, as the masters decreed it and as it has been handed down. The clay is prepared by adding charred husk, tiny bits of cotton and salt all ground up. This is done three times, each layer left to dry in the shade for two days. Twice thinly, the last layer thickest. The bronze too is made according to the old texts; the proportions must be correct to ensure the best finish. The amount is according to the weight of the wax: bronze eight times, silver twelve, gold sixteen. The mould is sunk in the earth here at the back of our workshops, in a crucible of clay. Mould is heated, wax runs out. Then bronze is heated in three stages: mild embers, flaming embers, then blazing. The bronze is poured in up to the mouths of the tubes and then we wait.'

His eyes stared through the ground as if he could see it.

'After twenty-four hours the mould is hauled out. Here is a half-broken mould.'

He showed me a shapeless charred lump out of which, rather like Michelangelo's giants emerging from their prisons of stone, the legs and front arm of a dancing Siva could be seen pushing their way from the hardened mould. One of the workmen, a thin, wiry man with watery eyes and a roasted nose, deftly hacked the top off a coconut with a machete, and offered it to me with a straw. I drank gratefully while the proprietor continued, absorbed in a tale he must have told a hundred times.

'When we have cleared the mould from the bronze, then the hard work begins. We have to model the rough cast; sometimes there are blemishes, but we pride ourselves that this does not happen often. Now these days our practice is to make the model rough and do a lot of carving later – eyes, face, details of clothes and so on. In ancient times the wax model carried all the detail and what followed was just finishing. Of course even the ancient masters could make a mistake; look carefully when you go into temples and sometimes you will see masks welded on to a face to cover a failure in the casting.

'When we are making idols for temples, all this procedure has to be done according to the correct rules and astrological rites: the auspicious day for the casting, the necessary puja to consecrate the image for religious use; open its eyes for *darshan*. But most now we make for middle-class living-rooms. Many rich people in Madras like a replica of a Cholan bronze on their cabinet, even movie stars. But we still make many for new Hindu temples here and abroad; we have a whole book of recommendations from satisfied customers in USA, Malaysia, Singapore, in Britain also.'

Back in the office he opened a cupboard and showed some finished images gleaming disconcertingly like chrome on a new car; quite unlike the soft browns, blue-greens and lead greys shading to a kind of gunmetal black, which you find in the patina of old works.

'Swamimalai has always been a centre for the making of fine idols and bell casting. It was an ancient home of Cholan craftsmen.

And of course has very good fine clay from the Cavery river. I am the seventh generation of our family of whom we have record as *sthapathis*.'

'Who were the best old masters?'

'Standard was very high. When you think even today there must be thousands of ancient bronzes surviving. Sometimes when I have puja in at temples, I make a mental note of very great work: Konierirajapuram *sthapathi* near here was very fine. But best were at Tiruvengadu. They were great artists who had a vision which added something to received religion. They were a family like ours: they were two or three generations, maybe just fathers and sons. For some reason they made the greatest masterpieces, like Rishabhavanmurti in Tanjore Museum, Siva as herdsman; and the Bhikshatanamurti, Siva as the divine mendicant. The best of all in my opinion is the half-man, half-woman Ardhanarisvara, also from Tiruvengadu. It is a unique image: impossible to copy. We have tried. Point is not so much a technical one. Though their technical ability was top quality. It has gone beyond matter of technique. Point is spiritual essence of art. Even if we could make exact copy in every detail, it would be inferior. Spiritual conditions no longer apply.'

SURYANARCOIL

I started back from Kumbakonam to Chidambaram by road. The driver was a kindly old gentleman I had found at the cab rank by the big tank. He had an antiquated Ambassador with squeaking wipers and a rattling asthmatic engine which had needed a push start from both of us in the middle of the street. In the sagging back seat the springs had gone, which made me feel as if I was sitting in a hole. Slowly we bumped and jarred along the country roads, stopping now and then to ask locals the way to obscure shrines from the *Tevaram*.

We crossed the leafy course of the Cavery: here a small stream like the Thames in the Windrush valley, a damp Arcadia with thickets of rattan cane and bamboo, overflowing with flowers, coco palms and acacias. By the roadside were huge banyans, *neem*, wild lime, laurel, wood apple and beech; in the gardens, banana, tamarind, mulberry and pomegranate underneath the rattling crowns of areca palms. Irridescent colours: orange fruit of *vilva*; yellow flowers of the *konnei* tree and, lifting above the trees at every village, the crumbling *gopura*s of ancient shrines, in faded pastels, sprouting tufts of grass and birds' nests.

At Konierirajapuram the paddies were flooded, and the narrow causeway road had been swept away, leaving a gaping crater of red mud. Soon a group of villagers arrived with a bullock cart loaded with stones to fill the hole. On the temple walls a big painting showed British district officers in pith helmets attending a temple festival in the 1920s. Inside were extraordinary tenth-century bronzes, some of them given by Sembiyan Mahadevi, the greatest Cholan royal patron, who is depicted on the nave wall worshipping Siva: a perfect small village temple, untouched. Not far off, over two flooded arms of the Cavery, enormous *gopura*s rose tantalizingly over the silent damp forests:

'Where's that?' I asked the driver.

'Tiruvidaimarudur.'

Once again that magical name. 'Can we go there?'

'Not possible,' he replied. 'Roads are flooded.'

In the depths of the countryside south of the river I came to Tiruvilimilalai, one of the sites most hymned by the ancient saints. It had a spectacular campus under a grey curtain of rain, an immense eroded red-brick perimeter wall dark with damp and lined with seated Nandis, and mud streets of pillared wooden Brahmins' houses, just as Appar described it in the seventh century. The huge tank had displaced steps and crumbling *mandapa*s. The front gate had cracked lintels and crumbling brickwork supported by bamboo scaffolding: trees were everywhere in the overgrown outer court along with the blackened ruins of a house. Three people were at the puja. 'We were famous in ancient days,' said a man sitting at the tank. 'This temple was a grand place when Rajaraja the Great was here,' he said, as if referring to recent history. 'But we have no trains and few country buses, and with no communications no one comes. Now this historical place is destroyed.'

My goal was Suryanarcoil, the Sun temple Rajdurai had told me to visit four years before. It lay up a warren of country lanes in thick palm forests and took some finding. A lovely tree-lined track with a floor of damp sand led up to the gate. On the left was a deep green tank the colour and consistency of pea soup. Stalls for coconuts and flowers. Twenty or thirty orange-clad sadhus. Some leapt up and hared across to me with an alacrity which belied their age. A moustachioed chap behind me dismissed them with a humph: 'Not sadhus, not holy men.' How anyone can tell beats me. 'Beggars?' 'Humph,' again. He's with his wife doing a honeymoon bus tour: 'We worship the planets with a view to acquiring peace, prosperity, wealth and longevity in this world. We believe they influence the destinies of human beings.'

Suryanarcoil is the only major temple of its kind in the south, a temple exclusively to the sun. It is completely surrounded by palm groves which crowd its walls and lean over the little swept courtyard. It has no prehistory. Inscriptions show the temple was built by Kulottunga I in the twelfth century as a response to the fashionable northern solar cults. The worship of the sun, of course, is one of the most ancient rituals of Hinduism, the chief item in morning prayer of every Hindu.

Outside, the cella is ringed by eight box shrines each on its own platform like little doll's houses stained black by offering lamps; these are for the other seven planets, preceded by the gatekeeper Chandikeshwarar. The pilgrims go round them in a clockwise direction.

The main cella is surmounted by the sun's disc flanked by lions, for the sun is the lord of Leo. (That is why Raj told me to come here, as Leo is my birth sign.) In front, where Nandi normally sits in a Siva temple, is a horse, the mount of the sun. The entrance was hung with a curtain of palm fronds; inside was a satisfyingly literal concretization of a set of ideas which could only ever happen, one imagines, in India. The long narrow cella is raised on a high platform. At the end stands the Sun, a young male figure hung with white flowers and wearing a white dhoti. He is faced by his guru Jupiter, a handsome and upright young man with a high forehead, open face, the epitome of knowledge and enlightenment. On his head are marigolds and red flowers, long garlands of fresh jasmine and small white hibiscus fall right down to the floor. Big flowers lie at his feet, bright red hibiscus, more jasmine. The wives of the sun stood to one side. His face was strangely familiar; I realized it resembled Rajdurai Dikshithar, the guru of my journey as it were, who had sent me to these places four years before. I almost expected a conspiratorial wink.

THE DANCE

I returned to Chidambaram and more storms. Rain beat down the bougainvillea outside the hotel foyer, where an old circular red British letter-box stands at the bottom of the steps. The hoot of a steam train, the local passenger to Cuddalore, huffing and puffing out of the station; the glint of the firebox through the drizzle. There was a tourist coach outside and the foyer was full of people shaking rain off their coats.

They were Malaysian tourists just arrived from Pondi, Tamils now living in south-east Asia (in the cultural zone of India's spirit empire, remember, which left its monuments from Java to Cambodia). They had come back to see Nataraja's temple, returning to their roots. They were all professionals, teachers of English, business people, all of them born abroad: 'My father was born here in Chidambaram,' said one. All were culture-shocked by south India:

'What do you think?' asked one woman hesitantly before admitting she found it all rather alarming. 'The first day, arriving in Madras, we experienced a bit of a shock. You see, Malaysia is so clean and efficient, but in Madras the first thing was that the stench was terrible everywhere. Here at least the air is fresh.'

They were on day four of a three-week trip; and some were worn out already. Their bus had broken down in Pondi and now they had a replacement coach with no air-conditioning, not much better than Mr Ramasamy's video bus. They sat in the restaurant mopping their brows, while the boys brought out vegetables and rice, at which they picked with some trepidation. Their programme was to eat, go to the temple for an hour at nine, come back for a short entertainment in the hotel, then take the bus on to Kumbakonam, as there is nowhere satisfactory to stay in Chidambaram. Then Tanjore, and two days in Trichy before going down to Madurai, Comari and the hill stations, doing the ancestral haunts. They sang the praises of Malaysia.

'India is the land of our fathers and mothers,' said the English teacher, a lady in her mid-thirties, wearing Western dress, 'but we are used to a multiracial land, a place where everyone works hard and everything is properly regulated. Malaysia is a highly advanced state; here it strikes us as chaotic, dirty, unclean, inefficient. The poverty is shocking. I really believe nothing much can have changed since my father's day. He said all India's problems are to do with health education and infrastructure. If they are not improved the rich will rise and the poor remain poor. Also, it's dangerous even, with all this growing communal trouble and the fundamentalism. In Malaysia we are multiracial and prosperous, no troubles: Muslims, Hindus, many cultures live side by side, united in our desire to build a good life. Our standard of living is such that we would never contemplate returning to this.'

The man next to her felt the same. He was a businessman in his early sixties I should guess; his father had been an indentured labourer under the British.

'Look, in Malaysia we have rules which everybody obeys. We go to school from four or five, and they tell you how to behave, how to do everything: where to go to the toilet, how to brush your teeth, how to live life. You cannot disobey the rules. It is a well-organized country. People obey the rules. Here just look at it. Every person has his own rules. Just watch the traffic, there's no right or left; people just go wherever they want. Look at the beach; it's a public toilet – they go anywhere.'

He shrugged his shoulders and spread his hands. 'Sure is an independent country,' he said without trace of irony; then realizing what he had said, he burst out laughing.

Around the table everyone nodded in agreement. I said I thought that ruling nine hundred million is different from ruling twenty million. India has been going through a profound revolution since 1947, a revolution caused by universal suffrage: democracy. No country this size had ever done that in history. Give it time. And given the scale of the problems, what an achievement it was to remain an open society. They clearly thought there was nothing which could not be achieved by judicious application of carrot and stick.

'We all find it vibrant and exciting,' said the English teacher. 'But I think we mostly agree already that it is a place to visit rather than to return to live. It is a great excitement to be in Chidambaram, where my father was born. But I couldn't live like this. Impossible. This kind of freedom is not freedom at all.'

The meal over, they threw jackets over their heads and piled back on to the coach to go to see Nataraja's temple. In the restaurant the rain ran down the windows while Rajendran cleared up the plates after them.

An hour or so later they came back. You could tell from their faces that it had been a moving experience, seeing for themselves the ancient traditions of Nataraja's temple, which is so revered throughout the Tamil diaspora. Exiles tapping a root, retrieving distant dreams, the ties that bound their grandparents and which their parents had chosen to cast off. As they reflected on what they had seen, you sensed the power of it for them: childhood tales, visions, smells, the repetition of the ancient gestures and words: the sound of the temple trumpet. The weight – and the spaciousness – of tradition.

In the meantime, in the restaurant, the tables had been pushed back, and a little stage set up. The Malaysians had asked that while they were in Chidambaram, the home of the dance, they might see a classical dance recital and this had been arranged. Presently the troupe arrived – teacher, dancers and three musicians, with drone *vina* and drums. They laid a white sheet on the little platform where they were to sit; then they lit incense and placed flowers on a low table with lamps and a bronze statue of Nataraja, to which these days the dancers pray before they begin.

The two dancers were beautiful young women. One in crimson, one in kingfisher; trails of jasmine were plaited into their long black hair; red gold in the nose and ears, stamped on the forehead and clustered at the throat. Their hands and feet were patterned with henna, so that when they lifted their feet they looked as if they had been stepping in blood. They wore silver bangles on their arms and heavy silver dancer's anklets which shook like rain with each footfall. In the unsteady light of the hotel generator we watched as the banal surroundings of the restaurant were transmuted by the little lamplit *mise en scène*.

The senior dancer began; she was still only about twenty I would guess. She had a bewitching smile and black shining eyes – 'eyes like spears', as saint Sundaramurti would say. (He fell in love with a dancing girl from Tiruvarur.) Her guru stood before her unsmiling, an old lady austerely dressed with severely parted hair brushed back tight against her skull: a Madrasi Miss Brodie. The girl knelt and touched her feet, a traditional mark of respect to one's guru; then she took up her opening position, struck the floor with her heels and the drum began.

The performance comprised songs from the traditional repertoire of the Bharata Natyam. The system of gesture is made up of the 108 main poses of the sacred dance, poses which are carved on the walls of the East Gate of the Nataraja temple and in the upper ambulatory inside the *vimana* of the great temple at Tanjore; poses which were already laid out in the first-century classical-dance treatise, the *Natya Shastra*. It is an art which goes as far back into the life of the south as it is possible to trace.

She turns her heels in and bends both legs out, back ramrod straight. She brings her flat right hand to her breast, then out, and turns it upwards. The right hand goes up to the face, the left down to the waist, then right down, fingers open. Now the head is cocked, mouth smiling and eyes gleaming. Chastely, tastefully, precisely, her body is miming desire: a girl who is torn by overwhelming passion (physical, spiritual) for her divine lover. 'My husband is calling. Shall I go to him, my beloved Lord?' Her feet beat the floor, her head, looking straight forward, now moves from side to side. In the audience some of the Malaysians have tears in their eyes as their video cameras whirr away recording the world they have lost.

In the Middle Ages dance was one of the great expressions of Tamil culture. Creation was a dance, god was a dancer and his temples were full of dancing girls dedicated to his service, *devadasis*. There were dancers in all the main temples, four hundred of them in Tanjore alone. The temple dance was part of a wider archaic tradition, which has distant parallels with the custom in the Bronze Age Near East of dedicating women to temples, sacred prostitution. All over India from the tenth century the custom grew. The popularity of tantric cults which promised liberation through sexual ecstasy added to the spread of the practice. In many parts of India the temples themselves were adorned with sculpture and painting depicting in the most unabashed way every possible variety of sexual activity, magically lustful couplings; not for them the chaste kiss of the Hindi movie. The custom has never died away completely. In many parts of India today, from the Harijan villages of Bihar to high-caste communities in Karnataka, the dedication of women to temples continues, but now linked more and more to the AIDS-stricken fleshpots of Delhi and Bombay.

In Tamil Nadu reformers worked against the tradition from the nineteenth century. The custom of dedicating women to temples was banned in the 1920s. Then the reformers moved against temple dancing itself, despite the fact that in many temples in Tamil Nadu there was a different kind of *devadasi*, women from families who had traditionally given their daughters to be ritual specialists, dancers and singers – 'ever-auspicious women', whose training and way of life could not have been further from prostitution. Before they left, as one of their parting shots, the British passed an act banning dancing inside the temples – amazing, considering what they had on their plate at that moment, with partition looming. 'However ancient and pure in its origin, there is no doubt the custom has led many women into a life of prostitution,' said the Devadasi Act of 1947.

However justified, the ban dealt a great blow to the continuance of the age-old dance which had been so tied to the temples and it destroyed the livelihood of the hereditary dancing families, who had maintained the religious content of the ancient repertoire. 'I don't know whether in our reformist zeal we've done anything to help stamp out prostitution,' wrote one of the legislators, 'but we have certainly killed off a great artistic tradition.' Now former *devadasis*, the 'ever-auspicious women' who had only ever worked as hereditary ritual specialists, were very reluctant even to admit to their past, and still less to hand on the now-despised tradition. In the anti-temple, anti-Brahmin mood of post-war Dravidian politics, the dance declined as an art to the point where its continuance was in doubt.

It was saved from an unlikely quarter. The dance had gone into secular concert halls as early as the 1930s and there had been a series of historic performances at the Music Academy in Madras which had opened the eyes of many educated Tamils to the value of the tradition which was about to be lost. So, as it died out in the temples, it was kept alive in secular venues. Then, in the sixties, in Tamil Nadu, some of the old dancers began to be tapped for their secrets and this eventually led to a huge upsurge of interest – as has happened all over the world when such traditions are about to disappear. Bharata Natyam has now become the best-known classical dance of India, recognized worldwide. Foreign women now flock to Madras to Kalakshetra to learn it. (It features in Louis Malle's haunting film *Inde Phantome*, banned by the Indian government.) In West Car Street in Chidambaram, the Shiva Sakti Dance School draws many local girls (and some boys) prepared to embark on the long, hard discipline necessary to master even the basics.

And in the process of this rediscovery, the dance is also being re-ritualized, its traditions reinvented. Denied temple performance, they bring Nataraja on to the stage instead. In their old age, the last of the pre-war dancers are now getting belated recognition: Bhanumathi, an old Kumbakonam dancer, has been honoured by the state; Tiruvarur Kamalam, a former dancer now living in Chidambaram, is helping to teach the new generation; girls like Mala's daughter Jaya are learning it as a fitting accomplishment, not as a sacred art. A recent chief minister, Karunanidhi, himself the movie scriptwriter son of a temple dancer, even suggested the time had come for the dance to go back into the temples. Others, though, say that time has already passed. One of the old *devadasis* of Murugan's shrine at Tirutanni, not long before her death a year or two ago, was quoted in the Madras papers as saying that she had no interest in seeing the art revived. The spiritual conditions which make it meaningful, she said, no longer existed.

SATURN

The monsoon season was coming to an end. More and more often the rain would stop for a few hours, and the sea breeze would chase the clouds away, leaving a blue sky and a town bathed in gentle sunlight. Then you start to feel the heat of the sun again, spirits rise; people leave their umbrellas at home and come outside at the golden hour, in clean shirts and fresh saris. Life takes to the streets once more.

Tamils are sociable people: they hate being in on their own, and when the rains last for too long they become withdrawn. Their idea of happiness is society; they walk down the streets holding hands; families live and sleep together in a single room. Mala could never understand it when I went back to the hotel to rest, as if I needed to be on my own.

'Why don't you take your rest here?' she would say, pointing to the mat at her feet, in the room crowded with neighbours and friends. 'Just sleep here with us while we carry on talking.' One of their worst fears is to be left alone. Unless one is a renouncer, why separate oneself from society? Hence when the rain pours and forces you indoors, it is the least favourite time. For Mala, the heat of the month of Adi is the best, when the warmth is saturating, and when you sleep outside and talk half the night. So with the first November sun there came a rush of happiness: it felt good to be alive. Right across Chidambaram people were jolly once more as the last pools dried up, and by the canal bridge the shanty dwellers were able to mend their huts, sweep the floors and mark out the kolams again on the earth at the threshold.

So one lovely November Saturday, as the last monsoon clouds clung to the furthest northern horizon and the sun cast a golden light over the tea stall in East Car Street, Mala and I went to the bus station early to take a journey to the coast, to visit the last stop on the journey given me by Rajdurai Dikshithar four years before: Saturn.

We took the bus to Tranquebar, an old Danish colony with a crumbling fort on the beach (the one earmarked by the Taj chain as 'a future five-star facility'). Opposite the bus stop, a stream and the eighteenth-century brick gate of the Danish town, a line of blue sea at the far end of main street, Lutheran churches. The bus stand was covered with political graffiti: elephant, cock, wheel, hand, rising sun, the emblems of today's parties reusing all the old religious symbols. At a little thatched stall we sat and drank sweet tea; above us was an imposing monument to a loyal Indian servant of the Raj, Rao Bahadur Ramasami Nadar (died 1922), 'erected in grateful loving memory by his friends and admirers: 25 Nov. 1926 stone laid by J.A. Thorne Esq. ICS Addl. District Magistrate, Tanjore'. Next to it a hand-painted sign advertised the Tranquebar Rationalist Forum (estd 11.07.1982) with the admonitions of Periyar (E.V.R. Naicker again, the anti-Brahmin, anti-caste, anti-Hindu rationalist and agitator): 'No God!! No God!! No God exist at all!!! Creator of God is a fool! Propagator of God is a scoundrel!! Believer of God is a barbarian!!! Relinquish God; remind Man!'

The afternoon bus took us up to Karaikkal. The road runs along a palmy shore with the sea glimpsed through the trees. At Karaikkal we waited at the bus stand near a little temple to the 'Mother of Karaikkal', the famous female renouncer saint and poetess who lived about AD 550, one of the sixty-three Saivite saints still known throughout Tamil Nadu. Mala told me her story.

'Once upon a time in this town, there was a merchant. His name was Paramadatta, which means "endowed with heavenly gifts". He had all the earthly good that a man could ever wish. Most of all, he had a beautiful and faithful wife called Punnidah-vatiyar, which means "She who is pure".'

'The same name as your eldest daughter?'

'The same. I named her after the saint. She was very devout, and always fed poor followers of Siva who came to her door.

'One day a wandering sadhu came to her house begging for

alms, and she had nothing to offer but boiled rice. Now her husband had recently received two beautiful mangoes from a friend, so she gave him one with the rice. When Paramadatta came back home and ate his meal, he asked for one of the mangoes, and he liked it so much he asked for the other as well. Punnidah didn't wish to tell him what she had done, so she prayed to Siva, and instantly found another mango, which she gave to her husband. It was of wonderful sweetness – supernatural indeed.

'To cut a long story short, when the miracle was revealed to Punnidah's husband – and it was not the only one – he came to the conclusion that she was touched by god, and he no longer dared make love with her, withdrawing his presence and his affections. Then, without telling her, he equipped a ship and on an auspicious day he sailed away to foreign lands, where he made a new life, and in time a new fortune.

'Some time later, pining for his native land, he returned to Tamil country, remarried in another town, and gave his baby daughter the name of his former wife. But now Punnidah's women relatives and friends got to hear of her husband's return, and they decided to take her to him. When they came face to face, he and his new wife and daughter prostrated themselves before her, and he called himself her slave and her his goddess. The women were angry with him and said he was mad: "Who but a madman worships his own wife?" He answered that he had seen her miracles with his own eyes; and that she had ceased to be his wife, but was divine.

'Punnidah was heartbroken. She prayed to Siva to remove her beauty: "Take away from me this beauty which I cherished for the sake of my husband alone," she said. "Remove from me this burden of the flesh and give me the form and features of one of your demon hosts who are always by your side to praise you" – the spirits who forever attend Siva in the cremation grounds he haunts. This he did. Then the gods rained flowers on her, and her relatives in awe paid her adoration and departed. Then she became a wanderer. No longer was she Punnidah, but Karaikkal Ammai-yar, the Mother of Karaikkal. Literally she became a *pey*, a demon. Finally, the story goes, she walked all the way to Mount Kailash, the Himalayan abode of Siva, and there she heard a voice telling her to return to Tamil Nadu where her devotion would be rewarded; where she would see Siva's dance of bliss and sit at his feet for ever.'

'Did she?'

'Yes. At Tiruvalangadu near Madras. There she spent the rest of her days. She composed poems about Siva's dance there which are still recited today. In every Siva temple in Tamil Nadu you will see her at the feet of Nataraja. And here at Karaikkal on full moon day in Ani month there is a festival, where in a hall by the temple, curd, rice and mangoes are given to the poor in her memory.'

Tirunallar is two miles outside Karaikkal; it is a busy little town famous for its ancient Siva temple. Siva here is 'Lord of the Darba Grass'; the temple priests will tell you the place existed in the four previous aeons under different names; and in its present incarnation for just the last few million years. The more historically minded will be satisfied to learn it was sung by Appar and the other saints from the seventh century onwards.

The temple is dedicated to Siva, but Saturn has a shrine inside the outer wall of the enclosure. He is popular all over south India: every Siva temple has a shrine to the planets, in which Saturn is the most frequented. He is the keeper of boundary, the extreme outer limit in Indian astrology, and is even more pervasive in influence than Yama, for even death must bow to karma, and Saturn is the Lord of Karma.

Small as it is, this is the most famous Saturn shrine in all India. The priests' wealth is legendary, founded on donations of the Tamil business fraternity across south-east Asia. The tradition here is of a form of sanctuary, a kind of karma-free spiritual zone; Saturn is temporarily unable to exercise influence on any person inside the precinct. According to legend Saturn was made powerless when King Nala placed himself under the protection of Siva; after he came here and bathed in the tank, he was released from an ancestral curse. Saturn promised not to touch those who pray here in Nala's name. This is propitiation pure and simple, for Saturn cannot be deflected.

To the right of the inner gate is a copper-ornamented shrine to Saturn, a small wizened old man, silver-chested. In the West we tend to see karma as guilt which arises from our deeds, especially bad deeds. But it is much more than that, for it is accumulated over generations of the individual's family and caste. It is a kind of coded essence: not exactly a genetic code, but a print given you by your family and your society; a history, if you like, in which genetics is one part. It is the essence of you, the stuff of you, which interacts with the stuff of the universe. Saturn (or what he symbolizes) is potentially the most serious influence over this; over the generations karma can build up and in our lives we may attract good deeds or bad – storms and cyclones, disease, death and pestilence, auspiciousness and inauspiciousness. All this is the domain of the Lord of Karma.

At the gate there were renouncers sitting waiting for alms, which are generously given here. Some were deformed, some performing austerities. Theirs is Saturn's domain too: pain, restriction, discipline and duty. The renouncer who stands on one leg for years or with one arm atrophied in self-generated penance is acting in ultimate obeisance to this Saturnine principle of things. To us their course is unacceptable, irrational. But for them it is a quest to break the bounds of this natural existence, they aspire to a transcendent absolute freedom, which to us is no freedom at all.

'Saturn is always said to be malign,' said the priest (who was not, by the way, sporting a Rolex). 'But he can be very beneficial if you never forget him. Adversity is testing. Discipline, endurance, the power to endure all sorts of privations, make a person austere and singularly profound in his mode of thinking. So without the help of Saturn one cannot become a high-order thinker. We say no one would choose the path of inner search, if Sani did not spread his influence.'

Which I suppose makes Saturn not an end to a journey, but in a sense the journey itself.

TO THE SEA

It was nearly sunset when we reached Poompuhar at the old mouth of the Cavery, where crowds still gather on full moons to bathe and stare out to sea. We arrived at the coast that Saturday evening in a soft light, to the roar of rolling breakers; along the strand were beached catamarans of split logs lashed with coir rope. Poompuhar is a popular place with holiday-makers and weekend trippers as well as pilgrims; food and trinket stalls line the road to the beach, and there is a strange art gallery full of stone sculptures celebrating the Roman-period Tamil epic *Silapaddikaram*, which is set here. *Silapaddikaram* is rather like one of the late Shakespearean romances: a tale of love and passion, mistaken identities, shipwrecks and sea changes and fateful coincidences. The young lovers are the captain's daughter Kannaki, she of 'a body like a golden creeper', and the merchant's son Kovalan, who was 'Murugan incarnate'. At the centre of the tale, malign as Desdemona's handkerchief, is the lost anklet which brings disaster on its possessors.

The tale takes place in the city of Kaveripatanam, which stood here before it was washed away by the sea or covered in dunes. The *'emporion Khaberis'*, as Pliny and Ptolemy called it, was celebrated in the Tamil epics as 'The city of Puhar, which equalled heaven in its fame and the Serpent World in its pleasures', a town crammed with foreign merchandise which came by ship and caravan – 'Himalayan gold, pearls from the south seas, red coral of the Bay of Bengal, the produce of Ganga and Cavery, grain from Ceylon and the rarest luxuries of Burma'.

Excavations here have given colour to this picture, turning up imported wine from Kos and Knidos, and jars of Spanish olive oil. On this beach merchants from Alexandria barbecued kebabs and downed sulphurous plonk from the Cyclades as they drew up their profit and loss in pepper, cloves, pearls, Chinese silk, coral, spike-nard, antimony, red and yellow orpiment and Argaritid muslins. All this was eighteen centuries before the first British ship, the Honourable East India Company's *Globe*, edged its way along this coast looking for safe anchorage on the surf-beaten strand of the Coromandel, that endless shore of pale sunburnt sand dotted with purple sandflowers and fishing villages. And that was in 1611, such a short time ago in the life of this land and its people: a blink in the eye of Brahma.

We sat on the beach where the breakers throw up fragments of Chinese porcelain, Roman glass and Company rupees rubbed smooth and faint by the waves which swirl amid the sea shells in a pearly phosphorescence. We watched the light change from opal into gold while urchin boys charged their scraggy ponies bareback up the dunes and smoke wafted under our noses from the vendors of chick-peas and sweetcorn. We met a wandering sadhu, in saffron cloth, with trident, flag and thick-rimmed spectacles: a sweet-spoken, balding man who had worked for Viyella and seen Nehru in Tanjore in 1957. He spoke about the beauty of English in which, just as in Sanskrit, 'one may say many things nobly and affectionately'. This was his cue to recite Shakespeare's Seven Ages of Man; having fulfilled his duties as a householder, he said, he was now in the last stage, not second childishness but an explorer, a world renouncer. 'My life is satisfied. After death, who knows? I have found salvation in living life.'

As we spoke, a coach party of young girls rushed across the beach laughing, to dip their toes in the water while the wind picked up the edges of their saris. One of them, in sky blue and gold, slipped in the undertow and stumbled into the foam, to the merriment of her friends. As the sun set, Mala bathed, lit her little lamp and let it go. Then she stood up, pushed back her wet hair, and stared out to sea, out to the point where the turbid brown flow of the sacred Cavery runs into the sparkling blue of the Bay of Bengal.

Part Three
THE TIME OF RIPE HEAT

7

Chidambaram

Two years later I went back to Chidambaram, a few days before
the full moon in Chitra month, which straddles April and May in
the Western calendar. Right in the middle of the heat. The train
down was a baking oven. Children's holidays had just started and
everyone was off on their summer break, so there was no space at
the Hotel Tamil Nadu. The best I could find was a bare room in
lodgings overlooking the temple gardens. There I sweltered
through the stifling nights of the hot season, waking before dawn
to monkeys chattering at my window. Outside was a townscape
of terracotta roofs and temple palms. Just below my room was a
little brick-paved yard with an old whitewashed wall which enclosed a well and a flower garden. There, each morning, in the
ethereal time after first light as the bells rang out from the temple,
a young woman in a top of brightest summer blue would come to
pick a basket of marigolds, an old man drew water in a wooden
bucket and a little boy brushed his teeth with a *neem* twig. This
blissful time lasts only an hour or so; then the heat clamps down
on the streets. By nine the sweat runs in pools in the eye sockets
and your shirt is wringing. It was not the ideal time to visit the
south. But to one born and raised in the cold north, it felt like
being close to some hot fecund essence of existence itself.

Things were moving and changing now, even in Chidambaram.
Everywhere on the rooftops there were TV aerials, and even the
odd satellite dish. In Mala's house all was still in place – the beds,
the metal box, the religious calendars, the *Panchang*, the picture of

the Mother, but here too there was now a small black and white Philips TV in the corner. There were Tamil programmes from Madras, but reception was poor, despite a new relay station in Kumbakonam. We watched the memorial show to the former pontiff of Kanchi, who had recently died in his hundredth year, the most revered religious figure in Hinduism, some said the greatest spiritual figure of this century. He was already famed India-wide for his wisdom some sixty years ago when he met the English writer Paul Brunton, a story told in Brunton's book *A Search in Secret India*. Now the tiny bespectacled mummy was being lowered upright into a pit of salt through a drizzle of static, Sanskrit mantras breaking up in the ether.

Reception was perfect, however, for the Hindi Metro channel, all pop music and action adventure. In the songs you could hear Heavy Metal electric guitar chords, reggae and even rap. The light entertainment programmes included games, quizzes and even a blind-date show.

There had been an outcry in Tamil Nadu when the new government channels were launched two years before, for Hindi language programmes had been foisted on them – a sore point in a state where there has been a long battle to keep Tamil as the first language and English, not Hindi, as second. It has been a continuing struggle since Lord Macaulay made English the official language of India, and the language for all higher education, on 7 March 1835: a fatal moment in Indian cultural history. Till then there had long been a pluralistic society in the north, which had always been open to foreign influences. (Persian was still the official language of government at that moment.) But in the south, with its deep continuities, for it had largely escaped the Muslim impact, it was another story. Until the nineteenth century Tamil cultural distinctiveness was preserved more successfully than in most other regions of India. Since then, there has been long exposure of the middle (and now lower) classes to Western influences and European and English culture. No doubt beneficial from some points of view, this could hardly be good for the creative preservation of the indigenous cultural literary heritage. But many foresaw that the arrival of TV and mass communications would deal the profoundest blow to the continuance of the old in the new.

The Tamils won the first battle of the TV age, as they did in the Education Acts and government decrees after Independence. Now they have their own daytime programme in Tamil, but they still go to Delhi for the national news at nine and then take Hindi programmes for the rest of the evening. It is also fertile territory for the satellite companies broadcasting Tamil channels from Hong Kong, Manila and Malaysia. Consumerism and world culture have suddenly come pouring into the living-rooms of the biggest middle class in the world, even in the south. And despite their traditional upbringing, Mala's children were ambitious to be a part of it.

Sitting watching trousered girls disco-dancing in a hair shampoo commercial in Hindi, it was hard to remember that not so many years ago we had sat in this same room watching fourteen-year-old Jaya dancing Bharata Natyam by lamplight. It had been one of Rajiv Gandhi's big ideas, to get a television set into every household in India. Only then, he thought, would India modernize. Now it has started. 'Reception is not yet reaching the villages here in Tamil Nadu,' said Mani. 'But it will come and then all will change.' TV shows don't have to be in thrall to the ancient taboos; international culture is open to all now and the values of the old world are bound to be rejected by a sizeable group of the young within a single generation.

In the morning Mala's oldest son Kumar came round to my hotel. He had now been back from Saudi for a few months. It had been a very unpleasant (and, one suspected, hurtful) experience, though one common to many from the subcontinent who go to work as guest workers in the Gulf. The promised money had been halved; food and extras deducted. The Saudis, he felt, had been undisguised in their racism towards their Asian workforce. Kumar had not been among the worst treated. Working as a stockman in a warehouse for a pharmacy, he had some status (he speaks excellent English and therefore could take responsibility for the stores). Others, though, were virtually bonded labourers. He had met one older Tamil there who had had so many deductions he had received only his keep – no pay – for two years. 'He will be lucky just to get home after four or five years, never mind make any money,' said Kumar. It was a shock to hear such a gentle and mild-mannered man speak the way he did, but like the rest of his family, Kumar is very honest and straightforward.

'In Saudi there was such hostility to us Hindus. When we arrived, we had our religious pictures confiscated. No puja was allowed – they do not allow temples or churches of any other religion on their soil.'

'So where did you pray?'

'Most people did not pray.'

'We are idol worshippers to them, unbelievers and inferior people. You felt some of them in their hearts actually desired to kill a Hindu. If they were alone in the desert with you they would like to do it and then boast of it to their people. But they treated Sri Lankans and Bangladeshis just as badly. I came back with 1000 rupees in my pocket. That's all. After nearly three years! At least maybe I learned how to be strong.'

When he came back to Chidambaram he stayed in his grand-father's house for a while, and licked his wounds. Then after a few months doing bits of work here and there, he raised the money to start a small business, a general shop selling Surf, carbolic soap, razor blades, Medimix Ayurvedic soap, batteries, soft drinks, bits and pieces. It cost him 20,000 rupees for the stock and the lease, and he borrowed the money from the family. He bought wholesale in town and sold for a few paise more out in the suburbs. It was a long day with a break over noon. The best business was early, between 6 and 8.30. At mid-morning we rode over on our bicycles.

The shop was in a rather unprepossessing area of the town. To get there you cycled down back lanes and muddy hollows away from South Car Street to a swampy area on the southern outskirts. A Vellala suburb, like the quarter where Mala lives. Here some new squat concrete flat blocks have been erected; some are not yet finished, though they are already taking on the look of ruins after a year or two's exposure to tropical heat and monsoon storms. The shop stands alone in an open space of bare earth between houses. Next to it there's a tiny Siva temple with a thatched forecourt sheltering a chirpy little Nandi.

We drank soft drinks, eyes narrowed with the fierce light coming up off the beaten track beyond the shade of his awning. By eleven it was not exactly bustling, but Kumar seemed content with progress. He looked trim and fit, wearing tie-dyed blue slacks and a crisply ironed navy-blue cotton shirt which showed off his beautiful dark skin; he sported a trim moustache and a red *tilak* dot between his smiling eyes. When I first met him, when he was a teenager, he had always seemed very diffident, somewhat suppressed, maybe even depressed. But I was mistaken. He is a very thoughtful person, extremely observant; there is little he misses. Maybe what I thought I saw back then was to do with the crises of his youth and adolescence, 'family problems', as his mother would say, especially the disaster of his father losing his sight. But now he was confident and patient. He had a plan of action which he was going to follow through.

'Eventually I would like to get a shop in one of the main streets, in the middle of Chidambaram. But investment there, for lease and stock, would be about six thousand dollars, more than one hundred thousand rupees – maybe two even. But I hope to do this. First I must build up this local business here in Sakti Nagar. Keep a clear mind. Watch the detail. In two years I will be strong. Then I can go bigger.' He reached into his shirt pocket and pulled out a business card carrying his name and his aunt's address.

'Also I am acting as an agent dealer for a new cleaning powder.

It is newly come to Tamil Nadu so it is not yet well known. It's a little like Vim. I am operating from my aunt's house in SPG Street, taking orders and delivering it personally. In time I will get a phone. Then maybe even a fax. But a fax is 40,000 rupees, and at the moment I am not big enough to need one. For the moment this will do. It is going well so far.' He smiled again his rather shy, winning smile. 'And after the time in Saudi I am so glad to be back here in my motherland.'

That May the whole of the state seemed to be on the move; the hottest month is the time of the biggest temple festivals in Tamil Nadu, and from the grandest to the smallest there are special celebrations, with processions, recitals and grand pujas. Every railway station and bus stand was covered with coloured posters giving details of the main events. These were gatherings on the scale of the great medieval fairs: a million outsiders were expected in Madurai to celebrate the sacred marriage; at Tiruvarur eight thousand people would be needed just to pull the temple car. Going down south the trains and buses were crammed with pilgrims. On the roads we saw walkers everywhere: At Vaithisvarancoil I met a man from a merchant family who had walked 150 miles from Karaikudi with his children, in a party of around sixty. 'This is the tradition among our community for the last two centuries or so,' he said. 'We walk by night, starting at dusk and stopping each morning towards dawn, resting through the heat of the day wherever we find shade.

'We do about forty kilometres a night,' he said. 'Then we make camp, sing old hymns of the *Tevaram*, sleep a little. We stay at Vaithisvarancoil three or four days over the full moon, and then leave on the Friday. I work for the Indian Overseas Bank as an officer in Madras. This time is a lovely communal event; we go back reinvigorated after brief experience of another world.'

Back in Chidambaram I took a bicycle out to Killai on Sea

through paddies burned brown by the scorching sun. There used to be a road lined with coconut trees from the temple to this spot, where they took Nataraja in procession on the festival day in Masi month, bathed him in the sea and gave him a rest in the hall on the beach, letting him enjoy the sea air. This custom only stopped fifteen years ago. This was the edge of Nataraja's domain. Until the nineteenth century the sacred land of Chidambaram extended between the two rivers and eastwards to the coast. You go out past the rice mills at Manallur, where Mala's father farmed paddy. You reach the sea at Pichavaram, close to Killai: local tradition says this was where Manikavasagar, the poet-saint, lived. The sea has now retreated. Salt flats, mangrove swamps, a big silted creek. There's an old brick-lined tank here with a great banyan – perhaps a descendant of the one mentioned in an inscription on the temple walls, in April 1128, 'giving shade to the pilgrims under its spreading crown'. The *mandapa* built anew that year is still here, though decrepit now and hung with creepers. A solitary spiny palm. A creek with beached boats made of split logs roped together. On a sandbar between a lagoon and a line of pounding surf, there is a fishing village of grass huts. Near by there are salt pans stirred in slow motion by men with long poles of bamboo, naked but for white turbans and loincloths, bodies black as ebony. Back at Killai, a sadhu sitting in the *mandapa* stares out to sea. He's walking to Cape Comorin.

Friday is a special puja night in Siva temples, and the last Friday I was there was a particularly festive day, following the full moon, with all the children on holiday. Thousands crammed the temple. The light was soft at six o'clock, the pavement still hot on one's bare feet. In the courtyard inside the East Gate, two women were brushing the flagstones with twig brooms. Before the entrance a crowd of people sat talking in the long covered walkway built eight hundred years ago by Kulottunga II to give shade to devotees. On the steps of the tank some bathers were hanging out their wet wraps; others were reading in the paved areas around the cloister; by the gate a couple of old sadhus in saffron waited for gifts; there was a man playing a flute outside the goddess shrine. The last sunlight glinted on the golden roof, throwing into relief the tracery of ancient inscriptions in flowery Tamil script; like faint, snaking wave marks on windblown sand they record the names of the old kings and benefactors, celebrating not victory in war but gifts of flowers and lamps, a garden of coco palms, milk for schoolchildren, the endowment of the shrine by the sea at Killai with its freshwater tank and its banyan tree.

That evening the sun sank into a small patch of cloud over the palm forests behind the Sivakami shrine. Then the temple's great bell began to ring; flights of swallows wheeled and swooped around the *gopura*s, and as the sun vanished, a warm wind came up, gusting gently across the courtyard, rushing through the East Gate, hurrying birds and people with it as the last chimes died away for the beginning of puja.

The TV was on when I got to Mala's for supper. We ate *dosai* and talked about the future: for India, for the Tamil country and for the family. They were not DMK people, despite everything; they had never been MGR people, though MGR was still popular in the villages among 'uneducated people'. Father shook his head: Nehru, Indira, Sanjay, Rajiv, he enunciated their names with a sense of respect and regret. A boy at Independence, he had grown up believing in their noble ideals. For him, the Gandhi dynasty represented the true direction for India; they were people worthy of admiration and loyalty, and their deaths represented the passing of an era, a period in his lifetime indeed. Of course it was still possible, Bharati chipped in, that Rajiv's daughter Priyanka might succeed in due course. The magazines were full of speculation, although she is said not to wish to follow in her father's footsteps. Many, though, still saw Rao as a caretaker till the crown returned. Mani was not convinced. The time had gone. Nehru's secular

India, the India he had grown up and lived through, was coming to an end, and a new India emerging. One he didn't like as much, even if it was truer to itself.

Mani's home village was not far from Mayavaram, twenty-five miles south of Chidambaram. Mani's father was the headman of the village, a landowner of the Vellala agricultural caste, the same social status as Mala's father. He had among his cousins an *oduvar* in the ancient shrine at Sirkali. His early years, from the end of the Second World War until 1951, were spent there; then he lived in Sirkali, where his family had land and the old house and garden of which Bharati had once spoken. It was the time after Independence when the DMK and the Dravidian movement in the south were pushing the causes of Tamil identity and autonomy, anti-Brahminism and atheism. The Vellalas, though, saw themselves as the 'real Dravidians', the pure Dravidian community of the soil, repositories of the old values. For this reason, Mani was always a Congress man; he was for Nehru's vision of a secular India and Indian unity in diversity. Also, I guess, though I never asked him, in some sense for a Gandhian ethic of hard work, self-sufficiency and morality, which fitted with the traditions of his caste.

Mani was housebound now. Not so long before my visit his sweet old friend, Mr Velu, had died, the man who had always been his guide, taking him to the temple every day without fail. Now Mani had no friend to chat with; he missed his conversation; he missed his trips out to the temple at puja time to listen to the trumpet and the singing of the *oduvar*s. So he sat at home and listened to All India Radio and the BBC World Service. (That summer, like so many Indians, he had avidly followed the South African elections.) But life was increasingly hard for him; especially as all his daughters had gone. Kumar was now living in his grandfather's house; only Balu slept at home. But he kept strange hours, and could be edgy and difficult as his efforts to get some kind of business going continued to be frustrated. The girls had tried again to persuade their parents to up roots and go to Madras, but still Mala would not leave Nataraja. So, increasingly her husband was forced into his inner world, bounded by that tiny space, in their cell-like room and the little passageway where he put his camp bed out in the heat of the summer to catch the little breeze which came from behind the tank and the latrine in the late afternoons. Now, he had only an awareness of light as against dark, seeing no detail in a land where every detail is meaningful.

In the alley the moon rose above the roof in a velvet darkness. After the meal Mala and I went to the temple for the last time. The Milky Way arched over the *gopuras* like a silver aureole. The courtyards were still hot from the day. Ganesh greeted me outside the Kanak Sabha. After our adventures on the video bus he never sees me now without a chortle. He was on duty, so no handshake – that would be ritually polluting. He asked me whether I would like to go inside. There was a little knot of people standing in quiet contemplation. From somewhere in the inner halls came distant Tamil singing. Sound seemed to be not audible but only visible in the movement of flames, flickering on the inside of the roof, the silvered thresholds and the brass utensils. Nataraja was smiling and covered with flowers. The ancient reassuring gesture of the open palm: 'Fear not; I am here.' By his side was the curtain sewn with gold leaves which concealed the empty room, god as nothingness. God nowhere but the human heart: the Secret of Chidambaram.

In front of the silver doors the *oduvar* arrived, briefcase under his arm. Softly and sweetly he began to sing a famous old song by Appar, the seventh-century Vellala saint, a quintessential Tamil song:

'Why bathe in the Ganga or the Cavery, or take a holy dip at Comari? Why bathe there at the mingling of the seas? Why chant the Vedas, roam the forests and wander through the towns? Why fast and starve, sit staring into the blue? One thing alone will save you: loving our gracious Lord . . .'

8

Madras

I went back to Madras with Bharati on the Saturday train. That night I had dinner at Ashvin and Prithvi's. She's now bureau chief for her magazine; his company is opening up to Germany and the USA. Ashok, their son, is sixteen now, a typical teenager, always on the phone to his friends. Tall and gawky, he paces the living-room in big trainers, with a permanent frown on his face; he is having an awful time with his exams, doing extra homework every night and all day Sundays. With the quota system for Brahmins your results have to be really excellent to guarantee a university place: '200 per cent,' he says ruefully. Their eleven-year-old daughter, Maneka, is assured, ambitious and determined. For them excitement is in the air, all is change now. Rao's government has lifted many of the restrictions on foreign imports and invest-ments, and foreign TV programmes. But the old stories still get the biggest audiences; the new Krishna soap has even outdone the incredible success of the previous blockbuster soaps, *Ramayana* and *Mahabharata*.

'It's terrible,' said Ashvin. 'But viewing figures are 200 million.' (Of course there are many more TVs now than in the late eighties when the *Ramayana* broke the world's TV box-office viewing figures.) 'And – wait for it – it's sponsored by Proctor and Gamble, or some other foreign firm. There's internationalism for you!'

Change has arrived. The younger generation eat meat; they don't cook it in the home, but they eat it in trendy restaurants. They know all the international trade marks: they want Nike shoes and Benetton shirts. They are now into the consumer revolution and there is no doubt it will transform the country. Even Hollywood is in now; they are showing US movies dubbed in Hindi.

Maneka is an ardent film fan: she loved *Jurassic Park*, which had already been running for weeks in Madras in English and Hindi.

'It is wonderful,' she said. 'I've seen it three times. Best film ever made.'

'Yes,' said Kamala. 'My near neighbours in Mylapore have just been on pilgrimage to Tirupati to see Lord Venkateshwara. They came back with the whole works; they had shaved their heads to give their hair to the god, scalps plastered with sandal paste, the kids too. And when they arrived back home the kids were wearing *Jurassic Park* hats! There it is in one image: tonsures and Dinomania! There you have the new India.'

Kamala is ever the optimist: 'Contradictions like this have always existed side by side in India. India is always able to assimilate, and it will again; it will simply metamorphose into some new form as wonderful and various as it always was! The people have common sense.'

'Just look what happened after Ayodhya,' she continued. 'When you were here last, prospects were really gloomy. Now things have stabilized. After the Ayodhya mosque was destroyed by the fanatics in December '92, there was great panic and worry, shame and self-examination in the newspapers. We all were terrified of the Muslim backlash. But the horrors we feared have been averted. After the Bombay bombings people realized this couldn't go on. Everyone is so money-minded these days they realized it would ruin things for everyone.'

So was there still a place for the old ideal, for Nehru and Gandhi's vision of India?

Ashvin shook his head. 'Look, let's be honest about it. Gandhi sold this image of eternal India: ahimsa, non-violence, and all that. But India is one of the most violent societies in the world. I'm not sure that Gandhi didn't resurrect something that was an aberration in our history and make it appear the norm. It was an ideal, not the reality.'

'Surely,' I said, 'it was more than that?'

'Anyway, that's all history now. Gandhi was wily, canny; this was his great quality. He understood the people. He focused the message which was right for the time. But it's one thing to fight a liberation struggle, to fight against the oppressor. You have to define yourself clearly, say what you are fighting for. Gandhi did this, defined us in terms of an image which we liked – and of course you Westerners liked it too. But fifty years on the message is more complicated. All their debates in the Anand Bhavan are irrelevant now. Nehru is irrelevant now. No one talks about him any more. The socialist-type experiment took us in the wrong direction. It delayed the growth of the country for much of the last fifty years. But it's over now. Material improvement is the only answer for India. People want to get on. None of us are Gandhians now.'

As I was leaving Prithvi was thoughtful. She had been doing a lot of travelling recently, to the States, Europe and the Pacific rim; she would be off again in a week or two. 'You know, it has made me think a lot about Tamil Nadu; I really think it is one of the best places in the world one could live. Maybe we were so impressed by things Western we didn't see what was under our noses. We have everything here. I just hope the kids think so too when they grow up.'

My taxi was outside, so we said our goodbyes.

'What about your Brahmin's thread, Ash?' I asked.

'Still in the drawer.'

'Made that trip down south yet?'

He laughed: 'Not yet. But I haven't forgotten. I will go to Tiruvidaimarudur. One day.'

9

Taramani Sunday

Mala's daughters' house is in Taramani, south Madras, a dusty new suburb over the Adyar river behind the ITT campus. Brick and cement dust swirling; there is new building everywhere. Five years ago it was fields with thatched houses; people grazed cows here and there was no bus link. Now there are streets of two-storey concrete houses in between the clusters of thatch. The cows, goats and bullocks are still there, tethered by the bus stand, picking their way round the pan and *beedi* store, and there are still beaten dirt roads, thick mud in winter, iron hard now. The girls live in the back part of a house and the landlady lives in the front with her old mother – they seem kind and friendly, and treat the girls like daughters. 'It is safe and secure here,' said Bharati, 'for three unmarried girls in a rough area.' They have a loo/washroom, a kitchen and a living-room, maybe ten feet by twenty, with a door which leads out on to the little balustraded yard. In the yard is a defunct water pump around which the household pile their water cans, jugs and buckets ready for the thrice-weekly water carrier from Madras. Unless you are rich, water shortages are a fact of life in Madras: only that week there had been stories of a cholera outbreak near here caused by illicit tapping of the main municipal water pipes. (The last outbreak in 1992 in Madras had been caused for the first time in the world by a new strain of bacteria for which there was no vaccine. Fortunately it had been contained.)

'We have taps, but they don't work,' said Bharati. 'The better class of people, they can just pay 150 rupees and buy a whole water van. We pay 4 rupees for the driver to fill our cans.'

In Chidambaram there was no shortage of tanks and wells and the water never ran out. Here you were quickly made aware that even having a bath or shower wasted water.

'It is the biggest problem with life in Madras,' said Jaya.

We sat down on the floor to eat.

Sarasu was reflective and hardly spoke. Her marriage plans had been on and off for three years. She had liked several of the men, but the horoscopes had not been good. Now the chart was fine but the prospective husband was in finance and Sarasu was worried because his family, though of the same caste, were of higher social status and would expect too much, despite her good job. I guessed she was also concerned about the demands in cash on her mother. 'It is the custom for the bride's family to give some gold to the boy's family along with the other parts of the dowry,' said Bharati. 'They want at least 45,000 rupees (£1000) plus 25,000 rupees in other gifts – scooter or whatever. Then there are the marriage costs, which must be born by the bride's family; the boy's family are insisting they want the marriage in Madras and mother wishes to hold it in Chidambaram. Hire of the marriage hall in Chidambaram costs 4000 rupees; in Madras it is nearly double; and where the cost of food for upwards of 600 people is 25,000 in Chidambaram; it is 50,000 in Madras. The whole will cost at least 100,000 rupees.'

Sarasu's concern was understandable. There had been other boys she had liked better, Moreover, Rajdurai had told Mala that Sarasu must marry by the following spring while the signs were auspicious for the wedding; otherwise things would best be put off for four years. At her age, with two younger sisters who also had to marry, this was out of the question. That kind of pressure seemed the worst thing of all, though I suspect that, underneath, Rajdurai, who is a kindly soul, was perhaps trying to encourage Sarasu to make a choice after so many delays.

Playing devil's advocate, I said why not break out altogether? Reject the idea of arranged marriages? With the amount of money invested in their dowries they could start a business together, open a shop. The three of them were so bright and personable, they would be bound to be a success. Then if they wished to marry, they could do it on their own terms; men would be queueing up to marry them for themselves. Their talent and their careers would be their dowries. My suggestion was greeted with polite laughs but no takers.

'Some people don't follow the horoscopes,' said Bharati. 'Some don't even marry in the same caste any more. Of course this happens more in Madras; you would not find it in the countryside or in a small town like Chidambaram. But here love marriages are becoming more common between different castes, as inevitably in modern society there is much more opportunity to meet and befriend people of different communities. And of course women are far more numerous in employment. We have friends of different castes and religions in the same firm. Now you even hear of marriage between Brahmin and lower castes. But not with us. Our community marries within the caste – Pillai or Vellala. You see, we are the traditional agricultural caste. One of our names means "do harm to no one". Along with the Brahmins and the Aiyangars (Vaishnavas) we kill nothing and we only try to do good. Others kill; lower castes and even some middle castes. We never will. Things are changing now, I admit. Even some Brahmins are seduced by Western ways. They will eat meat now. Perhaps not cook it at home, but they will eat it out at restaurants. They start to like it.' (Her eyebrows raised at the very thought of it.) 'You can see this happening. We have Brahmin friends at work and we see. Now in all this I think in time the dowry will change. More and more women have good jobs – look at the three of us. Still, I have a friend who is a doctor. She has very high earning potential. Even so, her father-in-law – whose son was an only child, an engineer – wanted a dowry from her family.'

We talked about their jobs. They all work six-day weeks. Working presumably also to save money towards their own dowries. Sarasu has a clerical job at a wholesale company which sell TVs and fridges, a big business now as the middle-class consumer boom takes off in Madras. Their Philips TV, and the one Mala has in Chidambaram, she got on discount from the company. She is out by 7.30 and gets back 9.30 at night. She turned down one good marriage prospect because, among other things, he insisted she should carry on working, when she had hoped to start a family straight away. Bharati is at a firm making transistors for TVs; she had a technical job at first (after technical college), and has been promoted to a supervisory position. Jaya is in a clerical job for a company manufacturing coated ribbons for computers (another growth industry in the Madras of the nineties). They go to work together each day, leaving home at eight o'clock and getting back after six.

'There's a small shop over the road where we can leave our orders for vegetables and basics and collect them at night. In the evenings we just stay in and watch TV, prepare food, talk. Sundays we have off. We get up lazily, very late; wash our saris, prepare food, clean the house, take everything down off the shelves and clean.'

The kitchen was about twelve feet by five: on the floor was a basket of purple onions, some vegetables, a bag of rice, pans and other utensils. By the door was a puja shelf – a small space cleared between the herbs and spices – with a lamp, incense, little cardboard box of camphor, and a row of pictures, which I asked the girls to explain.

Goddesses were the most prominent: Minakshi, Kamakshi and Thiruverkoddu Amman, all protectors of women. There were two or three pictures of Bhuvaneswari, a form of Sakti, 'who remains unmarried', hence the blood-red sari; they also had Lakshmi and Saraswati. ('She is for better education and knowledge,' explained Sarasu.) There were two pictures of the Mother of

Auroville. The others were Ganesh, of course, and a small Venkateshwara: as a Saivite family they are not particularly devoted to the Lord of Tirupati, who is an incarnation of Vishnu, though he reaches across castes, sects and even religions as the most popular and efficacious bringer of money and financial success in all south Asia. His is the world's richest shrine outside the Vatican, but he is an impersonal and distant deity compared with the old goddesses of the Tamil country.

Sarasu brought the food and we sat on the floor to eat. They still follow the old observances, even in the middle of the city. Each night when they get back from work they light the lamp for Lakshmi in the front room; and as they haven't got a back door, they close the door to the washroom and light a lamp in the puja place. And in the morning they make a little *kolam* on the front step.

As Bharati saw it, the way forward was to take the best of the modern and keep the best of the past. But this was coloured by an absolute commitment to traditional Tamil culture. And at the heart of this idea, it seemed, was a moral system exemplified by the values of their caste, of 'our community', which were seen as supportive and enriching. To a casual observer it might have seemed they were trapped in a system which denied them freedom, condemning them to act out its rules even when meaning was visibly draining from them and all around them people were adopting different values. But for them the caste was a system of mutual support, despite rules – such as dowry – which they acknowledged were oppressive.

In Madras their social life revolved around connections with the community: Jaya showed me photos of her dancing at the community hall – not a public performance, but one for their community association. They would never say so, but I sensed that they feel morally superior to the Brahmins – scrupulously honest where the Brahmins had too much opportunity for hypocrisy, in business, religion and even diet. They all knew Brahmins in Madras who have become Western consumers, not only of electronics and sportswear, but also in their eating habits. To them this was simply not acceptable. It went against all the norms of traditional society, of which they saw their caste as the true exemplars. Brahmins might have higher status in the real world of business, commerce, marriage and so on, but they themselves were the real Tamil caste of the soil. Their grandfather's house in Chidambaram, built 125 years ago by his grandfather, was a symbol and they were proud of that.

'Everything is changing these days,' said Bharati. 'But not us.' Sarasu agreed, with a smile which may have been glad, or may have been sad, I couldn't tell.

'Outwardly, of course, things must move on,' said Jaya. 'But not in the heart.'

Epilogue

Hard to believe, but it is now thirteen years since I waved goodbye to the girls on Taramani station and of course, for them, as for all of India, the intervening time has been truly momentous. Mala's father died soon after I left, almost as old as the century. He was a link with the ancient traditions of the Tamil lands and for the family it was truly the end of an era. Around that time, Mala left her cramped room near the East Gate and for a while rented a house in a sandy lane near the Ananteeswaram temple. By now her husband's sight was entirely gone, but they made ends meet, finally selling his house in Sirkali, though they never recovered the garden with its delicious mangoes. A couple of years later, Mala got her own house for the first time, a small old Brahmin house with a tiled roof which backed onto the temple gardens. The horoscope of the house was good, and, of course, she could hardly have been nearer to Nataraja: from the well in the back yard you can hear the temple bells.

For Mala's sons, the nineties were slow progress, neither really making enough to be able to contemplate early marriage and the duties of a householder. But as India's economy began to open up, so the prospects for their generation, even in a small southern town, began to improve dramatically. Kumar opened a shop for engine oil and accessories in the front of the family house, and was soon employing an assistant. After a first failure in business, Balu knuckled down to work in a garage, became a skilled mechanic, and started to earn good money. As for Mala's daughters, in the mid nineties Punnidha had another child, whom she named Arvind, after Aurobindo, the guru of Pondi. Her two boys worked hard at school and both, inevitably I suppose, are budding computer wizards. Sarasu, meanwhile, married the manager of a hotel in Madras, but she continued to work and earn rather than starting a family, as many middle-class women are doing now all over India: not for them the traditional roles accepted by their parents and grandparents

It was almost the end of the millennium before Rebecca and I finally took our daughters to Tamil Nadu. So much bigger now, Madras was in the throes of transformation into a modern city, and many of the old areas had been swept away, and replaced by high-rise office blocks. Even the city's old name had gone: for now we must call it Chennai. Our Madrasi friends' children were now at universities in America. Prithvi herself was running a dot com company; Kamala was on a dance tour in the States. Our old hotel in Madras too had experienced a makeover, with 'White Christmas' playing on the piped music in the foyer – in a city with one of the oldest classical music traditions in the world. I had a sudden intuition of the British past receding like the memory of a fantastic invasion.

We took the Cholan express down south. Past Cuddalore, we craned our necks to catch a first glimpse of the temple gopuras rising above the paddy fields on the right-hand-side of the train. Mala met us on the platform: her eyes shining with delight to see the girls for the first time.

She had booked us into a new hotel squashed between the goddess temple, the bus stand and the cinema, which guaranteed a round-the-clock racket at festival time when all temples start their amplified devotions at 4am prompt. But most of our days were spent at Mala's house with its little lightwell, surrounded by a colonnade of blue wooden posts. In the back, through the house, there was a yard with a well, a latrine and a small garden with a mango tree, where monkeys and chipmunks scampered. The kids helped Bharati grind spices and roll the mix for puri, they drew water from the well, and learned to eat rice by hand, using only the ends of their fingers, off a ribbed banana leaf. We visited grand-mother who asked after 'the old queen, George's wife: is she still going strong?' The girls loved disappearing into the nooks and crannies of her house, and in the yard the cow and her calf gave them endless delight.

At festival time we led Maya's husband ('tatta' to the girls) to the temple to visit Nataraja, where Ganesh Dikshithar, resplendent in his loincloth and stripes of ash, took the girls into the Chit Sabha. There in the flickering lamplight, peering at them through lenses as thick as window glass, he sweetly and patiently explained to widen-ing eyes the story of the sacred dance, and the mystic meaning of the empty room behind the curtain of golden leaves.

During the festival, East Car Street turned into the familiar glit-tering bazaar, where the girls bought packets of gaudy bangles for their schoolmates back home. From Mala's front door we watched the temple cars dragged through the processional streets, and the cows with painted horns garlanded with marigolds and pom-poms. It's a time when singers and musicians throng the town, and one night Mala brought back to the house some oduvars who had come all the way from Tinnevelly in the far south. After the meal they sang for us in her little puja space, softly, bass and tenor, songs of the beloved sacred places, Arur, Kuttalam and Tillai. Balu came over to see us from Cuddalore – he was doing very well now, his skills much in demand, and he'd put on weight – jolly, easy in his skin. Later we made trips into the countryside, to Tirupungur with its magnificent palm-fringed tank sprinkled with purple lotuses, and of course to Vaithisvarankoil, where we had tea and cake on the tank steps, and fed the temple elephant. When the time came to go, our eight-year-old cried as she watched the gopuras fall away behind the palm forests: 'I wish I could see Nataraja every day, Mum' she said.

The next year Jaya sent an e-mail with a plan: to meet up in New Year 2001, the year of Kumbh Mela. This mela takes place in North

India once every twelve years, at the junction of the sacred rivers Jumna and Ganga. Each time it has been by far the greatest gathering of human beings which has ever place, and each one has surpassed the previous one. This year somewhere between twenty and thirty million people were expected on the most sacred bathing night, the 24th of January, and incredibly, sixty million or more over the six weeks of the festival.

'According to the astrologers this will be the most auspicious mela in a hundred and forty-four years' wrote Jaya, who though a modern woman working for a computer firm still comfortably inhabited the old imaginal universe at the same time. 'Mum has said she will come. So why don't we all go together?'

In the midst of a busy life, with our kids at school, it was, no doubt, a crazy idea but it also promised one of those once-in-a-lifetime experiences. So we went out to Chidambaram for Pongal, and later that month, we made our way up to Allahabad.

Through a Tamil religious order, Mala had booked us into a tent in the holymen's sector, which we would share with several Tamil friends. Along with Mala and Jaya, there was Mr Parasmal, a pawn-broker from Madras, with his wife and their seventeen-year-old daughter Sangita; there was Rajesh, a shopkeeper from Mylapore, and Mr Selavadurai, a Malaysian devotee of Nataraja who had somehow become a member of Mala's family. Unbelievably, when one considers the size of the crowds, we made a successful rendezvous at Platform 8 on Allahabad station at about 4am two days before the big night. The Tamils were almost unrecognizable, swathed in woolly hats and shawls, for the north to them is like a foreign country: a freezing land where English is the only shared language for most people. Amid a seething tumult of pilgrims from all over India – turbaned Rajastanis, Biharis, Nepalis – we found a local motor rickshaw to take us into the camp. Though the mela site spread over fifty square kilometres along the sandy bed of the Ganga, to my astonishment, we found our enclosure with no trouble at all. Our tent comfortably held sixteen people. Inside, stuffed mats laid on the white river sand made it all rather snug and comfortable. Outside, there was a 'bathroom' – a standpipe behind corrugated sheets – a row of latrines with canvas curtains, and a cook tent where hot sweet mixed tea was brewed at first light to warm up pilgrims returning from the early dip in the Ganga. As for eating, it is the custom at such melas that ordinary pilgrims are fed by the great monastic orders, and no sooner had we arrived than Jaya and Sangita announced they were taking the kids off for breakfast: 'Mum, Dad, we were invited for breakfast by the holy men. They were very nice to us. And do you know what? They've got no clothes on!'

In the mornings the girls played in the sand under the washing line while gurus expostulated to their followers, and hymns to the Ganga blared out of the loudspeakers at almost ear-splitting volume.

As is the custom, we all took a dip at the Sangam, the junction of the two rivers. In ancient Indian belief, which is half forgotten now, this was the axis mundi, the navel of the earth – or to be absolutely strict about it, the thighs of the Goddess Earth: this is why the pilgrims sail out in their boats to the line of sandbanks which rises out of the water at the precise point where the coffee brown of Ganga meets the blue green of Jumna. This is the most auspicious point of all. The place of Creation.

And back in our tent that night, dried off and warmed up, our kids played London playground games and clapping rhymes, with Jaya and Sangita:

> 'A sailor went to sea-sea sea
> To see what he could see-see-see . . .'

While in the back of the tent, Mr Selvadurai laid out his little altar, tinkled his puja bell and quietly got on with his devotions, for that moment oblivious to the kids and all else around him:

'Om Nama Sivaya ...'
'... And all that he could see-see-see
Was the bottom of the deep blue sea-sea-sea'

After the mela, we made our way to Benares and said our goodbyes
at Kedar Ghat, where the Tamils had booked into a medieval pilgrim dormitory on the river. We said our goodbyes in a pool of
lamplight by a late night fruit stall. Mala and Jaya hugged the kids,
and Mala kissed them one last time: 'You are good children' she
said. Praise indeed from a Tamil mother. Jaya dabbed a tear from
her eye: 'I will e-mail you from the office next week' she shouted,
as we walked away, back towards the car, and our world.

To say we live in one world now, is a truism. But how wonderful is
difference, and how diminished we will be, if the global culture
takes hold everywhere, and destroys these other worlds; thought-
lessly rubbing out encoded identities which have grown over
sometimes thousands of years.

Back in Chidambaram life goes on, and the town is doing well: a
couple of nice new hotels, electronics shops, a block of swish retirement apartments for devotees; they have even laid the streets with
tarmac. Now of course India is booming. Third biggest economy in
the world (and rising) and the south is getting many of the gains and
fewer of the drawbacks. In all the recent government surveys Tamil
Nadu has risen up alongside Kerala as one of the top Indian states
in terms of standard of living, education, security of person and
property, and quality of life.

In the last couple of years both Mala's sons finally felt able to
marry: Kumar to the daughter of an old Vellala farmer – a salt of the
earth kind of man; Balu to a sparkly village girl, not a Vellala, who
has already given birth to a son. And after rejecting a number of
suitors, Bharati last year finally married a man from an old Vellala
family in Mayavaram – she is in her mid thirties now, so quite late
by Tamil standards. So Jaya is the last to remain single, working in

Chennai, while Mala juggles the family savings for one last dowry.

At the temple, the Dikkshithars still meticulously keep up the traditions and rituals of Nataraja, though they find it hard to maintain the giant campus, their weighty inheritance from the past, with its thousand- and hundred-pillared halls, its gopuras tanks and courtyards. Ganesh Dikshithar, like everyone concerned about the state of world, is hoping to do another special puja, a ten-day ritual for world peace (which will cost a small fortune in cloths, sandal paste and food) as he says in his newsletter, 'to energize the whole universe, to bring about ecological balance and promote long-term prosperity'. Radu phoned me from Holland recently after my last television programmes went out. He is spending much more time there, he's running a course on Hinduism, and he has privately published a book on the mystic secret of Chidambaram which is on sale on the stalls in East Sannadhi.

And I nearly forgot: not so long ago Kumar sent me a message from Mr Ramasamy, the video bus impressario, who had stopped by the oil shop. He has more plans – a pilgrimage to the far north of India, to the ice caves of Amarnath and Badrinath and the glacier of Gangotri, a one month epic. And of course, there is the now annual trip to Tiruchendur and Palani. 'Why not bring the kids? As you know, it is more fun than the movies' said Mr Ramasamy, 'except we have the movies too! So book early, Mr Michael, to avoid disappointment!'

Indian Gods and Goddesses

In the south, leaving aside the plethora of village gods and goddesses, the most popular deities are Siva, Vishnu, Murugan and Sakti (the goddess)

Siva is the wild god, creator and destroyer. He has many affinities in his attributes and temperament with the Greek Dionysus, a god of ecstasy and abandon, androgyne and aescetic. Of Siva's many aspects, those mentioned in this book are these: Ardhanari (half-man, half-woman); Bairava (a terrible form: the protector of the universe); Bhikshatanamurti (the enchanting mendicant); Dakshinamurti (lord of the south; the teacher of knowledge) and Nataraja (lord of the dance). Nataraja's main cult centre is in Chidambaram: but the seven different phases of the dance also have separate shrines across Tamil Nadu. In the Saivite holy family Siva and his wife Parvati have two sons, Ganesh and Murugan. The jolly elephant-headed Ganesh (Vinayaka to Tamils) is loved all over India and is especially invoked at the start of any enterprise. Murugan is perhaps the most popular god in Tamil Nadu and is often described as the god of the Tamils. He has his own independent cult, including the six famous 'abodes', the three most important of which appear in this story. Saivites, incidentally, wear horizontal stripes of white ash on the forehead, often combined with the red dot of the goddess.

The second of the big three is Vishnu. He is the necessary balance to Siva's essence. Where Siva has many frightening aspects and is the lord of destruction, Vishnu is benign: he represents the principle of duration, the power that holds the universe together. He has had various animal and human incarnations, when he came to the world to punish the wicked; the most famous are Krishna and Rama; some would add Buddha. In addition, Vishnu has local forms, in the south Venkateswara (Balaji) of Tirupati, the richest shrine in the world, and Ranganatha on the island of Srirangam in the Cavery river, which is probably the largest temple in the world. Vaishnavites wear vertical stripes of sandal and vermilion.

The goddess, Sakti, is popular all over India but especially so in the south; she is held to symbolize the all-pervading energy, the creative force of life. Her most important aspect is as the wife of Siva: she chiefly appears here as Kali (the frightening one) and Parvati (the benign wife and mother). She also has important local incarnations such as Sivakami in Chidambaram; Minakshi in Madurai; Kamakshi in Kanchi; and Mariamman everywhere in the villages. Sakti worshippers wear a red dot on the forehead. In the Middle Ages Saiva cults arose which made great play on Sakti worship. They said that god is manifest through the world only through the medium of Sakti, the goddess. According to them she is the agent and the material cause of creation. The universe is Sakti, unconscious matter, and all material objects as well as conscious souls are nothing but limited manifestations of her. Siva only has his power through Sakti, and the effort of all spiritual quest (for such Saivites) is to find Sakti and attain union with it/her. There are still sects, known as tantric, which follow this path.

Glossary

ahimsa	non-violence
chai	tea
choultry	resting place for travellers or pilgrims
darshan	vision, seeing, especially of a deity
devadasi	'slave of god' – women dancers dedicated to service in temples
dhal	lentil curry
dhobi	laundry-man; traditionally washes by hand on a stone in the river
dhoti	an ample wrap for men, tucked in so that it hangs down at the waist
Dikshithar	here a hereditary priest of the Chidambaram temple
Divali	the autumn festival of lights
dosa (pl. *dosai*)	ground rice and lentil pancake
ghat	steps or landing place on a river bank; also the mountain range between Kerala and Tamil Nadu
ghee	clarified butter used in cooking and as oil for temple worship
gopura	the characteristic Tamil temple gateway
Harijan	'child of god' – Gandhi's name for the untouchables
iddly (or *idli*)	fluffy balls of steamed rice
Kailash	a mountain in western Tibet, in Hindu mythology the abode of Siva
kolam	an auspicious pattern of rice powder laid out in front of the door each morning
kun kum	red powder worn on the forehead in worship of the goddess
lathi	a wooden baton used by the Indian police

linga	a sign or token; as the phallus, the symbol and aniconic image of Siva
lungi	the simplest form of loincloth, the poor man's dhoti
mandapa	hall in a temple
muth, mutt	monastery for Hindu renouncers
nageswaram (or nadeswaram)	the long reedy trumpet used in Tamil temple music
Navarati	the religious festival in September/October; in Madurai, the festival of the goddess Minakshi
neem	a sacred tree whose bitter bark, fruit, leaves and seeds have various attested medical uses
oduvar	professional singers of hymns from the Tevaram (*q.v.*) at Siva temples in south India
paddy	strictly, rice in the husk; generally, growing rice. (Our word 'rice' comes from the Tamil *arisi*, husked rice.)
pan	a digestive concoction made of betel nut, lime paste and tobacco
Panchang	the south Indian religious almanac
Pillai	another name for the Vellala, the agricultural caste in Tamil Nadu
pipal	the poplar-like Indian fig tree, *Ficus religiosa*, often found in the heart of a village or in temple grounds
prasad	literally, grace; offerings (usually edible) given to the deity and returned, touched with divine grace, to the devotee
puja	the act of worship
raga	a scale in Indian music
sadhu (or saddhu)	holy man
Saiva	pertaining to Siva; worshipper of Siva
sambhar	vegetable curry eaten with *dosa*s or *iddly*
Sangam/*sangam*	the classical period of Tamil literature; the academy
sthapathi	craftsman or maker; here, the bronze caster
tantric	pertaining to the sexual theories of some Saiva sects (see appendix, Indian Gods and Goddesses, p. 242)
Tevaram	the hymnbook of the three great Tamil Saiva saints, Appar, Sambandar and Sundarar, who lived between AD 570 and AD 730
tilak	forehead mark

tirtha	literally, crossing place; hence any holy site
ulema	Islamic religious authorities
vadai	savoury doughnuts
Vellala	the old agricultural caste of Tamil Nadu
vilva	a type of tree which is sacred to Siva
vimana	the pyramidal central shrine in Tamil temples